SOME MINOR CHARACTERS IN
THE NEW TESTAMENT

SOME MINOR CHARACTERS IN THE NEW TESTAMENT

BY

PROFESSOR A. T. ROBERTSON, Litt.D.,

CHAIR OF NEW TESTAMENT INTERPRETATION IN THE SOUTHERN
BAPTIST THEOLOGICAL SEMINARY, LOUISVILLE, KENTUCKY

BROADMAN PRESS
NASHVILLE, TENNESSEE

ISBN: 0-8054-1516-5 (complete set)
4215-16
0-8054-1514-9 (this volume)
4215-14

To

JOHN R. SAMPEY

My Beloved Friend
and Colleague for
Forty Years

These chapters have appeared mainly in *The Expositor* (Cleveland), *Church Management, The Moody Monthly, The Biblical Review,* and *The Record of Christian Work,* and are reproduced with the consent of these journals.

PREFACE

These sketches of various persons in the New Testament not treated formally in my other books have been an interesting by-play in my life-work. There are enough more for another volume. It has not yet been possible for me to write out the contemplated book on Simon Peter. A score of other volumes have cried out in me that may or may not see the light of day. The New Testament is the most gripping book in all the world for sheer human interest and charm.

A. T. ROBERTSON.

CONTENTS

CHAPTER I

NICODEMUS THE TIMID SCHOLAR

IT is the Fourth Gospel alone that tells us about Nicodemus and we catch only three glimpses of him (John 3:1–21; 7:45–52; 19:38–42). But his character is drawn with deftness and clearness. Each time he acts in perfect accord with the pictures drawn in the other places. The bold outline is not difficult to trace. He was a Pharisee and member of the Sanhedrin. These two items tell a great deal. The Sanhedrin had both Pharisees and Sadducees in the membership in nearly equal proportion. But the chief priest who presided over the meetings was Caiaphas, a Sadducee. There were many kinds of Pharisees. They are described in my Princeton lectures, *The Pharisees and Jesus.* Most of them were hostile to Jesus, but some were friendly and more open-minded.

Nicodemus is the first Pharisee who manifests a kindly spirit toward Jesus. Evidently he was a man far above the average in endowments of nature. He felt the appeal of Jesus at the very time that the men of his class were lined up against him. He was not willing to join in the outcry against Jesus because he had made a protest against the abuses of the temple worship. As a

1

matter of fact the Sadducees were more responsible for the graft and coarse merchandise carried on right in the temple precincts (John 2:14), the enclosure (*to hieron*), not the sanctuary (*ho naos*). But the soul of Jesus rose in revolt at the desecration of his Father's house right before his eyes (2:16). The Jews challenged the authority of Jesus after they had fled before his wrath. But Jesus stood his ground and gave them as a proof of his Messianic authority the promise of his Resurrection which they did not understand. What did Nicodemus think of this claim of Jesus? We are not told, but we do know that many were carried away by the spectacle of a new rabbi from Nazareth who challenged and routed the whole ecclesiastical organization in Jerusalem. It was daring and it was magnificent, but it meant relentless hostility on the part of the Sanhedrin towards this revolutionary upstart who had charged them with connivance at desecration of the temple of God and who had actually said "My Father" in justification of his deed.

But Jesus was cautious and unwilling to credit this sudden enthusiasm which was without prop·r understanding of the real nature of the Kingdom of God which he was proclaiming and of his own relation to it. John's Gospel (2:23-5) contains an arresting statement of Christ's knowledge of human nature and of each man in particular. He means that Jesus understood men in a way not true of other men. Hence Jesus would not trust himself to these loud and impulsive believers (2:24).

They believed (aorist indicative, punctiliar action) on Jesus, but he refused to believe in them (imperfect indicative of the same verb, *pisteuo*).

It was in this critical atmosphere at the passover that Nicodemus, the Pharisee and member of the Sanhedrin, paid Jesus a secret visit by night, probably to his tent on the Mount of Olives. It required some courage at such a time when the men of his class had already taken an open stand against Jesus as an ignorant upstart and deceiver for a man like Nicodemus to show any interest in him. He did not wish to lose caste with his colleagues in the Sanhedrin. He did not court controversy. He was evidently a shy man as many scholars are. Nicodemus was a scholar in Jewish lore, probably a graduate of the theological school of Hillel in Jerusalem. It has often required courage in schools of learning for a scholar to take an open and active interest in Christ and in Christianity. There is fear of one's cult that is very real to-day. The situation in the schools of America is very much better than it was a hundred or more years ago among teachers and students. There are some teachers in our schools who take pleasure in ridiculing the deity of Christ and organized church life. But there have always been many scholars, more now than ever, who rejoice in glad and full worship of Jesus as Lord and Savior. School life brings a great many problems for the intellect and the soul. It is true that Nicodemus came to Jesus by night, but he came. He felt that Jesus had something that he did not possess and that he wanted. Nicodemus had watched the work of Jesus in Jerusalem and had deliberately made up his mind independently in spite of the prejudice against Jesus that he had the approval of God on his work.

It is possible that John, the author of the Fourth Gospel, was present and heard the conversation between Nicodemus and Jesus. Nicodemus explained why he had come: "Rabbi, I know (he says 'we,' probably literary plural, and he calls him 'rabbi' by courtesy, though Jesus was not a school man) that you have come from God as a teacher (a marvelous admission from the Jewish rabbi) ; for no one is able to go on doing (present infinitive *poiein*) these signs which you are doing, unless God be with him." It was not just one miracle, but a great many that Nicodemus had tested himself. The proof to Nicodemus was conclusive that Jesus wrought these signs by the power of God. Later the Pharisees will suggest that Jesus was in league with Beelzebub and wrought his miracles by the power of the devil. But even then they did not deny the reality of the cures. The signs merely enraged the enemies of Jesus who had already prejudiced the case against him. But Nicodemus was a Pharisee who did his own thinking and was anxious to be fair. He was not opposed to new truth just because it disturbed the equilibrium of his traditional theology. He wanted to get at the facts and so came to Jesus instead of merely listening to the misconceptions circulated about him and his work. If sceptics to-day would only go to Christ himself, with the right attitude of heart, they would find fresh light for many problems.

The answer of Jesus touches the real difficulty of Nicodemus of which he was not himself aware. As a Pharisee Nicodemus was looking for a political Kingdom under a political Messiah. But Jesus proclaimed a spiritual Kingdom, the reign of God in the heart that began with a new birth. "Verily, verily, I tell you, unless one be born again (or from above), he is not able to see (get to see, ingressive aorist infinitive) the Kingdom of God." But this idea was a shock to Nicodemus. He did not see that Jesus was speaking of a different sort of Kingdom and hence he thought only of physical birth when Jesus spoke of being born again or from above. There is no one so hard to teach as the man whose mind is already filled with error. So Nicodemus made a reply that seems stupid to us, but was intensely real to him: "How can a man be born when he is old? Is he able (surely not) to enter a second time into the womb of his mother and be born?" The gulf between Nicodemus and Jesus seems impassable. It is a tragedy to see a choice mind like that of Nicodemus befogged by error so patent.

But Jesus perseveres with patience and persistence. He tries a new form of his statement. Pure spiritual birth like the new birth was plainly outside of the range of the mind of Nicodemus. He was a Pharisee and used to symbolism in rites and ceremonies. Hence Jesus put the thing in a way that seems to have helped Nicodemus, though it has raised a fresh problem for modern men: "Verily, verily I tell you, unless one be born of water and of the Spirit, he is not able to enter the Kingdom of God. That which is born of the flesh is flesh, and that which is born of the Spirit is spirit. Do not wonder that I said to you, 'You must be born again.' The wind blows where it wills, and you hear the sound of it, but you do not know whence it comes and where it goes. So is every one who is born of the Spirit." We are puzzled by the placing of "water" here before "Spirit" as a necessity to entering the Kingdom of God. But Nicodemus was troubled about "Spirit." He was thinking only of the physical birth. On the whole it is probable that by "water" Jesus refers to baptism. John the Baptist preached repentance and practiced the baptism of those who confessed their sins. When Jesus repeats the point to Nicodemus he drops any mention of water: "You must be born again." This looks as if it was mentioned once in order to help Nicodemus understand that Jesus referred to spiritual birth as symbolized by baptism, not that baptism was essential to the new birth. Some, indeed, take "water" here to refer to the physical birth, since Jesus goes on to explain the two kinds of birth, physical and spiritual. In that case there would be no reference to baptism at all. Clearly it is the necessity of the new birth alone that Jesus is explaining to Nicodemus. Jesus tries to help Nicodemus again about the nature of the new birth of the Spirit by using the word for spirit (*pneuma*) in its original sense of wind with all its mystery of movement. Surely Nicodemus would now be able to grasp the idea of Jesus.

But Nicodemus could only make the rather dazed reply: "How can these things come to pass?" It was clearly beyond his intellectual horizon. So Jesus turns on Nicodemus with a rather sharp retort, but with the utmost kindness: "Are you the teacher of Israel and yet you do not know these things?" That question would cut to the quick, but Jesus meant that it should cut because the mind of Nicodemus with all his candor and sincerity seemed incapable of grasping spiritual truth. He was bound still in the clasp of Pharisaic formalism and ceremonialism. Jesus gave Nicodemus this electric jolt to shake him free if possible. So Jesus went on: "Verily, verily I tell you that I am speaking what I know (literary plural) and I am bearing witness to what I have seen, and yet you do not accept my witness." Here Jesus claims experimental knowledge concerning the spiritual realm. That is a scientific method and it should have appealed to a scholar like Nicodemus. But Jesus proceeded: "If I told you the earthly things and you do not believe, how will you believe if I tell you the heavenly things?" The new birth belongs to "the earthly things," taking place here on earth. "The heavenly things" include the Incarnation, the Atoning Death of Christ, God's redemptive love and grace (3:13–17). There was no reply from Nicodemus. It is not clear precisely where the words of Jesus cease and where the Evangelist goes on with his narrative. But evidently Nicodemus felt that he had gone into water beyond his depth. He was silenced, but apparently not yet convinced. Incredulity still held him fast. He could not reconcile the things that Jesus had said with his theological system. It would require time for Nicodemus to think through the problems raised by his interview with Jesus. One can imagine Nicodemus cautiously going away in the dark with many a shy glance to see if any one had observed his presence at the tent of the Rabbi from Nazareth.

It is probably a year and a half before we have a further note about Nicodemus in John's Gospel. It is at the feast of tabernacles just six months before the end of Christ's ministry when he appears in Jerusalem after a considerable absence. Jesus was there at a feast mentioned in John 5:1 and the feeling against him rose to fever heat and the Jewish leaders actually tried to kill him because he not only violated their rules about the Sabbath, but he actually made himself equal with God (John 5:18). Hence he remained away from Jerusalem. But now he did come and found the people divided in sentiment, though the friends of Jesus were awed through fear of the Sanhedrin (John 7:13). Finally the Sanhedrin sent officers to arrest Jesus and bring him before the body for trial (7:32). But, when they came, they did not bring Jesus. In amazement the Pharisees asked: "Why did you not bring him?" (7:45).

The officers, Roman soldiers as they were, calmly replied: "Never man spoke like this man" (7:46). Then it was that the Pharisees lost all control of themselves and said to the Roman officers: "Have you also gone astray? Did any one of the rulers believe on him or of the Pharisees? But this crowd that do not know the law are accursed." It would be hard to find elsewhere so much venom in so few words. They shouted their scorn at Roman officers being led off by an ignorant upstart from Galilee. Nobody but the *am-ha-aretz* (like our "clod-hoppers" or uncouth backwoodsmen) had followed Jesus. Not a single one of the leading Pharisees or rulers had believed on him. This last statement was an unconscious challenge to Nicodemus who had kept his secret well. He had slowly come closer to faith in Jesus as the Messiah, though he had taken no public stand for Christ. But manifestly Nicodemus winced under the words that not one of the rulers or of the Pharisees believed on Jesus. Nicodemus was both a Pharisee and a ruler and now he did secretly believe on him. Was he ready to take an open stand in the Sanhedrin for Jesus and own him as the Messiah of promise? Not that and not yet. He knew that, if he did, he would be ostracized and driven from the Sanhedrin. Later John will say: "Nevertheless, however, many of the rulers did believe (aorist tense) on him, but because of the Pharisees would not confess (imperfect tense) him that they might not become outcasts from the synagogue, for they loved the glory of men more than the glory of God"

(John 12:42-3). These are stinging words, it is true, but they correctly describe the attitude of men of the official class whose judgment was convinced that Jesus was the Messiah, though they lacked the courage to say so and pay the price of such courage. The lines were clearly and sharply drawn against Jesus in Jerusalem. What was Nicodemus to do? What did he do? He was unwilling to remain silent. He was afraid to avow his faith. He took a middle course. He would at least stand up for the legal rights of Jesus as he would for those of any man. So he ventured to raise a point of law. He put it clearly and sharply and all saw at once the bearing of the point: "Does our law condemn the man except it first hear from him and get knowledge of (ingressive aorist) what he is doing?" The very form of the question expects the negative answer. It was a sound legal principle and absolutely unanswerable. No one tried to answer it. Instead of that the other members of the Sanhedrin stormed at Nicodemus: "Are you also of Galilee? Search and see that no prophet comes out of Galilee." They passed by the matter of common justice mentioned by Nicodemus and made a personal thrust at him. They sneer at him as a mere ignorant Galilean like the mob and actually say that no prophet comes out of Galilee, an obvious untruth. But religious hatred knows no bounds. Nicodemus apparently lapsed into silence. He had cleared his conscience and had made himself a marked man. He would be under suspicion, though he kept his place in the Sanhedrin by keeping still as before.

Nicodemus is not heard from again till Jesus is dead upon the Cross. Two members of the Sanhedrin come forward late Friday afternoon to give decent burial to the body of Jesus. Joseph of Arimathea had been a secret disciple "because of fear of the Jews" (John 19:38). He was a rich man with a new tomb and he had not consented to the dreadful deed of the Sanhedrin (Luke 23:51). He asked Pilate for the body of Jesus that it might not be buried in the potters' field. Then it was that Nicodemus, another secret disciple in the Sanhedrin, stepped forward and took his stand by the side of Joseph of Arimathea. He brought a mixture of myrrh and aloes. These two men of scholarship and wealth now in the hour of deepest shame for Jesus openly avowed their love for him and confidence in him. How they felt now about his claims to be the Messiah we do not know. But they at least took up their cross when the apostles had fled. They gave Jesus dignified and honorable burial in Joseph's new tomb to the north of Jerusalem in the garden (John 19:41). The tomb was hewn out of a rock (Mark 15:46) and may have been the one now shown there near Gordon's Calvary. They rolled a great stone against the door of the tomb and went their way (Matt. 27:60). One may wonder if Nicodemus did not have many a pang in his heart that he had waited so long to take an open stand for Jesus at whatever cost.

At any rate it was some comfort to make small amends for his tardy confession by what he had now done. There are always those who will lay flowers on the coffin who gave none during life. And yet we must not be too harsh in our judgments of men. God sees the whole and we see only a part. Nicodemus was in a difficult place as many a man is to-day. He did at last show his colors for Christ.

CHAPTER II

ANDREW THE MAN OF DECISION

It is the Fourth Gospel that tells most about Andrew, though we catch glimpses of him also in the Synoptic Gospels. He is not one of the outstanding figures among the twelve apostles, but he is very far from being a figurehead. He is a good specimen of the man of average gifts who had more than ordinary energy and who uses what gifts he has steadily and zealously. He comes from Bethsaida of Galilee and has a Greek name like Philip. The Greek language was spoken in Galilee as well as Aramaic and this fact may account in part for his name. He was not a Greek, for he was the brother of Simon Peter (Cephas). The name means "manly" from *aner*. We have the same proper name in English as that of Dr. Basil Manly, one of the first professors in the Southern Baptist Theological Seminary. It is clear that Andrew deserved his name and lived up to it. His father's name was John. He was engaged in the fishing business in Capernaum with his brother Simon and the brothers James and John. They were partners together and had hired men to help in the work. There must have been a regularly organized company including Zebedee the father

13

of James and John. In Capernaum Andrew lived with his brother Simon who was married (Mark 1:29).

HE FELT THE PULL OF JOHN'S MISSION

Andrew was attracted to Bethany beyond Jordan by the preaching of John the Baptist as so many others had been. It is even possible that Andrew and Simon came with the crowd that included Philip of Bethsaida and Nathanael of Cana. These towns were near to Nazareth and one may wonder if Jesus, the carpenter of Nazareth, came along with the same caravan. At any rate they are all at Bethany beyond Jordan at the same time when John the Baptist bears his remarkable and stirring witness to the Messiahship of Jesus on two successive days as the Lamb of God that takes away the sin of the world and as the Son of God (John 1:29–51). Andrew along with the rest felt the pull of John's mission and message. He had come close to the Baptist on one of the days at Bethany, so close that he could hear distinctly the Baptist's striking testimony to Jesus as the Messiah.

Andrew has the further distinction of being the first one who followed Jesus as Messiah. That is honor enough for any man. To be sure, the Baptist had done so, but that is different. The Baptist was the forerunner and had proclaimed the coming of the Messiah before he saw Jesus on the banks of the Jordan. He had recognized Jesus and had bap-

tized him and now he had publicly identified Him
as the Messiah after denying to the committee from
the Sanhedrin that he himself was the Messiah.
But there was as yet no rush of the people after
Jesus. The Baptist said: "In the midst of you
stands one whom you know not, one coming after
me, the latchet of whose sandal I am not worthy
to untie" (John 1:26). But where was He? One
day Andrew and another of John's disciples, who
was apparently John the brother of James, saw
John the Baptist point to Jesus of Nazareth with
a look of rapture and of longing that sent Andrew
and John after Jesus. It was a new experience for
Jesus and He turned sharply upon Andrew and
John and demanded what they wanted. The new
followers wanted further conversation, not controversy, and Jesus invited them to come and see
Him in His stopping-place at Bethany. It was a
memorable occasion, for they spent the day with
Jesus from ten o'clock in the morning (Roman
time), all that day (accusative case in the Greek,
extent of time). Andrew decided quickly to act
on the words of the Baptist and John joined him.
This quick decision is characteristic of Andrew.
If the Baptist meant what he said, the thing to
do was to leave the Baptist and go to Jesus.

HE STARTED THE PROCESSION OF THE CENTURIES

That is the way the testimony of the Baptist
struck the practical Andrew. He had come from
Galilee to see and hear the Baptist whose fame

had filled all the land. And now the Baptist had
sent him after one from Nazareth which is not
far from Bethsaida, his own town. To many this
would have been an insuperable difficulty as it
was a stumbling block to Nathanael (John 1:46).
Probably Andrew did not know at the moment
who Jesus was nor that He came from Nazareth.
He acted solely on the enthusiastic witness of the
Baptist whose disciple he had already become. But
that day with Jesus in his tent or in his khan
opened a new world to Andrew. He gave Jesus his
whole heart. The Baptist was right as Andrew now
knew by personal experience. Andrew had led the
way along the path that millions were to travel
in the coming ages, the "Jesus road" as the Indians
call it now. Andrew took the Baptist at his word
and started the procession of the centuries. In
every movement some one is the first to act, the
quickest to respond, to take the decisive step, to
cross the Rubicon.

But Andrew also is the first who won another
to Jesus as Messiah. He not simply is the first
who did it, but he did it as the first thing after
his own conviction that Jesus was the Messiah.
The correct text is *proton* which means the first
thing that he did, but some manuscripts read
protos, which would mean that he was the first
who did a thing like this, probably implying that
John did it also with his own brother James, but
after Andrew saw Simon. Both things are true
of Andrew. He was the first to win a convert and
he did it before he did anything else. It is note-

worthy also that his first convert was his brother Simon. There are proverbial obstacles in the way of spiritual approach to those who are kin to us or who are closely connected by business ties. But Andrew did not hesitate a moment. It was a startling piece of news that he had to tell to Simon and he made it short: "We have found the Messiah." The Baptist had raised expectations on every hand about the Messiah, but he had not pointed Him out to the people at large. Andrew and John had been fortunate enough to catch the Baptist in the act of identifying Jesus as the Messiah. Now their own experience confirmed the witness of the Baptist. It was momentous, if true. But was it true? Simon was a disciple of the Baptist, but he had not seen Jesus and he was sceptical, no doubt, though he knew that the Baptist had announced that the Messiah was at hand.

IT WAS NOT EASY

It was probably not easy for Andrew to get Simon to come to see Jesus. He was evidently unable to convince him without doing so. He was too wise to risk it all on argument. Somehow he brought Simon to Jesus. That was more than half the battle. Andrew was acting again on his own initiative. He was blazing a new trail. He was learning how to lead his own brother into the love and knowledge of Jesus Christ. He had no rules to go by and no teacher to guide him. But he won his man to Christ. If Andrew had done nothing

else in his life than this one act, he would deserve
the gratitude of Christians through all the ages.
He brought Simon to Jesus and opened the way
for the wonderful career of the man who, after
the death of Jesus, sprang to the front as the
leader of the apostles and who has left such a
deep mark upon the history of Christianity. The
greatest act of many a life is just this thing, to
win one great soul to Christ. It is practically always done by personal work and it is work that
any one can do. Andrew at this time was just a
layman, not a preacher.

So Andrew became a disciple of Jesus. Disciple
means learner under a teacher. He was not yet
one of the twelve apostles, but he was apparently
with Jesus at the wedding at Cana (John 2:2),
in Capernaum for a brief space (John 2:12), at
the first passover in Jerusalem (John 2:13, 17).
Like the other disciples he saw at Cana the mani-
festation of the glory of Jesus in His first miracle
that increased their faith. He saw the first clash
of Jesus with the Jerusalem ecclesiastics and recalled with the other disciples the saying of the
Psalmist (69:10) : "The zeal of thine house shall
eat me up." But, also like the rest, he did not comprehend what Jesus meant by raising "this temple
in three days" till after the resurrection of Jesus
(John 2:22). But these early days of the kingdom
of God on earth were wondrous to Andrew who
had had his share in starting the ball to rolling.
He may not have met Nicodemus, but he did wonder with the others that Jesus would talk in public

with a woman at Sychar in Samaria (John 4:27) and at the strange passion for souls that took away the hunger of the body (4:32).

THE CALL TO SERVICE

But Andrew had not yet given up his business as a fisherman. It was not until Jesus saw the two pairs of brothers washing their nets by the Sea of Galilee that He gave them a definite call to give up their business and to devote their time exclusively to His service, to the work of winning souls: "Come ye after me, and I will make you to become fishers of men" (Mark 1:17). That call has come to many laymen since Jesus invited Andrew and Simon, James and John, to stop making money and to make men. So "they left all and followed him" as learners and preachers, not yet as apostles in the technical sense. Soon Andrew, who lived with Simon and his family in Capernaum (Mark 1:29) saw ample proof of the power of Jesus in the very home where he lived. The mother-in-law of Simon was healed of a fever and that evening at sunset "all the city was gathered at the door" (Mark 1:33) of Andrew's house to see Jesus heal the procession of the sick as they passed by. Andrew probably shared in the perplexity of Peter early next morning when the crowds came again and found Jesus gone to a desert place to pray. It is plain that Andrew's part in the work was quiet. He saw Jesus defy the Pharisees from Jerusalem when He healed the paralytic let down through the roof of the house of Andrew and Peter (Mark 2:2).

It is small wonder that Andrew was included in the number of the twelve apostles carefully and prayerfully chosen by Jesus. He had already proven his worth to the cause of Christ. In the four lists of the twelve Andrew always appears in the first four. Mark's Gospel and Acts put him in the fourth place, while Matthew and Luke name him second just after Simon Peter. It was soon plain to all that Simon was more gifted than his older brother Andrew who yet had brought Simon to Jesus. There is nowhere a trace of jealousy on the part of Andrew toward Simon. He probably knew the weaknesses of Simon only too well as brothers always do, but he found joy in the prominence and leadership of Simon, and kept on doing his humble work.

A PRACTICAL TURN OF MIND

But it was not work that was useless or that any one could do. When the disciples propose to Jesus that he send the multitudes away on the slopes near Bethsaida Julias, Jesus proposes to Philip that something be done to feed them. Philip was at a loss as were the rest except Andrew who with his practical turn of mind made the suggestion to Jesus about the lad with five barley loaves and two fishes (John 6:8f.). The suggestion seemed like a forlorn hope even to Andrew, but the point is that Andrew made it. He would not give up without giving Jesus all the facts. Jesus at once took hold of the suggestion of Andrew and made it the starting point for working the wonderful miracle of feeding the five thousand. Andrew stands in clear light here. It is just the man like Andrew, more often a woman, who sees a little thing that can be done that turns the scale. To be sure, Andrew did not work the miracle. Jesus has all the glory for that, but Andrew found the boy who had the few loaves and fishes that the Master Workman used.

WISDOM FOR AN EMERGENCY

Once again Philip shows his estimate of Andrew as a man of wisdom for an emergency. It was the last week of the public ministry in Jerusalem, on Monday, the day after the triumphal entry. Jesus is in the Temple teaching when some Greeks, who have come up to worship at the feast of the Passover, possibly God-fearers if not proselytes, approach Philip with a desire to meet Jesus of whom all at the feast are now speaking: "Sir, we desire to see Jesus." Now Jesus is just at hand, but Philip does not introduce the Greeks to Jesus, as we should do to-day with strangers who desire to meet the preacher. Instead of that Philip consults Andrew (John 12:22) as the one most likely to help him with light on this problem of bringing Greeks to Jesus. One wonders if Philip had not seen Jesus at work in Phoenicia when the Syro-Phoenician woman won her case with Jesus and

when in Decapolis among the Greeks Jesus
wrought miracles. But this is in Jerusalem right
in the midst of the Temple. The middle wall of
partition rises before Philip and between him and
the Greeks as it rose before Simon Peter later on
the house-top in Joppa (Acts 10). The problem
was too great for Philip and it was too great for
Andrew. So both Andrew and Philip come and
tell Jesus, but apparently do not bring the Greeks.
Andrew's wisdom failed Philip on this occasion.
It was not equal to the task of removing race and
religious prejudice. Race hatred and national
jealousy and religious rivalry to-day create acute
problems that tax the wisdom of the world. No
one has understood this matter so profoundly as
Jesus whose heart was so greatly agitated by the
dilemma of Andrew and Philip. Jesus knew that
only His Cross could break down the wall of prejudice between Jew and Greek. What Andrew and
Philip thought of the agitation of Jesus we do
not know nor what the Greeks understood by the
tragic words of Jesus: "And I, if I be lifted up
from the earth, will draw all men unto myself."
But we know to-day that nothing but the love of
Christ can make men of many nations love each
other and be just toward all.

THE LAST WE HEAR OF HIM

Andrew appears only once more by name in the
Gospels. It is on the Mount of Olives after Jesus
had, as they passed out of the Temple for the last

time, foretold the destruction of the wonderful building of whose beauty they had spoken to Jesus. The disciples evidently talked about these strange words as they passed on out of the gate and through the valley of Jehoshaphat and up the slope of the Mount of Olives. When Jesus sat down on the summit of the mountain, "Peter and James and John and Andrew" asked Jesus privately the meaning of his language (Mark 13:3f.). Here Andrew is mentioned last in the list of four by Mark. Whether Mark obtained his information in chapter 13 (the "Little Apocalypse") from Peter is not known. But no special significance need to be attached to the position of Andrew's name. He had evidently joined in the discussion on the way up the mountain.

There are many legends in the apocryphal writings about Andrew, all of which will be passed by in our picture. He is represented as preaching in Bithynia, in Scythia, in Greece, among the Kurds. There is an apocryphal "Acts of St. Andrew."

The only item of real value is the statement in the *Muratorian Fragment* which says: "The Fourth Gospel was written by one of the disciples. When his fellow-disciples and bishops urgently pressed him, he said: 'Fast with me for three days, and let us tell one another any revelation which may be made to us, either for or against.' On the same night it was revealed to Andrew, one of the apostles, that John should relate all in his own name, and that all should review." Whether this incident is true or not, it is in harmony with what we know of the character and work of Andrew.

The story is that he was crucified in Achaia by the proconsul Eges whose wife had been estranged from him by the preaching of Andrew. Part of the cross of Andrew is now shown in Rome for those who can believe it to be genuine. A piece of his arm is reported to be in Scotland so that he is the patron saint of Scotland.

But the numerous legends cannot destroy the clearness and force of the picture of this noble man who was the very first to take a stand for Jesus as the Christ.

CHAPTER III

HEROD THE GREAT PERVERT, AS PRESENTED IN THE GOSPEL OF MATTHEW

THE interest of New Testament students in Herod the Great grows primarily out of the fact that Jesus was born in Bethlehem before his death in B. C. 4. Luke expressly states that the angel Gabriel appeared to Zacharias "in the days of Herod, King of Judea" (Luke 1:5). He does not say in so many words that Herod was still reigning when Jesus was born, but he implies it (Luke 2:1-4).

But in Matthew 2:1-23 Herod cuts quite a figure in the narrative concerning the birth of Jesus. The picture here drawn of Herod the King of Judea fits in precisely with the extended account of this ruler in Josephus, *Antiquities,* Books xiv-xvii. We are not concerned in this article to tell the whole story of Herod the Great, "Herod the Great in Sin" as Amelie Rives calls him in *"Herod and Mariamne,"* save as that story throws light on his conduct about the birth of Jesus.

Herod has had champions ever since Nicolaus of Damascus, whose extensive eulogy contributed so much to the pages of Josephus. The Emperor Augustus thought well of him for the most part and once planned to enlarge his domain since he was a man of such big soul. But in the end he lost caste with Augustus.

See how Matthew presents Herod when he hears of the birth of the new King of the Jews from the wise men from the east: "And when Herod the king heard it, he was troubled, and all Jerusalem with him" (Matt. 2:3). Books xvi and xvii of the *Antiquities* of Josephus throw a tragic light on these simple words. The third period of Herod's career, his decline and death, is told here (B. C. 19–4). Herod's two sons by Mariamne (Alexander and Aristobulus) were the heirs to the throne as belonging to the Maccabean line. Mariamne was the granddaughter of Hyrcanus II. The return of these two sons from Rome, where they had been sent to mingle in court circles, was the occasion of jealousy on the part of Salome, Herod's sister, who had an intense dislike for the Maccabees. Antipater, Herod's son by Doris, joined in the schemings that led finally to the death of both Alexander and Aristobulus. Antipater was named successor, but grew impatient and acually plotted to get Herod out of the way that he might get the throne the sooner. As a result, he was thrown into prison and finally put to death. Herod, before the death of Antipater, had made Antipas, his son by Malthace, his heir. It was apparently at this juncture, before the death of Antipater, that the visit of the Wise Men so disturbed the old and irritable tyrant. The idea of a new king, not one of his sons, upset Herod the Great very thoroughly. All Jerusalem was likewise disturbed.

The city was apprehensive about fresh manifestations of cruelty on the part of Herod the
Great. The Roman Emperor and judges had
winked at the death of the two sons by Mariamne
(Alexander and Aristobulus). Augustus had made
his famous pun on the death of these young men:
"I would rather be Herod's hog than his son"
(his *hus* than his *huios*). But that was not the
beginning of Herod's cruelty. He had obtained
Antony's consent to the death of the Maccabean
Antigonus whom the Parthians had set up as
king and high priest. He had put to death forty-
five of the leaders in the Sanhedrin, sparing Pollio
and Sameas. He had secured the drowning of the
young high priest Aristobulus, the brother of
Mariamne, grand-daughter of Hyrcanus II whom
he married to consolidate his hold on the throne
and the Jewish people. He had finally caught the
aged Hyrcanus in a plot with the Arabians and
secured his death. By the help of his sister, Salome,
he had his beloved wife Mariamne put to death on
trumped-up charges. He almost lost his mind for
grief after the death of Mariamne. Then Alexandra, the mother of Mariamne, was put to death.
The sons of Baba were likewise slain at the demand
of Salome, to get the Maccabean adherents out of
the way. Salome gratified her spite against her
own husband, Costobar, by his divorce and then
death. These family disturbances kept the court
circles in Jerusalem in a turmoil and the people
generally on the *qui vive*. Nobody knew what

Herod was likely to do when in one of his tan-
trums over family affairs. Josephus several times
facetiously says that about this time Herod's
family affairs grew worse and worse. There was
suspicion on every side and nobody trusted anybody. Small wonder, therefore, that all Jerusalem
was troubled over the new disturbance in the mood
of Herod the Great, one of the most whimsical and
cruel and selfish tyrants of all time.

Herod first "gathered together all the chief
priests and scribes of the people" and "inquired
of them where the Christ should be born" (Matt.
2:4). He probably knew something of the Messianic
expectation of the Jewish people, but had apparently taken no personal interest in the matter.
He was an Idumean by birth and a nominal Jew
since the Idumeans had been conquered by John
Hyrcanus I. But he was actually without religious
interest or concern. His present agitation was not
due to personal interest in the birth of the Jewish
Messiah, but purely to the peril to his own wishes
about his successor. The appeal to the Jewish
ecclesiastical leaders was to secure information
for his own conduct, not with a view to helping
the wise men in their worship of the Messiah.

The sly shrewdness of Herod about the request
of the wise men is in precise accord with his conduct concerning the reports about the various
victims of his jealous rage. "Then Herod privily
called the wise men, and learned of them carefully what time the star appeared" (Matt. 2:7). He
appeared on the surface to approve of the aim

of the wise men and to desire to coöperate with them, though he had already given way to his violent emotions among the members of the household and court circles. "And he sent them to Bethlehem and said, Go and search out carefully concerning the young child; and when ye have found him, bring me word, that I also may come and worship him" (Matt. 2:8). There is an obvious untruth in the words of Herod. He had not the remotest idea of worshiping the Babe in Bethlehem if the wise men succeeded in finding the Messiah there according to Micah's prophecy. But he wished the wise men to think so and to make a report to him of the result of their search in order that he might then know how to proceed. Josephus gives ample proof of like duplicity on the part of Herod concerning the death of young Aristobulus and how Alexandra, the mother, was not deceived by reports of the "accidental" drowning of her son nor by the hypocritical tears of Herod and the grand funeral. So also Mariamne was not deceived by the double-dealing of Herod in his orders to have her put to death if he was not spared by Antony and then by Octavius. Matthew leaves us to infer that the wise men from the east, strangers to Palestine and to Herod, might have fallen into Herod's trap if they had not been "warned of God in a dream that they should not return to Herod" (Matt. 2:12). They may, to be sure, have heard something about the jealousy and cruelty of Herod's character since all Jerusalem was troubled. The dream would simply confirm the vague fears already entertained. At any rate "they departed into their own country another way," and Herod was left to draw his own conclusions about the young Messiah whether he was really in Bethlehem or not.

Joseph also probably was only too familiar with the reputation of Herod the Great. It is likely that the wise men told Joseph of the inquiry and command of Herod and of the dream which led them to leave Jerusalem and Herod to one side on their return home. At any rate the dream that came to Joseph was definite with a clear picture of the purpose of Herod: "Arise and take the young child and his mother, and flee into Egypt, and be thou there until I tell thee: for Herod will seek the young child to destroy him" (Matt. 2:13). There was no disobeying a clear command like that, even in a dream sent by God. It fell in precisely with all that was known of the imperious will of Herod who was unwilling to brook a rival even after his death. It began to look to Herod as if all his plans might go awry and no one of his sons might succeed him. Joseph lost no time in getting out of Herod's way with Mary and Jesus. He remained in Egypt with his precious charge till the death of Herod (Matt. 2:14). Under the circumstances that was only common prudence, but Joseph had direct revelation from God to strengthen his purpose.

But Matthew notes that the execution of the warning was none too soon, for Herod was not long in seeing that he had been outwitted by the wise men. A trickster is always angry when his

trickery fails to work. "Then Herod, when he saw
that he was mocked of the wise men, was exceeding wroth" (Matt. 2:16). The palace, no doubt,
was a dangerous place even for the inmates who
had learned how to avoid Herod in a time like
this. He knew by intuition that the wise men had
somehow seen through his suave phrases and had
purposely avoided making a report to him concerning their search for the young Messiah. It
might be possible, to be sure, that they had not
succeeded in finding him. But then again they may
have been unwilling to tell him because they had
learned something of his conduct towards members
of his own family. Herod was not willing to take
any chances about so important a matter which
might mean the thwarting of his own will. He did
not know that a pretender to the throne had been
born in Bethlehem, let alone the name of such a
child there. It still seems incredible to some modern men that on mere suspicion Herod should
have done so cruel a thing, for he "sent forth, and
slew all the male children that were in Bethlehem,
and in all the borders thereof, from two years old
and under, according to the time which he had
carefully learned of the wise men" (Matt. 2:16).
He felt sure that the babe was not over two years
old, though exactly how old he did not know. Hence
he gave a blanket order for the slaughter of all
the little boys as old as two years. We have no
means of knowing the precise number that were
slain, probably about twenty. The size of the community would certainly call for that number of in-

fant boys. This slaughter of the innocent little boys would be incredible in the lives of most tyrants and criminals, but it causes no jar to one familiar with the life of Herod the Great as told by Josephus. It is objected by some writers that the account in Matthew's Gospel lacks confirmation by Josephus. The reply to that criticism is that this incident was a small item in the long life of Herod and had no particular interest to Josephus. What Josephus does tell about Herod makes the narration by Matthew highly credible. The talk about this latest exhibition of cruelty on the part of Herod would soon die down. The children that were put to death were probably for the most part in the homes of more or less obscure people who were not considered to have any particular rights by the king. It is revolting to us to think of the willful murder by a king of these helpless and harmless babies who lost their lives for the sake of and, in a sense, in the place of the Babe Jesus who had been taken away to Egypt. They were put to death because of the insane jealousy and anger of Herod about the birth of the Messiah in Bethlehem as Herod feared, according to the prophecy of Micah and the inquiry of the wise men. Probably Herod soon forgot the slaying of these little boys as too small a matter to occupy the thoughts of a king.

He was in serious trouble himself. He had a loathsome disease and sought in vain the benefit of the healing waters of Callirhoe. It is a pitiful picture that Josephus draws of the closing days of

the famous king of the Jews. He actually tried
to kill himself in order to get out of his misery.
He was determined that he should be mourned at
his funeral and seemed to know that nobody really
loved him, not even Salome, his sister who had
made him gratify her own hatreds and prejudices.
He gave command that a number of prominent
men should be slain in the event of his death in
order that there would certainly be general mourning in Jerusalem. His directions concerning a
splendid display at his funeral were carried out
very strictly. But there was no real grief at his
departure. He was despised alike by his own family
and by the Jewish people who felt that his successor could not be any worse than he had been.

The death of Herod the Great was B. C. 4 and
gives the proof that the birth of Jesus was before
that date. Joseph at once faced the problem of
returning to Palestine. He had feared to risk a
return while Herod was alive because his agents
might find it out and seek to kill the child Jesus.
"But when Herod was dead, behold, an angel of
the Lord appears in a dream to Joseph in Egypt,
saying, Arise and take the young child and his
mother, and go into the land of Israel; for they
are dead that sought the young child's life" (Matt.
2:20). Only Herod had died, so far as we know,
though it is possible that some of the assassins
sent by Herod to Bethlehem may have died also.
It is more likely, however, that the plural "they"
means only Herod who is referred to in this general way. The way now was open for the return.

So "he arose and took the young child and his mother, and came into the land of Israel" (Matt. 2:21). The first interest of the state authorities in the birth and life of Jesus was active hostility. Another Herod, Agrippa I, will later put James, the brother of John, to death and imprison Simon Peter (Acts 12:1). It has not been easy for the state to understand how to treat Christianity fairly. Real religious liberty has come at last in the United States and is needed by all the world.

Once back in Palestine Joseph found that Herod had changed his will again before he died. When Joseph fled from Bethlehem, the successor was to be Herod Antipas. "But when he heard that Archelaus was reigning over Judea in the room of his father, he was afraid to go thither; and being warned of God in a dream, he withdrew into the parts of Galilee, and came and dwelt in a city called Nazareth" (Matt. 2:22–3). We find in Josephus that at the last Herod had changed his will once more in a fit of uneasiness. No one of his sons was to get the whole kingdom as had been expected. All the schemings were in vain after all. Alexander and Aristobulus and Antipater were dead. Under the new will Archelaus, his son by Malthace, was to get Idumea, Judea and Samaria with the title of Ethnarch, while Herod Antipas, another son by Malthace, was to be Tetrarch of Galilee and Perea, and Herod Philip, his son by Cleopatra, of Jerusalem, was to be Tetrarch of Iturea and Trachonitis. It is plain that Joseph preferred Herod Antipas to Archelaus. The outcome showed the wisdom of Joseph, for Archelaus turned out to be the worst of Herod's sons, now that Antipater was dead. Joseph "was afraid to go thither" to Bethlehem under the rule of Archelaus. He was evidently apprehensive lest Archelaus carry out the plan of Herod the Great and slay the child Jesus on his return to Bethlehem. This fear was confirmed by the warning in a dream. One may wonder why Joseph planned to go back to Bethlehem instead of to Nazareth where he had his home and his business. It may be that Joseph felt it was proper for the Messiah to be reared in Bethlehem where he was born and where David had lived as a youth. In Bethlehem also no question would be raised by gossip about the birth of Jesus and the recent marriage to Mary. In the nature of the case Joseph and Mary could not tell the neighbors in Nazareth what the angel Gabriel had told them. But the change of rulers made Joseph and Mary decide to take no risk about the life of the child. It was far better to endure the wagging tongues of neighbors than to place the life of the child Jesus in jeopardy in Bethlehem.

It is surprising to see what a part the wickedness of Herod and his family played in the early events in the life of Jesus as recorded in the Gospel of Matthew. Because of Herod's jealous fears the little male children of Bethlehem were slain, the child Jesus was taken to Egypt and kept there till the death of the tyrant. Because of the character of Archelaus Jesus lived in Nazareth instead of Bethlehem and was called a Nazarene.

Archelaus is called king by Matthew, 2:22, in popular parlance, though he did not actually obtain the title. His title as Ethnarch was challenged by Salome and Herod Antipas. Salome failed in her effort to upset Herod's will and Archelaus became Ethnarch with the promise of the higher title in case of good behavior. But he did not make good and in ten years was recalled and Roman procurators ruled the province of Judea. There is little doubt that Jesus refers to the expedition of Archelaus to obtain the kingdom in the parable of the pounds in Luke 19.

It is plain that the picture of Herod the Great given in the Gospel of Matthew is of a piece with that drawn at length by Josephus. He was a selfish and a cruel man who really cared little for others save as they contributed to his own pleasure. He tried in a frantic manner to win the favor of the Jews by gifts in time of famine and by erecting fine buildings, especially the new temple in Jerusalem. The people distrusted his plans about this and would only agree to the tearing down of any portion when Herod was ready to replace it. The work, begun in B. C. 20, was not really completed till A. D. 65, but it bore Herod's name and was a very wonderful structure.

Herod was a Hellenist in his sympathies and tastes and introduced Greek games and built theaters and places for gymnastic exercises. As a result, he was disliked and distrusted by the Pharisees. He angered the Jews also by rebuilding Samaria which he called Sebaste. He made Cæsarea

so attractive that the Romans made it the political
capital of Palestine. Herod was a political opportunist of the first rank. He curried favor with the
Romans and won the favor of Augustus to an as-
tonishing degree. His Hellenizing practices were
very irritating to the Pharisees, but he stood well
with some of the Sadducees.

Herod undoubtedly had great talents of a certain sort. But ambition and lust reigned in his
life. He had ten wives and was an absolute auto-
crat in his home and in his kingdom.

Distance lends enchantment to the view. After
his death and the Roman procurator has taken
the place of Archelaus, we find a party of Herodians
whose policy was to restore the rule of the Herods.
They hated the Pharisees very much, but came to
hate Jesus more and were willing to conspire with
the Pharisees to put Jesus to death (Mark, 3:6).
Jesus warned the disciples against "the leaven of
the Pharisees and the leaven of Herod" (Mark
8:15). On the last Tuesday in the Temple the Herodians combine with the Pharisees in trying to
catch Jesus with the issue of giving tribute to
Cæsar (Mark 12:13; Matt. 22:16).

Herod was a past master in intolerance and he
was living up to his past when he acted as he did
toward the magi and the babes in Bethlehem. The
Roman Emperor Augustus was responsible by his
new periodical census for the birth of Jesus in
Bethlehem, though Augustus little knew that the
chief interest in his census on the part of future
centuries would be precisely this item connected

with it. It can be said about Herod the Great that he did not know that he was stepping athwart the plans of Almighty God in his angry whim to kill the babes to prevent the expected Jewish Messiah from breaking his own will. Both Emperor and King seem like puppets on the stage in the larger purposes of God and yet each was true to his own nature and environment. No doubt the devil tried to use Herod to get rid of the child Jesus as he did use Judas and the Jewish ecclesiastics to compass his death at a later period. Herod was willing enough to play the devil's part as he had often done before. But God would not let Jesus die before his "hour" had come. That problem confronts each of us in the midst of malevolence and accidents on every hand. We can see the restraining hand of God in the sparing of the child Jesus, though Herod's guilt was just the same. But that is not to say that we can always see the hand of God in the path of the tornado, the earthquake, or the shipwreck. The picture of Herod is black enough in Josephus. It is made a bit blacker by the second chapter of Matthew's Gospel.

CHAPTER IV

CAIAPHAS THE BLINDED ECCLESIASTIC

CAIAPHAS challenges the interest of modern men because he was the high priest during the ministry of Jesus. He presided at the meeting of the Sanhedrin which tried Jesus and he took the lead in the opposition to Jesus towards the end. One wishes that there was more information available about his life. He was high priest from A. D. 18 when he was appointed by Valerius Gratus till A. D. 36 when he was removed by Vitellius. But he held his place for eighteen years which fact shows that he knew how to get along with the Roman officials. He was the son-in-law of Annas (Ananus) who was high priest from A. D. 7 to 14. Annas continued to be called high priest even after he was no longer in possession of the office (Luke 3:2, John 18:19–22; Acts 4:6). As a matter of fact Annas was the dominant force in the priestly party. In Luke 3:2 we find that "in the high-priesthood of Annas and Caiaphas" John began his ministry. In Acts 4:6 Annas is named before any one else: "And Annas the high priest was there, and Caiaphas, and John, and Alexander, and as many as were of the kindred of the high priest." Five of the sons of Annas, besides his son-in-law, Caiaphas, succeeded him as high priest. It is small wonder, therefore, that he continued to dominate the Sadducees even though no longer in office. While Caiaphas was the titular head, Annas was the moving spirit among the Sadducees.

But Caiaphas cannot be excused from his responsibilities in connection with Jesus. Caiaphas recognized the high standing of Annas by sending Jesus to him first (John 18:12-23), while he was gathering the Sanhedrin together for the full meeting and John's Gospel calls Annas here high priest. But Caiaphas in no sense tried to dodge his own leadership as the nominal high priest. We see Caiaphas in bold outline on three occasions in the New Testament.

When Jesus raised Lazarus from the grave at Bethany just east of Jerusalem, some of the Jews who had come over to comfort Martha and Mary (John 11:19), went and told the Pharisees what had happened (John 11:46). There was no effort to discredit the stupendous miracle. Jesus had said just a little while before: "If they hear not Moses and the prophets, neither will they be persuaded, if one rise from the dead." So now the Pharisees are not convinced of the Messianic power and claims of Jesus by the raising of Lazarus. Rather they see peril to their own position as the people flock to the side of Jesus. The situation calls for instant action on the part of the Sanhedrin to stop Jesus from raising dead people right at the door of Jerusalem. "The chief priests therefore and the Pharisees gathered a council" (John 11:47). It was a special meeting of the Sanhedrin at the call of both Sadducees (chief priests) and Pharisees, enemies and rivals in the Sanhedrin who are now united in face of the dangerous prestige of Jesus because of the raising of Lazarus in the presence of so many witnesses, many of whom had already believed on Jesus (John 11:45). The general sentiment was voiced: "What are we doing, for this man is doing many signs? It we let him thus alone, all men will believe on him and the Romans will come and will take away both our place and our nation" (John 11:47f). It was very adroit and fully justified the suddenly called meeting of the Sanhedrin. It was plain to all that the only way to save the nation was for the rulers to keep their positions. They piously put place before patriotism with frank naïveté. The Sadducees and Pharisees in the Sanhedrin have an instinctive feeling that the success of Jesus placed in jeopardy their own offices and the very existence of the nation. They looked upon Jesus as a dangerous revolutionist whose ambitions would probably embroil the nation with the Romans who would be only too glad of a pretext to destroy the city of Jerusalem. As a matter of fact the Romans did come and they took away the nation and robbed the rabbis of their place in the Sanhedrin which perished with the destruction of the temple, though it was revived later in Galilee with some modifications. The rabbis were right in the feeling that their very existence as a court was at stake. It is at this point that Caiaphas, the high priest, is first heard with a piece of oracular wisdom characteristic of the professional ecclesiastic who cares more for his own selfish interest than for anything else: "You do not know anything at all (probably true) nor do you consider that it is expedient for you that one man die in behalf of the people and not all the nation perish" (John 11:49f). Caiaphas spoke as the incarnation of selfishness, and put to the test by his subtle proposal the self-interest of all the other members of the Sanhedrin. He made the definite and concrete suggestion that the thing to do was to get Jesus out of the way in order to save the nation from the Romans. His plan was adopted by the Sanhedrin and after some weeks carried out, but it did not save the nation from the Romans. In fact, Jesus will one day predict the ruin of the nation for the very reason that they have decided to kill him. Worldly wisdom is not always wise, but often otherwise. Caiaphas proposed the easy way out, as many a deacon has done in a church trouble by pushing the pastor out in order to save the church. That may be best sometimes, but by no means always. It certainly did not so turn out about Jesus. Incidentally, Caiaphas uses the Greek preposition *huper* in the substitutionary sense, because he adds, "and not all the people perish." He actually offers Jesus as an involuntary sacrifice in order to save the Jewish nation. No question of right or wrong is raised. Whether Jesus deserves such a death or not is quite beside the issue. He can be made to contribute to the welfare of the Sanhedrin and of the nation by killing him. The philosophy of Caiaphas is that of many another pious scoundrel. He is perfectly willing to obtain peace by the ruin of another man. Caiaphas appears in an utterly despicable rôle that is in no sense relieved by the interpretation of the Evangelist that, as high priest, the language of Caiaphas had a prophetic meaning concerning the atoning death of Christ (John 11:51–2). That is all true enough, but Caiaphas did not mean it and he must be measured by his own motive which was wholly selfish and mean. His argument made an impression and stuck to his name (John 18:14). He carried his point and the Sanhedrin decided by formal vote to kill Jesus (11:53). They had planned it for a long time. Now it was only a matter of weeks. They made public proclamation for any one who saw Jesus come to the passover to reveal his whereabouts that they might arrest him (John 11:57). Perhaps this notice was posted as a placard in the temple courts. When the crowd gathered at Bethany to see Jesus and Lazarus, the rulers decided to kill both of them (12:10f).

Caiaphas comes to his glory at the trial of Jesus. The demonstration in favor of Jesus during the Triumphal Entry made the Sanhedrin pause in the attempt to kill Jesus during the passover feast because of the sympathy of the Galilean populace. So they held a meeting in the court of Caiaphas and decided to put off the death of Jesus till after the feast to avoid a tumult of the people (Matt. 26:3–5). In simple truth Caiaphas was frightened by the unexpected popularity of Jesus as the crowds in the temple hung on the words of Jesus

(Luke 21:37f). It was Judas who came to the help of Caiaphas at this juncture and pointed out how Jesus could be arrested in the Garden of Gethsemane at night while at prayer and be tried and condemned before the people stirred in the morning. It was a clever scheme to make Jesus lose popular sympathy as a Messianic hero by a *fait accompli* with Christ as a condemned criminal. This could all be done "in the absence of the multitude." The treachery of Judas no doubt appeared to Caiaphas as a dispensation of Providence in favor of the Sanhedrin (Luke 22:3–6). No wonder he was glad, and sealed the bargain with Judas by paying him the price of a slave.

It is plain that the task of getting Jesus condemned by the Sanhedrin fell to Caiaphas. Judas had Jesus arrested and turned him over bound to Annas first (John 18:13), while Caiaphas gathered the Sanhedrin together in his house (Matt. 26:57; Luke 22:54). Then Annas sent Jesus on to Caiaphas (John 18:24). Caiaphas presided and conducted the trial which was a prosecution rather than a trial. There was no indictment and no warrant and no opportunity for Jesus to have a lawyer or witnesses. The purpose of the Sanhedrin was to convict Jesus, not to find out the truth about him. Moreover, they sought for false witnesses in order to put Jesus to death (Mark 15:55; Matt. 26:60). The farcical trial took place at night instead of by day. Besides, the Sanhedrin no longer had the power of life and death as Caiaphas knew perfectly well and admitted to

Pilate (John 18:30). It is not made clear why the Sanhedrin condemned Jesus to death anyhow since it was futile without the approval of Pilate. But Caiaphas did not tell Pilate that the Sanhedrin had already condemned Jesus to death (Luke 23: 2; John 18:30). Pilate actually offered to turn Jesus over to them for trial (John 18:31), but they protest that they cannot put him to death and do not say that they have already condemned him to death. They do at least say that he ought by their law to die because he made himself the Son of God (John 19:7). Why then did the Sanhedrin go through the farce of a trial? Perhaps as protest against the Roman usurpation. Perhaps also as a means of gratifying personal resentment against Jesus who had defied them so utterly before the people.

But even so, the so-called trial by Caiaphas was a failure. The only testimony against Jesus with a semblance of truth was given by two witnesses who contradicted each other. It was a desperate situation and it would have ended the matter with the freedom of Jesus by a judge who cared for the facts and for truth and justice. But Caiaphas had staked all on a verdict now that by the treachery of Judas he had Jesus in his power. So with bluster and bravado this prejudiced ecclesiastic put Jesus on solemn oath before the Sanhedrin concerning his claim to be "the Christ, the Son of God" (Mark 14:61; Matt. 26:63). Caiaphas had no legal right to treat a prisoner thus. The whole trial violated Jewish legal procedure at every step.

But Caiaphas would stop at nothing. Jesus did
not have to reply and convict himself by his own
testimony. But he did reply on oath that he was
the Messiah, the Son of God (Mark 14:62; Matt.
26:64). If he had kept silent now, as he had done
before, that would have been interpreted as denial
that he made such a claim. Hence Jesus took his
life in his hands in his answer. It was not blasphemy for the Son of God to claim to be the
Messiah. But the Sanhedrin would not agree that
Jesus of Nazareth was the Messiah, the Son of
God. Hence they called it blasphemy and condemned him to death which was now illegal for
them and which judgment they could not execute.
The Sanhedrin showed their glee at the result by
conduct worthy of hoodlums or of "rough-necks"
as they mocked and buffeted Jesus (Mark 14:65;
Matt. 26:67f; Luke 22:63-5).

Caiaphas had carried his point against Jesus before the Sanhedrin and now had the far more
difficult task of getting a conviction from Pilate.
The Roman governors at least had to keep up the
semblance of justice. Pilate bore an evil reputation and the Jews had many counts against him.
All this made him afraid of the power of Caiaphas
who could report him to Cæsar. But even so,
Caiaphas did not have an easy time with Pilate
who several times announced the innocence of
Jesus and ought to have set him free. He would
have done so but for the persistence of Caiaphas
and of the Sanhedrin. They had adroitly accused
Jesus of claiming to be "Christ a King" (Luke

23:2), and Pilate had to examine that charge though he soon saw that Jesus was no rival of Cæsar as a political ruler. At the end Pilate was disposed to set Jesus free, but the Jews cried out that they would tell Cæsar on him if he did (John 18:12). Then Pilate surrendered and Caiaphas and the Sadducees actually boasted of their loyalty to Cæsar: "We have no king but Cæsar" (John 18: 15). Caiaphas played a desperate game and carried it on to the end and took the blood of Jesus on his own head and the heads of the people and of their children (Matt. 27:25).

Caiaphas appears in the book of Acts also. The Sadducees took ill the bold preaching of Peter and John that Jesus had actually risen from the dead (Acts 4:2). The Sadducees took the lead in the death of Jesus though the Pharisees were the first to attack him and his teachings. The Sadducees are the first to arrest the apostles while for a time the Pharisees held off. The emphasis on the doctrine of the resurrection at first stressed the cleavage between the Sadducees and the Pharisees at this point. It might appear from Acts 4:6 that Annas was even more active in the persecution and arrest of Peter and John than Caiaphas. But certainly Caiaphas did his share in the formal meetings of the Sanhedrin. Peter boldly accused the Sanhedrin of the death of Jesus, "whom ye crucified" (Acts 4:10). Caiaphas and the rest resent the courage of Peter, but are helpless in the presence of the healed man and are full of scorn of the name Jesus (4:17f). The prohibition against preaching the resurrection of Jesus was useless and the Sadducees tried another arrest (Acts 5:17f), but Peter and the other apostles bluntly defied them: "We must obey God rather than men" (5:29). This time Gamaliel came to the rescue of the apostles and revealed a breach between Caiaphas and Gamaliel, or between the Sadducees and the Pharisees, on the doctrine of the resurrection.

It is probable that Stephen appeared for trial before Caiaphas also (Acts 9:1), though the glory or shame of Stephen's death rests with the Pharisees rather than with the Sadducees. Stephen stirred up the Pharisees as Peter had the Sadducees. The two parties came together again as in the trial and death of Jesus. So then the united Sanhedrin made short work of Stephen and did not wait this time for the approval of Pilate who may have already been recalled with no successor yet on hand. At any rate it was a case of mob law, or lynch law, that did not wait for a judicial process. Gamaliel made no protest in behalf of Stephen and Caiaphas let the Pharisees have their way as they would not in the case of Simon Peter.

It is probable also that Caiaphas gave Saul the papers to go to Damascus to arrest and bring before the Sanhedrin the Christians in that city (Acts 9:1). If so, Caiaphas presided in the numerous condemnations of men and women to death for the crime of being Christians under the leadership of young Saul. As this was a Pharisaic persecution, the leadership passed from Caiaphas to Saul, but there is no evidence that Caiaphas failed to coöperate with the zealous Pharisee who was trying to put an end to Christianity, an end much desired by Caiaphas.

Caiaphas remains a typical ecclesiastic who is blinded by prejudice and privilege. The light of the world shone around him and before him, but he could not see. If he had been blind in his physical eyes, it would not have been so bad (John 9: 41). He had spiritual blindness though he professed to be the spiritual leader of his people. There are none so blind as those who will not see. If the light within Caiaphas was darkness, how great was that darkness (Matt. 6:23). Caiaphas was an obscurantist who tried to stop the sun from shining. The religious reactionary always steps out boldly in front of the march of God through the ages. But in the end he is run over by the inevitable shining of the light which cannot be held back and which shines on forever. The furthest star shines on though millions of light-years away. But Caiaphas stood right in front of the Sun of Righteousness and denied that he saw anything. As a matter of fact he did not see what was before him. The eyes of his heart were not opened so that he could see. Having eyes he saw not and ears he heard not.

CHAPTER V

PILATE THE UNJUST JUDGE

THERE is no doubt at all about the weakness and the cowardice of Pilate. The story of the trial of Jesus shows the feebleness of the character of Pilate as recorded in each of the Gospels. Munkacsy's great painting, Christ before Pilate, seizes upon this feature with consummate power. Pilate there really appears to be on trial before Christ, as he is, in fact, condemned by the moral judgment of the world for his treatment of Jesus.

But late legends condone the conduct of Pilate and even credit him with becoming a Christian and he is enrolled among the saints in the Coptic Church. In particular, his wife, who is given the name of Claudia Procula or Procla, is identified with the Claudia of 2 Timothy 4:21 and October 27 is her calendar date in the Coptic Church. The message of Pilate's wife that he should have "nothing to do with that righteous man" (Matt. 27:19), probably explains the favorable opinion held by some Christians concerning Pilate's wife. It is best to pass by all the apocryphal accounts of Pilate such as the references in the Gospel of Peter (second century), the Gospel of Nicodemus (fourth century) containing the Acts of Pilate, and also pass by the Acts of Peter and Paul with the alleged (but spurious) letter or report of Pilate to Tiberius. The extant Acts of Pilate are spurious, though credited by some people to-day.

It is enough to draw our picture of Pilate from the Gospels and from Josephus and from Philo. It is plain from these writings that Pilate incurred the dislike of the Jews on many grounds (Philo, *Ad Gaium*, 38). Here Agrippa tells how Pilate hung gilt shields in the palace of Herod in Jerusalem on which were inscribed the names of the donor and of him in whose honor the shield was set up. The Jews were enraged at this and wrote to Tiberius who ordered Pilate to remove them. Philo quotes Agrippa as saying that the threat of the Jews "exasperated Pilate in the greatest possible degree, as he feared lest they might impeach him with respect to other particulars of his government—his corruption, his acts of insolence, his rapine, and his habit of insulting people, his cruelty, and his continual murder of people untried and uncondemned, and his never-ending, gratuitous, and most grievous inhumanity." This description can be discounted as partly Jewish hatred. But Josephus (*Ant.* XVIII. iii. 1; *War* II. ix. 2, 3) related how Pilate angered the Jews greatly by directing the Roman soldiers to go to Jerusalem carrying the usual image of the emperor on the standards. To the Jews this meant emperor worship and they made violent protest to Pilate in Cæsarea and threw themselves on the ground, preferring death to the violation of their laws. Pilate only then relented as he had not contemplated wholesale massacre. He outraged the Jews again by using money from the temple treasury (*corban*) to build aqueducts into Jerusalem (*Ant.* XVIII. iii. 2). Luke 13:1, tells of some "Galileans whose blood Pilate mingled with their sacrifices." Barabbas led a sedition which illustrates the unsettled condition of the country, Mark 15:7. Pilate was finally deposed by Vitellius, Propraetor of Syria, for killing so many Samaritans in suppressing an uprising over the promise of an impostor to show on Mount Gerizim the sacred vessels hidden there by Moses. This false Messiah was thus the indirect cause of his removal. Vitellius ordered Pilate to proceed to Rome to report to Tiberius, the Emperor, who died before his arrival. That was March 16, A. D. 37. Pilate was Procurator of Judea A. D. 26 to 36.

Little is known of his family history. His first name is not given, only his second name, Pontius (a famous Samnite name), and his third, Pilatus (probably "armed with a pike"). He was a Roman citizen and belonged to the equestrian class. He probably had military experience. The procurator was an imperial official and responsible to the emperor. He was subordinate to the Propraetor of Syria. The Sanhedrin retained many judicial functions, but not the power of life and death which they once had. The ruler of Judea had to be a man of some ability and skill, for the Jews were a difficult race to rule. Souter holds that he was "doubtless in many respects a competent governor." But he failed in his great crisis. Many men can do well when all goes well. But it is the hour of trial which reveals a man's real caliber. Pilate stands convicted as an unjust judge by his own words and by his own conduct. One is reminded of Christ's parable of the judge who feared not God and regarded not man who boasted of his arrogance (Luke 18:2–5). Only this unjust judge did yield to the widow's plea. Pilate, on the other hand, stifled his own sense of justice for political and personal reasons. He went against his own conception of law and right in order to save his place. It seems only retributive justice that he lost it at last because of a false Messiah.

In order to make good this charge against Pilate it is only necessary to make a careful study of the data in the Gospels concerning the trial of Jesus. No one of the Gospels tells all the story. Mark's is the shortest as it is the earliest account. John's narrative is much the fullest and furnishes an easy framework for the details in the Synoptic Gospels. The author of the Fourth Gospel was present during the trial and so had first-hand knowledge of the proceedings. Hence the Fourth Gospel makes plainer what is told in the Synoptics. Those who deny the historical worth of the Fourth Gospel have here something to consider. All the Gospels are used in this picture of Pilate.

When Jesus is brought to Pilate by the Sanhedrin, he naturally asks for a definite charge (John 18:29). They probably tell him that they think him guilty, though there is no indication that the

Sanhedrin told Pilate of the trial and condemnation of Jesus by them. At any rate they make no mention of it. They had condemned Jesus for blasphemy, but they do not refer to that charge at all. They first take a bold stand that they would not have brought Jesus to him if he were not an evil-doer (John 18:30). Pilate did not wish to be bothered with petty cases and allowed the Sanhedrin a great deal of latitude anyhow. Hence he said: "Take him yourselves and judge him according to your law" (John 18:31). They had the right to try minor cases. But the Sanhedrin reveal their animus by saying: "It is not lawful for us to put any man to death" (ib.). Hence Pilate called for specific accusations. The Sanhedrin make three: a general charge of sedition as a perverter of the nation, forbidding to give tribute to Cæsar, and calling himself Christ a King (Luke 23:2). These charges are all of a political nature and compelled attention at the hands of Pilate. The first is very vague and the second is flatly untrue, for Jesus had seen through the craftiness of the spies sent to trap him on that very point (Luke 20:20–26). The third is true as Jesus means his words, for on oath he had confessed to the Sanhedrin that he was the Christ, the Son of God (Matt. 26:63). But the Sanhedrin condemned Jesus for blasphemy because he claimed to be the Messiah the Son of God, not because he asserted that he was "Christ a King" in the political sense. The Sanhedrin know that Pilate will take the word "king" in a political sense whatever he may think of the epithet "Christ." If he ignores the charge that Jesus sets himself up as a rival to Cæsar, Pilate will be accused before Cæsar and lose his position and probably his life. Cæsar will brook no rival and no rebellion. The Sanhedrin know perfectly well that Jesus makes no such claim though the Triumphant Entry gave them the specious excuse for the charge. The multitude had hailed Jesus as King in the hearing of the Pharisees (Luke 19:30f). A year before in Galilee the crowd had wanted to take Jesus by force and make him king (John 6:14f).

So Pilate was compelled to notice this charge. He took Jesus within the palace and asked him pointedly: "Art thou the King of the Jews?" (John 18:33). The first interview between Pilate and Jesus reveals the weakness and helplessness of Pilate. He does not comprehend a kingdom not of this world, whose citizens will not fight, and which is confined to the realm of truth (John 18:34–38). Pilate feels sure that this peculiar kingdom of truth, whatever it may be, is not in conflict with that of Cæsar. Pilate had probably heard of Jesus before as Herod Antipas had in Galilee, but his own judgement is now clear after this first interview that Jesus is a harmless enthusiast, perhaps erratic, even a bit unbalanced in his devotion to what he called truth, but clearly no rival of Cæsar in any political or legal sense. Hence Pilate steps out of the palace and announces his decision to the Sanhedrin and the multitudes who have now assembled at the beginning of day: "I find no crime in him" (John 18:38; Luke 23:4). In this first phase of the

Roman trial Pilate at least shows no prejudice against Jesus and renders his decision in accordance with the facts as he finds them, though he is unable to fathom the mystery of Christ's person and claims.

The rulers were thunderstruck by this defeat of their plans of hate and death. They repeated their accusations with many additions, so that Pilate turned to Jesus to see if he had anything to say in reply to their charges (Mark 15:4). But Jesus remained silent to the amazement of Pilate (Matt. 27:14). The rulers saw that the sympathy of Pilate was with Jesus and that they had to overcome his first decision. They renew with energy the charge that Jesus is a disturber of the people all the way from Galilee to Jerusalem (Luke 23:5).

Pilate now makes his first serious blunder. He had made his decision, but he lacked the courage to stand by his conviction of duty towards the prisoner in the face of public clamor. He eagerly seized a chance to avoid responsibility at the mention of Galilee. That would throw Jesus under the jurisdiction of Herod Antipas who happened to be in Jerusalem at that very time. Herod Antipas had been jealous of Pilate and curious to see Jesus. So Pilate saw a chance to get rid of a troublesome case and at the same time please a native ruler who was hostile to him. It looked like a masterstroke to Pilate in his predicament. He knew that Jesus was innocent and he did not wish to condemn him, but if he stuck to his decision already rendered, the Jews would take it very ill and get him in serious trouble

with Cæsar. With great glee Pilate sent Jesus off
to Herod Antipas (Luke 23:6–12). The Galilean
tetrarch had evidently gotten over his guilty fears
that Jesus was John the Baptist come to life again
(Mark 6:14–29). Now he wanted Jesus to perform
miracles for his entertainment like an oriental
juggler. But the dignified silence of Jesus baffled
Herod and the chief priests and scribes. So Herod
made a mock of Jesus and sent him back to Pilate.
But he and Pilate became friends as a result of the
incident.

Once again Pilate had Jesus on his hands. The
dodge had failed and now Pilate must act. He
seized upon the failure of Herod to condemn Jesus
to defend his previous decision of the innocence of
Jesus which he reaffirmed (Luke 23:13–16). Pilate
boldly announced that he would chastise him and
release him, a sop to Cerberus, for he had no right
to scourge an innocent man, except that Jesus was
not a Roman citizen. In the eyes of Pilate Jesus was
merely a slave with no inherent rights of any kind.
He was more concerned to conform to the forms of
Roman justice and legal jurisprudence than he was
to be merciful or even just to Jesus. Souter reminds
us that "Pilate had a tender enough conscience or
a sound enough idea of justice to try to save this
'slave.'" Yes, but he did not save him. He struggled
with the forces of evil around him and yielded at
last to public clamor and injustice, a thing that a
just judge never does. He had the reins of justice
in his own hands. It was far more important for
justice to be done to a prisoner than for the judge

to retain his office. Pilate bethought him of the custom of releasing a prisoner at the passover. He knew that for envy the rabbis had delivered Jesus to him (Matt. 27:18). He knew also something of the popularity of Jesus with the multitudes. Besides, his wife had sent him a message about a troubled dream that she had had because of Jesus. She warned him to have nothing to do with Jesus (Matt. 27:19). He even dared to call Jesus, "the King of the Jews," as he gave them the choice between Jesus and Barabbas (Mark 15:9). But the chief priests countered this appeal to popular favor by diligent work among the rabble to ask for Barabbas instead of Jesus. Barabbas was himself a sort of hero with a certain element of disorderly disposition. He had led an insurrection and was guilty of murder (Mark 15:7). A successful robber often makes an appeal to the popular imagination. But Pilate pressed the point and demanded which of the two the people wanted to set free. Then with a great shout they all cried out: "Away with this man, and release unto us Barabbas" (Luke 23:18). So Pilate had failed again with this ruse. He had hoped to use the people against the Sanhedrin to justify his release of Jesus.

So once more Pilate has to decide what to do with Jesus. He had Jesus scourged with the hope that this would be enough. He then thought he would get the people into a good humor and make them laugh a bit in the hope that they would still rally to the support of Jesus. So the soldiers arrayed him in a purple garment with a crown of

thorns on his head and in mockery hailed him as
King of the Jews. Pilate brought Jesus thus be-
decked out to the people and said: "Behold, the
man" (John 19:5). "What shall I do unto Jesus
which is called Christ?" (Matt. 27:22). The people
saw no humor in the situation. The chief priests
led the shout in reply: "Crucify, crucify him"
(Luke 23:21; John 19:6). Pilate argued the matter:
"Why, what evil hath this man done? I have found
no cause of death in him" (Luke 23:22). But they
cried out exceedingly, "Crucify him!" (Mark
15:14). It was now plain to Pilate that he had lost
his appeal to the people against the rabbis. It was
still his prerogative to stand by his just judgment
that Jesus was innocent of any crime. But the populace had now sided with the Sanhedrin and had
made it harder for Pilate to stand up for justice. So
in a pet he yielded with a stultifying incrimination
of himself: "Take him yourselves and crucify him,
for I find no crime in him" (John 19:6). It is impossible to imagine a more contemptible decision
by a judge. In all history it has probably never been
surpassed for sheer stupidity. He gave Jesus up to
the wolves in order to save his own life. He accused
them while excusing himself and asserting the innocence of Jesus. But he accused himself also, for
he was the judge, not the Sanhedrin, not the mob.
His surrender is a travesty upon justice and the
acme of judicial cowardice.

The Jews now claim that Jesus ought to die
according to their law "because he made himself
the Son of God" (John 19:7). This was said to com-

fort the conscience of Pilate who had yielded to the
Jews against the plain dictates of Roman law. But
the description of Jesus as "the Son of God" disturbed Pilate again. He recalled his wife's warning
and the peculiar claim of Jesus about the Kingdom
of Truth. Once more Pilate, moved by his fears,
sought an interview with Jesus (John 19:8–11).
But Jesus was silent at first until Pilate boasted of
his power to release or to crucify Jesus. This boast
convicts Pilate again. He did possess this power
and hence there was no escape from responsibility
and guilt. But, guilty as Pilate was, Judas was
more so.

Once again Pilate came out and sought to release
Jesus, that is, sought to persuade the Jews to be
willing for Pilate to release him. There was never
a moment after the trial began when Pilate could
not have ended the farce by a firm stand. The real
decision was in his own hands. All along Pilate had
been afraid of what now happened. The Jews
bluntly said: "If thou release this man, thou art not
Cæsar's friend; every one that maketh himself a
king speaketh against Cæsar" (John 19:12). The
shadow of this charge had been in the background
all the while. Now it had stepped forth into view.
The hour of final decision had come as Pilate now
knew. It was six o'clock in the morning (John
19:14). The crowd shouted again: "Crucify him!"
Pilate feebly countered, "Shall I crucify your
king?" (John 19:15). The chief priests (Sadducees) now answered: "We have no king but Cæsar."

He had made them confess loyalty to Cæsar at any rate, but he lost his own self-respect and the respect of mankind.

The very effort of Pilate to prove his innocence shows his own consciousness of guilt, washing his hands and saying: "I am innocent of the blood of this righteous man" (Matt. 27:24). The people helped his feeling by saying: "His blood be on us and on our children." It is, alas! There is guilt enough for all of them, for Judas, for the Sanhedrin (Sadducees and Pharisees), for the rabble, for the nation, for Pilate. Each had his share in this crime of the ages.

There is a legend that the body of Pilate after his suicide was finally buried in the territory of Lausanne and that, when heavy storms are on Mount Pilatus, the ghost of Pilate comes out and washes his hands in the vain endeavor to wash out the stain of the blood of Christ. But the stain will never disappear. He knew Roman law and knew that he was violating it in turning over Jesus, an innocent man, to the rage of the Jews. He had his great moral opportunity and fell down before it. It is idle as it is futile to find excuses for his conduct in the scheming of the Sanhedrin and the clamor of the rabble. There are always excuses for crimes. The difference between a man of character and a weakling is precisely this: Let justice be done though the heavens fall. Pilate preferred for justice to be done, provided it did not hurt him. There are too many men in public life like Pilate. They are open to graft, to influence, to patronage, to partisanship. They would rather do right and what is best for the country, but the election is coming and they want votes. Pilate is the unjust judge of all time. He acquitted the innocent prisoner and then turned him over to the rage of the rabble to save his own miserable neck.

CHAPTER VI

THE RICH YOUNG RULER: A YOUNG MAN WHO MISSED THE HIGHEST

(Mark 10:17-31; Matthew 19:16-30; Luke 18:18-30).

THE Rich Young Ruler is an example of the young men to-day who come near the highest things and then fall back to a life of failure.

Some hold that he was Saul of Tarsus, who afterwards came to Christ. According to this view Paul alludes to his previous knowledge of Christ before his conversion in 2 Corinthians 5:16 when he says: "wherefore henceforth we know no one according to the flesh: though we have known Christ according to the flesh, but now no longer do we so know him." A fascinating theory is this which has attracted a number of scholars including the late James Hope Moulton. But the phrase "according to the flesh" (*kata sarka*) naturally means "as the flesh looks at Christ" rather than "Christ in the flesh." Dr. Edward Shillito, of London, is probably correct in the sharp contrast that he draws in an imaginary conversation between Paul and the Ruler, who possibly were schoolmates and met in Rome when Paul was a prisoner for the Christ whom the Young Ruler had rejected. Each looked with pity on the other as their lives had drifted so far apart, but Paul towers far above him. In truth nothing at all is known of him save what the Synoptic Gospels tell us.

There is a great charm in the young man that won the heart of Jesus at first sight. Mark (10:21) records that Jesus fell in love (ingressive aorist tense) with him when He looked upon him for the first time. Jesus looked this young man full in the face, and His heart leaped out toward him. He yearned for him as a disciple and follower. The Rich Young Ruler had come to his hour of destiny.

He was an outstanding youth in his community. He had wealth. He had political office. He had social standing. All these pre-requisites he had, besides the charm of his engaging personality. It is small wonder that he so completely won the heart of Christ. He would win the praise and affection of every lover of the best in human life.

Yet he was not happy. He had great unrest. He knew by the witness of his own heart that he was not perfect as he longed to be. Every young man has a problem. Some have many. Every young man is a problem to his loved ones. It is a pity that it is so difficult to get to the hearts of many young men. The very finest spirits are sometimes so reticent and shy that one cannot penetrate the outer surface.

But this one had heard of Jesus as a wonderful teacher, who understood the ways of the soul. By chance Jesus came his way in His journeys. Here was his great opportunity. He was not going to let it slip. So he came eagerly running and fell on his knees before Jesus. He brought his problem to Jesus instead of concealing it or seeking to forget it. He was sure that Jesus could tell him what to do for his heartache and soul hunger. "Good Teacher, what shall I do that I may get (Matthew), or inherit (Mark and Luke) eternal life?" The *summum bonum* of life was eternal life. All the rabbis taught that. They held out that hope as the price of a life perfect in details, a boon to be bought by obedience to a world of ritual observances. He was willing to do anything within reason to satisfy the ethical demands of his teachers. So he put his problem right up to Jesus. He was not affected or sophisticated. He was sincere and called for serious treatment.

Jesus met him squarely with a challenge. He had greeted Jesus with courtesy that might be mere politeness. "Why do you speak of me as good? No one is absolutely good except God." This reply is not a disclaimer of deity on the part of Christ, but a direct thrust at the young man's real attitude towards Christ himself. "You know the commandments!" "If you wish to enter into life, keep on observing the commandments." Jesus was meeting the young man on his own ground.

"What sort of commandments?"

Jesus reminds him of the outstanding ethical ideals in the Ten Commandments about murder, adultery, theft, false witness, honoring father and mother, with the summary of it all in loving one's neighbor as oneself.

There was disappointment in the reply of the

young ruler who had anticipated some great and
original contribution to rabbinical ethics, on a par
with Hillel's negative form of the Golden Rule.
Each great rabbi made at least one great contribution to the *Torah*. The young man expected
Jesus to make a great deliverance that would
throw the needed light upon his own darkened
soul. Instead of that he had heard only the common-
places of the Mosaic Covenant, upon which he had
been brought up from his mother's knee. "These,
every one of them, I have observed from my youth."
He had learned the *Torah* when a child, these pre-
cepts in particular, and had tried to obey the law,
yet he realized vaguely that something was amiss.
There are parents in plenty who would be intensely
happy if they knew for certain that their sons
knew and lived up to the demands made by the Ten
Commandments. No special code of morals has been
invented for them. The standard for rich and poor
is all the same.

There is sincerity in the cry of the young ruler,
"What lack I yet?" He did not wish to lack anything if he could help it. How near the kingdom of
God this young man seemed to be. He was seeking
Jesus and eternal life at His hands. He was eager
to follow the leadership of Jesus. He was hanging
on the words of the great Teacher who looked on
him intently and fell in love with him. "If you wish
to be perfect, one thing still fails you." Think of
that. This young man lacked only one mark of perfection. His grade in school language would be
ninety-nine. Most young men would be content with

far less than this. Some young men think it not *au fait* to be brilliant in school, diligent in work, or remarkably pious and moral, but this young man wanted the highest within his reach, or thought that he did.

He was in the grip of one of the deadliest sins and did not know it until Jesus turned the flashlight of truth upon his soul. "Go, sell all whatever you have and distribute to poor people, and you will have treasure in heaven. Then come on and follow me all the way." Now the young man had his shock. The mental reaction of the wealthy young man was visible in his countenance, for his face became sad and revealed his utter disappointment in Jesus. He was greatly grieved that Jesus had made this demand of all things on earth.

Without his property he would be as a common day-laborer if not a pauper and a beggar. He took it all in after a moment of intellectual illumination as he faced his opportunity and crisis. He felt sure that Jesus had misjudged him. It was true that he was very rich, but that was no crime. Job had been very wealthy as was King David. Jesus himself had rich disciples, like the Bethany family and later Joseph of Arimathea. The Jews looked on wealth as proof of the favor of God and poverty as a curse. The young man was puzzled beyond expression. The New Teacher had cut across the path of all his training and conviction. He did not know that he was covetous. He probably gave alms regularly. He did not know that he worshiped mammon. Jesus did not mean that no one could be His disciple who

did not first give away all his money. He did not
mean that this was the only sin that could imperil
a man's life. He did not mean that all men were in
the grip of this particular sin of greed. But He
made this stiff test of this particular young man
because he was in reality in the grip of the money-
devil. He was worshiping the almighty dollar.
Many people to-day do not consider covetousness a
vice at all, but rather a virtue. When did you ever
know a man to be excluded from church on the
charge of covetousness? And yet few sins are more
blighting to the soul. The finer traits shrivel up
under the blasting effect of the exaggerated love of
money. Jesus evidently means the young man who
posed so near perfection to see that he had violated
the very first of the Ten Commandments. He loved
money more than he did God. There are many com-
placent church members to-day who would receive
a severe jolt if they realized that they actually
loved money more than they did the cause of Christ.
The preacher to-day is placed in an embarrassing
position about money. If he exposes the "skin-
flints" for their stinginess, they will try to make
him resign or at least criticize him for always talking about money instead of preaching the simple
gospel of grace which they conceive to be devoid of
any financial obligations. A pastor should be faithful in exposing the sin of covetousness and in warning men of the peril to the soul in the love of gold
with its grasping greed.

Jesus promised the rich young ruler treasure in
heaven if he would break the power of money over

his own life. Each of the Synoptic Gospels preserves this item. Jesus used the same figure elsewhere, as in Matthew 6. The word for treasure (thesaurus) we have preserved in our English. To have treasure in heaven is an appealing figure. We can lay up treasure in heaven by the right use of our money here. The only way to take money to heaven is to give it away here.

Jesus demanded the surrender of all his wealth. Jesus wanted no half-hearted service from this gifted young man. He demanded his whole heart, his whole life, his whole wealth. The young man was called on to lay all upon the altar. "Then come and go on following me," said Jesus. "Follow me all the time and all the way to baptism, to the cross." It was the call to the high and the heroic. That appeal has always found a prompt and enthusiastic response from young men through all the ages. But it meets a loyal acceptance from those who have come to Christ and who have left self behind. This one had come to Christ for advice and was willing to pay any reasonable price for the eternal life that he so much desired. He would probably have agreed to go on a long pilgrimage to some sacred place, to live a life of abstemiousness for some considerable time, to fast and to pray, to pay a good deal of money by way of alms or for kingdom work. He was undoubtedly prepared to do much and to meet Jesus half way. But he was not ready to go the whole way and to put all at the service of Christ even to win so great a prize as eternal life. Jesus demanded that there be no private reservations, no secret places in the heart reserved for self, no exceptions in what he gave up. It was a drastic demand that searched the inmost recesses of the young man's life. He was willing to give up all the sins of which he was not guilty. He only hesitated about this one sin which he had thought was a virtue, this one defect in his life which kept him back from perfection. Beyond a doubt many a man is held back from the service of Christ because he is unwilling to give up the pet sin or sins which he hugs closely to his heart. It often happens that such a man talks much about the intellectual difficulties in Christianity, about the things that he cannot understand and cannot believe, about the doubts raised by scientists or by theologians and what not. At bottom they are all excuses to hide the secret or open sin in his own life.

An hour before this young man had come running up to Jesus with all deference. Now, with a broken and disappointed heart he turned away from Jesus and went back to his money and to his life of selfishness. He was saddened beyond words that Jesus had made such an impossible demand. There are people to-day who say that Christianity must be toned down to meet the views of the modern "youth movement," that university men and women to-day will not have the Jesus of theology and will put up only with the Jesus of history, a mere man at that, who will condone the life of "modern" men and who will not make demands of young people of culture and enlightenment to which they will not accede. Jesus to-day meets a threat from certain self-appointed leaders who defiantly proclaim that they will not follow Jesus "unless." But to-day, as when the Rich Young Ruler rejected Jesus, it is impossible to conceive of Jesus as granting "ifs" in order to win the nominal service of young people of wealth and culture. Jesus Christ asks for all or for nothing. He asks for the whole of life. He does not ask that we stop thinking, but that we think rightly. Our age greatly needs the warning of this brilliant young man.

He went away from Christ and, so far as we know, he never came back. He made the final, the irrevocable choice. He chose his life of ease and pleasure to the consecration demanded by Jesus. One thinks of Saul of Tarsus who was challenged on the road to Damascus and gave up all for Christ and who became the great Apostle to the Gentiles. Paul became poor and made many rich. The Rich Young Ruler met his crisis and missed his greatest opportunity in life.

There is the sad reflection that Jesus Himself, the Saviour of sinners, failed to save this young man whom He loved so much. As the Physician of souls, Jesus diagnosed the young man's case rightly. He put his finger on the sore spot, but the young man refused to submit to the operation. We come up against the age-long problem of divine sovereignty and human free agency. There is nothing new to say about it. God has to be sovereign else He is not God. Man has to be free else he is not a free moral agent. But God respects the rights of the individual and his personality. In the last analysis, if a man wills to serve the worst and to be the slave of sin, he can so decide.

It is not surprising that preachers to-day sometimes fail to win young men of the highest promise. We make mistakes ourselves and do not possess the consummate wisdom and power of Jesus in winning souls. And then we strike the same hardness of heart that had this young ruler in its grip. But it is a tragedy, whenever it happens, to see so fine a man lost to the highest and the best.

Christ's failure to win the young man deeply moved his own soul. He looked around (Mark) and said to the disciples, after the young man had gone: "With how much difficulty do those who have wealth enter the kingdom of God." The disciples were doubtless saddened also by the choice of the young man. But the saying of Jesus surprised them, for the Jews regarded money as a mark of divine favor and not a hindrance to the life of faith. Jesus explained: "It is easier for a camel to go through the eye of a needle (surgeon's needle, Luke says) than for a rich man to enter the kingdom of God." This illustration depressed them still more. "Who then can be saved?" The thing looked hopeless for all. Then Jesus looked on the disciples again in pity and admitted that it was impossible with men, but added that God can do the impossible. God can save a rich man just like any other sinner. Peter added the naïve remark that they had left all to follow Christ, which was quite true. Each of the Twelve Apostles had given up his business in order to follow Christ. In some cases there may have been opposition in the home circle. Jesus appreciates to the full the sacrifices that they had made and promises fullness of blessings in this life "along with persecutions" and in the coming age eternal life. It was a solemn time of testing as Jesus added: "Many first ones will be last and many last ones will be first."

CHAPTER VII

MARY MAGDALENE THE MISREPRESENTED WOMAN

GET a misunderstanding started and it is almost
impossible to stop it. Correction never overtakes
the original slander. There is absolutely nothing in
the records of the Gospels as ground for the notion
that Mary Magdalene was a harlot who was won to
Christ. There are real objections to that view which
will be stated later.

The worst form of the slander involves Christ
also and pictures Mary Magdalene as the paramour
of Jesus. It is difficult to be patient or to be courteous towards one who offers a slur upon the character of Christ. Evil to him who evil thinks. Certainly
Jesus needs no defense from this slander, nor does
Mary, but she has been attacked in so many ways
that it is only fair to her memory to answer the
slanders. No one doubts the power of Christ to rescue and to change a woman of evil life. He has done
it time and again with women and men and he can
work that miracle of grace to-day. But the possession of this power is no proof that it was actual fact
in the case of Mary Magdalene.

One of the later legends says not simply that
Mary Magdalene had been a harlot, but relapsed
into her former mode of life and "abused all her

admirable gifts to tempt others to sin" (J. B. Mayor, Hasting's *Dictionary of the Bible*). This late legend is even worse than the way some articles have treated her as the synonym of the repentant and converted harlot so that the very name *Magdalene* to-day has come to carry that meaning. The name is now applied to houses of reform for fallen women. It is too late to change the current of actual usage, but we can at least be free from the sin of misrepresenting so noble a woman as Mary Magdalene.

Let us trace the story. The name "Magdalene" is probably due to her coming from Magdala (or Magadan of Matt. 15:39), a town some three miles from Capernaum at the southern end of the Plain of Genneseret. All that the epithet means is that she was Mary of Magdala, or Mary the Magdalene, to distinguish her from the other Marys. Several rabbis in the Talmud are termed Magdalene. There is the ruin of a miserable village to-day called *Mejdel*. Tristran (*Bible Places*, p. 260) says "Magdala is only the Greek form of *Mighdol* or watch-tower, one of the many places of the name in Palestine." The ancient Magdala was a wealthy city and the Talmud says that its tribute had to be carried to Jerusalem in wagons. The town had a bad reputation, like Corinth, and the rabbis gave this as the cause for its final destruction. It was celebrated for its dye works and was a Sabbath day's journey from Tiberias. But it is folly to translate the term Magdalene the same as harlot. How about the rabbis called Magdalene?

Some of the rabbis say that Magdalene means a plaiter of hair and that women of loose character made a point of wearing long plaited hair like the sinful woman who wiped her tears from the feet of Jesus with her hair (Luke 7:38). Surely this is a fanciful reason for maligning the character of Mary.

It is argued also by some that Mary Magdalene had seven demons cast out of her, which proves that she had been a woman of evil life. Jerome (*Vit. Hil. Erem*) does speak of a *Virgo Dei* at Majumas as possessed of *amoris daemon*. Some of the Jews did consider demoniac possession as involving immorality, probably true of some, but it is a large jump to conclude that therefore it was true of Mary. Jesus spoke of the man from whom a demon was cast out and into whom the demon came again with seven other demons worse than the first, so that the last state of that man was worse than the first (Matt. 12:45—Luke 11:26), but it is a leap in logic to conclude that therefore this was true of Mary and that she had a sevenfold possession of passion instead of a sevenfold endowment of grace. The one possessed of a demon was regarded and treated by Jesus as the victim of the evil spirit, not as an accomplice in vice. Jesus did not blame these victims for their sad condition. The divided consciousness, peculiar frenzy, and long fits of silence of the demoniac make it wholly unlikely that Mary was a harlot. Her condition was bad enough. Recall the case of the wild man who had two thousand demons in him and how uncontrollable he was be-

fore he was healed. Surely Mary Magdalene had
grounds enough for deep gratitude to Jesus.

Those who treat Mary Magdalene as an abandoned woman identify her with the woman of the
street who slipped into the house of Simon the
Pharisee with an alabaster box of myrrh and stood
at the feet of Jesus, weeping, who wet his feet with
her tears and wiped them with her hair, who kissed
his feet and anointed them with the myrrh. There
is no question concerning the character of this
woman. She was a woman of the town and the pious
Pharisee was amazed that Jesus, passing as a
prophet, should be so ignorant as to allow such a
woman to take liberties of this nature (Luke 7:39).
But Jesus did know of her many sins and had forgiven her. Her great love was due to the forgiveness
she had received. Was she Mary Magdalene? If so,
why did not Luke say so? It is hardly conceivable
that Luke would have concealed the name of the
sinful woman in chapter 7:35–50 and then adroitly
introduced Mary Magdalene in 8:1–3 either to keep
his readers from identifying her with the sinful
woman or to suggest by inference that she was.
Either alternative is quite out of harmony with
Luke's method and manner. Of course, Luke may
not have known of the evil life if that were a fact,
but the Fourth Gospel does not give the slightest
indication of such a past life. The introduction of
Mary Magdalene in Luke 8:1–3 is plainly that of
a new character with no connection with the sinful
woman of the preceding paragraph. Mayor says
that Luke could easily have said in defense of Jesus

that the sinful woman had been under Satanic influence and freed of demons and hence was showing her gratitude. But she is simply termed a sinner. If Mary Magdalene had been a common harlot, would she have been allowed to travel with Jesus and his company? Mayor asks if it would not have been placing an additional temptation in the path of one known to be unusually weak. If the Messiah were known to allow one of notorious character to travel in his group over Galilee, some might draw wrong conclusions about them all. Luke probably did not know the name of the sinful woman and closes the incident about her at the end of chapter 7. Mary Magdalene was "a healed invalid, not a rescued social derelict" (L. M. Sweet). We do not find that Mary Magdalene did anoint the feet of Jesus. She is introduced in Luke 8:2 as a new character with no connection with the sinful woman at all.

Let Mary stand upon her own feet in the group of women in Luke 8:1-3. This is a notable company, the first organization of women for the support of the gospel of Christ. What would have been the fate of Christianity if it had appealed only to men like Mithraism, its chief rival in the second and third centuries? These women had all been healed of various diseases and had particular grounds for gratitude to Jesus. They were ministering with their property for the support of Jesus and his group of twelve preachers. It required courage and circumspection for these women to carry out this laudable enterprise and they prob-

ably incurred criticism. Apparently they had all
been healed of evil spirits and weaknesses, but
Mary Magdalene had special occasion for consecration because seven demons had gone out of her. The
number of women is not given, though Luke says
that they were "many." Blessings on these women
who were the first to rally to the call of Christ for
money.

Legend goes further with Mary Magdalene and
actually identifies her with Mary of Bethany as
well as with the sinful woman of Luke 7 and on
even less basis of fact. It is argued that the name
of the host in each of the two anointings is Simon,
but this was a very common name. In one case it is
Simon the Pharisee who sneers at Jesus, his guest.
In the other case it is Simon the leper who gives a
feast in honor of Jesus. The one anointing is by a
woman who had been a sinner, the other by Mary
of Bethany, who does it with her mind on the death
of Jesus. She alone showed any comprehension of
that tragic event coming upon them. The Pharisee's
complaint is about the ignorance of Jesus. The
other complaint is about the wastefulness of Mary
of Bethany. A mere detail is that in both cases there
is an anointing and wiping of the feet of Jesus with
the hair. Clearly Luke does not describe Mary
Magdalene in Chapter 7 under the guise of a sinful
woman, for he introduces her as a new character
in 8:2. Least of all does he mean in 10:38–42 that
Mary of Bethany is Mary Magdalene and certainly
not the sinful woman of Chapter 7. Martha and
Mary, her sister, are given their first description by

Luke in 10:38–42. The Mary of Bethany here bears no similarity at all to Mary Magdalene. Luke alone, in chapter 7, gives the anointing apparently during the Galilean ministry while Matthew and Mark and John give the one at the close of the ministry during passion week. It is only by a patient examination of all the confusion created by legend in the light of actual Scriptural data that one can sweep aside the cobwebs spun through the centuries. All three of these women had abundant cause for gratitude to Christ, but that does not mean identification. Legions of other women were also grateful. It is impossible to think that John in the Fourth Gospel confused Mary of Bethany and Mary Magdalene, either from ignorance or on purpose. It is hard, besides, to think of Mary Magdalene as the sister of Martha.

There seems to be no end of speculative confusion in ancient writings. One tries to identify Mary Magdalene as the daughter of the Syro-Phœnician woman. Another suggests that there were two Mary Magdalenes, one in Matthew and the other in John. Baring-Gould suggests that the starting point of most of these legends is due to the traditions about Marius who defeated the Ambrons and Teutons at Aix B. C. 102. At Les Baux where Marius encamped, an ancient sculpture of three figures is called *Tremaie* which Gilles interprets as Marius, his wife, Julia, and the prophetess Martha. But tradition has taken this to include Mary Magdalene. There is another *Trois Maries* sculpture at

Camargue. So legend grows spinning out fanciful details.

Mary Magdalene is a clear-cut figure in the Gospels, if painters would only take her as she is there depicted. She does not appear again in the narrative till we see her standing at the Cross of Jesus with the mother of Jesus, her sister, and Mary, the wife of Cleopas. She was one of the watchers of the Cross. The mother of Jesus was taken away from the Cross to the home of the Beloved Disciple (John 19:26–27), but the other women ("many other women") remained "beholding from afar" (Mark 15:40) the dreadful tragedy, these faithful women who had followed Jesus all the way from Galilee (Matt. 27:56; Luke 23:49). These women were at the Cross when all the apostles but John had fled in terror. The other of the sons of Zebedee was there, but John and James were not there. Mary Magdalene was apparently the leader of this group of women in the sad vigil at the Cross of Christ.

When Jesus was really dead, "Mary Magdalene and Mary, the mother of Jesus, beheld where he was laid" (Mark 15:47). Mark uses the imperfect tense (*etheoroun*) and it was therefore more than a casual glance, a prolonged and anxious watch as Mary Magdalene and the other Mary were "sitting over against the tomb" (Matthew 27:61). They observed how his body was "laid" (Luke 23:55) and then returned and rested during the Sabbath day (Luke 23:56). It was a sad and sorrowful Sabbath. Some-

how the women managed to go through the gloom
of that dark day. The women apparently knew
nothing of the Roman guard which Pilate had put
at the tomb.

Late on the Sabbath day Mary Magdalene and the
other Mary went to see the sepulcher (Matthew
28:1; Luke 23:56). After the Sabbath was over (at
sundown) Mary Magdalene and Mary, the mother
of James and Salome, bought spices, that they
might anoint him (Mark 16:1). Then they waited
till next morning while it was yet dark and Mary
Magdalene and the other women started from Bethany with the spices. When they reached the tomb to
the north of Jerusalem, the sun had risen (John
20:1; Luke 24:1; Mark 16:2). According to John's
account, Mary Magdalene ran in her eagerness and
arrived at the tomb before the rest. She stopped
long enough to see that the stone was rolled away,
without looking into the tomb. She draws the conclusion that there had been a grave robbery. She
suspects the enemies of Christ of having done
this despicable thing. At any rate it was clearly a
man's job. Mary Magdalene hurries on without
waiting for the other women to tell Peter and John
her fears: "They have taken away the Lord out of
the tomb, and we know not where they have laid
him." She was mistaken in her interpretation of
the empty tomb, but it was a natural error. She followed on after Peter and John and arrived after
they had departed.

Mark, in the disputed close of the Gospel (16:9),
says that Jesus "appeared first to Mary Magdalene

from whom he had cast out seven demons." This testimony, though probably not a part of Mark's Gospel, yet has the confirmation of John's Gospel. Some critics wish to discredit this first witness to the resurrection of Jesus. It is urged that she was a paranoiac and was in the habit of seeing things. Because of her previous condition at the hands of the demons she is pictured as a nervous wreck. Certainly she does not act then as if she was a victim of tremors and hallucinations. She did not expect the resurrection of Jesus from the dead and she does not imagine that fact as the explanation of the empty tomb. She was the last at the Cross and the first at the tomb and shows keen interest in the empty tomb as a probable desecration. Her witness does not come from a woman who is a nervous wreck.

John's Gospel (20:11–19) gives the marvelous picture of Mary in her interview with the risen Christ. She was standing outside weeping as she paused a moment before looking into the tomb. Peter and John had gone and Mary knew nothing of John's intuitive conclusion that the Lord was risen (John 20:8). She finally stooped and looked through her tears into the empty tomb. Amazed she saw two angels in the tomb, clad in white, sitting one at the head and the other at the foot. For some reason Peter and John did not see these angels, though the other women had seen them (Mark 16:5–8; Matt. 28: 5–8; Luke 24:4–8). Luke speaks of "two men," while Mark mentions only one "young man sitting on the right side." Matthew

calls this *man* an *angel*. It is not pertinent therefore to say that Mary Magdalene just imagined
that she saw the angels. What about the other
women? Mary Magdalene knew nothing at all of
their experience. Mary Magdalene told the same
story to the angels that she had given to Peter and
John. Her fear was that enemies of Christ had
robbed the grave of the body of Jesus.

Why did Mary Magdalene turn back at this juncture? Her eyes were full of blinding tears and not
expecting to see Jesus, the Risen Christ. In the case
of Cleopas and his companion their eyes were
holden so that they did not recognize Jesus (Luke
24:16). Mark has it that Jesus appeared in "another form" (16:12). At any rate Mary has a new
idea no more right than the other one. She suspects
that the gardener has merely moved the body of
Jesus to another tomb for a fresh burial in this
tomb. There is the utmost pathos and tenderness in
her words: "Sir, if thou hast borne him hence, tell
me where thou hast laid him, and I will take him
away." Her mind is still all bent on honoring the
body of Jesus with no hope of his resurrection. That
was her reply to the question of Jesus: "Woman,
why weepest thou? Whom seekest thou?" There is
no indication of the sudden revelation that came to
Mary Magdalene first of all. It came clearly from
no psychological peculiarity of Mary Magdalene.
Her mind was all turned in another direction.

In moments of great tragedy, of sorrow, of joy,
one can say very little. Words come with difficulty
and fail to express the deep emotion felt. Jesus said

simply, "Mariam" as the Greek has it, the Aramaic form of the name. He spoke it with the accent that she knew and loved. There was no mistaking his voice, now that she saw with undimmed eyes. Her mind was no longer holden and Jesus was not in another form. When he stood before her, her theories of grave robbery and then of the removal of the body by the gardener vanished like mist before the sun. And yet what can she say? There was only one word to utter. It was "Rabboni," likewise in Aramaic, "My Lord," "My Rabbi," "My Master." This word told it all. Mary Magdalene confronted the Risen Christ with dignity, with faith, with joy.

Mary Magdalene did not restrain a natural impulse to take hold of Jesus, to put her hands upon him, to cling to him in joy. But this was going too far. Jesus did allow the other women to clasp his feet as they worshiped him (Matthew 28:9). So he said to Mary Magdalene, "Cease clinging to me." He explains why he is still here: "For I am not yet ascended to the Father." It is not as it once was and his body is in a transition state before he is glorified. Probably Mary Magdalene could not comprehend this clearly, though she did not demur.

But Jesus had a message for Mary to carry to the brethren: "Say to them, I ascend unto my Father and your Father, and my God and your God." He has brought a new conception of God as Father and now he links the disciples with him in the glorious fellowship. It is the Son of God in a sense not true of others, but Jesus calls us his *brothers* with the same Father, God.

It was a message of mystery and of joy. Mary Magdalene added some words of her own as she told it. It was the most wonderful message ever brought by merely human lips, "I have seen the Lord." This was her crown of glory. It should have brought untold joy to all, but they were not ready to believe Mary's story. They "disbelieved" her (Mark 16:11), possibly thinking Mary had the demons back again. They were mourning and weeping (Mark 16:10), but the talk of the women was "idle talk" (Luke 24:10, 22).

Mary Magdalene's story was confirmed by that of Simon Peter (Luke 24:34; I Corinthians 15:5) and that brought conviction. But she was right before Simon Peter bore his witness. John has evidently taken joy in painting the noble picture of Mary Magdalene as she carried the glad news of the Risen Lord. She is the first herald of the Gospel of the Risen Christ, the message that has brought cheer to the world.

CHAPTER VIII

Epaphras the Newsbearer

News is one of the most important things in the world. The great newspaper world rests upon the promulgation of news. Many a man has to decide what is news before he puts it in his papers. The taste of the public about daily, weekly, monthly, and quarterly journals, is whimsical and changing. Even the government has to place limits on the circulation of certain kinds of journals, yellow and rotten. In Athens when Paul was there, he found the fidgety whimsical fever for the very latest items of news. But all the same the gospel in Greek is good news, the news of salvation, the glad tidings of God's love to men in Christ. The Greek word for preacher is "herald" and the real preacher finds his joy in telling the story of Jesus to men. The peril of the present-day preacher is that he tells the old story in a hum-drum way so that the news element vanishes. That is the great opportunity of the missionary that he has people before him who have not become tired of the message, who may not have heard it before. Kanamori of Japan will not let people hear his three-hour sermon who have heard it before. He tries to tell the whole gospel in one sermon. We cannot do that to-day, but it is within one's power to make what we do tell fresh and gripping and winning.

Epaphras came to Paul in Rome from Colossae, where he lived and worked, "Epaphras, who is one of you" (Col. 4:2). We do not know whether Epaphras was born in Colossae or not, but certainly he came from that city to Rome. His name is a shortened form of Epaphroditus, but he is certainly not the Epaphroditus from Philippi (Phil. 2:25). It was common then, as now, for men to have similar names.

Paul had not visited Colossae (Col. 2:1). It is probable that Epaphras had heard Paul in Ephesus or that Paul's message had been carried over Asia to Epaphras by those who heard Paul in Ephesus. Paul had said to the elders of Ephesus that for three years night and day he was in Asia and was with them all the time (Acts 20:18, 31). He may have made brief excursions into the province of Asia, but that is not the natural meaning of Luke's report. And yet Luke says that both Jews and Greeks in all Asia heard the word of the Lord (Acts 19:10) and Demetrius told his fellow-craftsmen that "almost throughout all Asia this Paul had persuaded and turned away much people" (Acts 19:26). It seems plain therefore that, directly or indirectly, Epaphras was a convert from Paul's work in Ephesus.

But he was more than that. The correct text in Col. 1:17 speaks of Epaphras as "a faithful minister of Christ on our behalf" instead of "on your behalf." This is the reading of the oldest Greek manuscripts and is clearly correct. So then the meaning is that Epaphras was Paul's representative in Christ, his delegate in the gospel since he could not go himself. Paul while in Ephesus had sent Epaphras to evangelize Colossae as well as Laodicea and Hieropolis (Col. 4:12 and 13), in a word the Lycus Valley. Epaphras had labored much and successfully in this important region of Asia and Paul had great agony of heart about them (Col. 2:1). They had not seen his face, but he had sent Epaphras to them and Paul is grateful for God's blessing on his work. The correct text in Colossians 1:7 makes it plain that Epaphras was the first missionary to them, "even as ye learned from Epaphras." The word "also" is not genuine. Epaphras did not just add to what they already knew as "also" would imply and as is true of most preachers from the nature of the case. He was the very first to tell the story of Christ in this great valley. He was the missionary who was the instrument in winning these people to Christ.

And he did his work well. Paul calls him "our beloved fellow servant" and "faithful minister of Christ" (Col. 1:7). He was an exponent of Paul's gospel and a faithful interpreter of Christ to these important cities in the Lycus Valley. The very zeal of Epaphras for Christ and his strong love for Paul led him to come to Rome to tell the great Apostle to the Gentiles the story of conditions in Asia. Epaphras had done what he could to stem the tide of false teaching that swept into this region. Paul at Miletus had told the Ephesian elders of the grievous wolves that would cause havoc after he had gone (Acts 20:29). So Epaphras goes to Rome to tell Paul, prisoner as he was, the sad situation in Colossae. Men called Gnostics had come who were misleading some of the followers of Christ by their subtle philosophy and affectation of superior learning. These men had a theory of matter as wholly evil and so they held that God could not be the Creator of evil matter. Hence they postulated the hypothesis of *œons* or intermediate agencies that came in below God until one was found far enough away from God to create matter without contaminating God and yet with power enough to do the work. If one wonders at such philosophic foolishness having a following, he has only to recall theosophy to-day and "new thought" and so-called "Christian Science" to understand how gullible some people are. This Gnostic view of creation came in from Persia with a dash of Essenism and confronted Christianity with its Christ. At once some of them said that Christ was one of the lower *œons*. That degrading view of Christ alarmed Epaphras and it alarmed Paul, who wrote the powerful little Epistle to the Colossians to magnify the Headship of Christ in the realm of nature and of grace. Epaphras bore this sad news to Paul and he told it to Paul in such intelligent fashion that Paul grasped the whole situation and expounded the emptiness of this false philosophy and the peril to the faith and lives of these who fell under the spell of these who became either ascetics or libertines. It is a credit to the intelligence and the courage of

Epaphras that he voluntarily turned to Paul as the only man who could handle this great issue.

So Epaphras came to Rome and apparently fell a victim to the Roman hostility to Paul. He calls him "our beloved fellow-bondsman" (Col. 1:7) and "my fellow-captive in Christ Jesus" (Philemon 23). It is possible to take these phrases in a metaphorical sense, but the latter phrase is far more naturally understood in a literal sense. It is used of Aristarchus (Col. 4:10) and of Andronicus and Junias (Rom. 16:7). Paul calls Timothy a "bondservant of Christ Jesus" (Phil. 1:1) and elsewhere save in Col. 1:7 only of himself. It seems more likely that Epaphras showed so much eagerness to be with Paul that he incurred the displeasure of the authorities in spite of Paul's liberty to see his friends (Acts 28:30) or perhaps he voluntarily assumed captivity with Paul as Aristarchus may have done in order to be with Paul the more constantly. At any rate he was not the bearer of the letter to the Colossians as would have otherwise been the case. He was apparently a sharer of Paul's imprisonment.

Epaphras had by no means lost his interest in the saints in the Lycus Valley. He had given Paul a most favorable report of the progress and faith of the churches there which stirred Paul's heart to gratitude and thanksgiving when he heard it (Col. 1:4–9). Epaphras had told of their faith and love and hope and grasp of the word of truth. The story of Epaphras made Paul pray with renewed zeal that they might have full knowledge of Christ

as an antidote to the false and superficial teachings
of the Gnostics. But Epaphras himself kept up his
agonizing prayer for the Colossians that they may
stand firm and be fully established in the will of
God. So Paul includes the salutation of Epaphras
as the one who has done most for them as disciples
of Christ and who deserves most at their hands
(Col. 4:12 and 13).

So we may think of Epaphras a prisoner with
Paul left behind in Rome while Tychicus and
Onesimus the converted runaway slave bear the
letters to Philemon in Colossae (Col. 4:7–9) and
another circular letter to Hierapolis (Col. 4:16)
which we now call the Epistle to the Ephesians.
Onesimus comes with some embarrassment because
of uncertainty as to what the attitude of Philemon
will be toward Onesimus. Paul throws his whole
heart into the plea to Philemon that must have won
acquiescence. But Tychicus was unhampered. He
will tell the whole story about Paul's situation in
Rome (Col. 4:7). Paul has sent Tychicus for this
very purpose that the Colossians may get fresh
information in fuller form than Paul can put into a
letter. Tychicus will comfort their hearts by the
way that he gives the probabilities about Paul's release. He asked Philemon to reserve a room for him
(Philemon 22). Let us hope that after his release
he did reach Colossae and saw Philemon, but this
is all speculation.

But the Colossians would wish to know also
something about Epaphras. Tychicus could tell
them why he was not able to come back and speak

for himself. He would be sure to tell of his loyalty to the Colossians and how nobly he had presented the whole case of their faith and of the peril in which they were because of the Gnostics. Epaphras had been a wise and faithful interpreter to Paul of the conditions in the Lycus Valley. They were fortunate in having such a man as Epaphras as their minister and now as their pleader with Paul. Their case was in good hands.

We are not able to follow the story of Epaphras any further. There is a tradition that he did return to Colossae and become bishop of the church there. Another tradition is that he suffered martyrdom and that his bones were buried in the church of Sta. Maria Maggiore in Rome. One can only hope that the Colossians did see again the face of this faithful servant of Christ and that Paul also carried out his wish to come. But a veil of silence rests on all this as also on the question whether John Mark ever reached Colossae or not (Col. 4:10). At any rate Paul had sent to the Colossians, probably by Mark himself, a note of kindly commendation. Mark is now in Rome with Paul and sends his greetings with the rest. Epaphras disappears from our knowledge, but he did his work. He was the bearer of good news to the Lycus Valley and to Paul. So let us to-day pass on the glad tidings of Jesus our Lord and Savior.

CHAPTER IX

The Samaritan Woman Who Started a Revival

THIS nameless woman is not the only woman who has started a revival of religion. There was Lydia, the first European convert in Paul's ministry, whose conversion led to the founding of the first church in Macedonia, and under Lydia's influence it became the first church that gave financial support to Paul's missionary campaign. It is a great mistake to think women have only of late been active in Christian work. Many a revival through all the centuries has been due to the consecration, prayer, and work of a single woman, sometimes a woman on a bed of affliction who kept in touch with the throne of God.

In the case of the Samaritan woman (John 4:5–42) there were apparently insuperable difficulties in the way of anything that she could do to help on the Kingdom of God. Race prejudice was bitter between the Jews and the Samaritans. The Jews hated the Samaritans all the more because they were half-Jews just as some people to-day give an added touch of dislike to neighbors who are kin to them. Later James and John wanted to call down fire from heaven to consume the Samaritans who did not welcome them when they were going to-

wards Jerusalem (Luke 9:51–56). This woman is
greatly surprised that Jesus should rise above this
hatred and ask a favor of her, a Samaritan. It is
a tragedy to-day that race prejudice and national
jealousy play so large a part in the life of nations
and of individuals. The Christian leaven of love
has not permeated modern life to such an extent
that men will usually be just to those of another
race or nation.

But this Samaritan was a woman besides being
a Samaritan. She felt a sense of inferiority on both
grounds and she herself spoke of these two obstacles (John 4:9). The Jews showed their dislike of
her as a Samaritan. And men (both Jews and Samaritans) reminded her that she was only a
woman. One of the prayers of the rabbis preserved
to us was an expression of gratitude to God that
the rabbi was not a woman. Even the disciples
were astonished (continued to be amazed, imperfect tense *ethaumazon*) that the Master was talking with a woman (John 4:27) in public where
anybody could see him. It was not considered good
form for a rabbi to speak with a woman in public.
It was actually said by rabbis that a husband
would be sure of *gehenna* if he talked too much
with his wife. And yet the disciples did not dare
to ask Jesus why he had not conformed to this con-
vention, much as they wished to do so. All the
liberty that women enjoy to-day they owe to Jesus
who broke the shackles of bondage by which they
were bound.

This woman at first failed to understand the

parable of water, quick as she was in wit and repartee. Jesus met her on the common ground of the water from Jacob's well which she had come to draw at the evening hour (6 P. M., Roman time used in John's Gospel). He was weary from the day's journey and was sitting on the curbstone of the well when the woman came up. Jesus asked for a drink of water from the well, but, woman that she was, she had to have the independence of Jesus explained in his asking a favor of her. But he quickly changed the topic and affirmed that she would have asked him for living water, if she had really known the gift of God. She states her difficulties, of course, in the way of her understanding this Jewish stranger. He had no bucket and no rope and the well was deep. Surely he did not claim (*me,* expecting a negative answer) to be greater than Jacob who gave them the well. But Jesus is patient with this woman and explains that she will never thirst again, but there will be in her a fountain of water bubbling up into eternal life. Imagine the woman's keen interest in spite of her apparent dullness about spiritual things. The metaphor of Jesus was still too deep for her. Still she bantered back to Jesus that he would please give her this kind of water that she might not have to come every evening to this well and draw the water for her family. The woman is still the water carrier in the Orient.

Many a preacher has quit when he finds one so dense as this woman, but Jesus persevered. He gave her a sudden personal thrust: "Go call your

husband and come here." Clearly she was now em-
barrassed at this unexpected turn of the conversation with this stranger. She was reluctant to heed
his request for it involved exposure of her own life
and there was no telling what this stranger would
say when the two were together before Jesus. Perhaps she felt that her husband would be no match
for this stranger. So she countered by a technical
splitting of hairs as a dodge: "Sir, I have no husband." She thought perhaps that this hedge would
protect her against any further probing of her own
life which she did not wish to discuss. Imagine her
surprise when Jesus bluntly said to her. "You said
well 'I have no husband,' because you have had five
husbands, and now the one that you have is not
your husband. This is strictly true what you have
said." The woman was amazed again at the insight
of the stranger into her own wicked life. But she
has one more line of defense, one that many sinners have tried when the preacher becomes personal and touches a sore spot. She shows a sudden
interest in theology and wants to change the subject to the old dispute between the Jews and Samaritans about the true place to worship God.
She confesses that the stranger is a prophet, meaning this as a compliment, and seizes upon this dis-
covery as her way of escape from further personal
inquiries of an embarrassing nature. The Jews had
their temple in Jerusalem, still wonderful in its
glory. The Samaritans had lost their temple on
Mt. Gerizim which rose majestically above, as she
spoke. But the Samaritans clung to this mountain,

as the handful of them do yet, as the only place
where God should be worshiped. So the woman
with quick repartee raises this famous theological
problem with a sigh of relief. But it was of short
duration, for Jesus explains to her that God is
spiritual and is not confined to one temple or one
mountain and must be worshiped in spirit by men
wherever they are. Jesus definitely, however, said
that salvation was of the Jews.

The woman probably had a sense of weariness
and of disappointment as she replied: "I know
that Messiah comes, who is called Christ. Whenever that one comes he will announce all things
to us." She loses her sudden interest in theology
and falls back upon the Messianic expectations
common to both Jews and Samaritans. The episode would probably have ended right here but
for the startling words of Jesus: "I am he, the
one who is speaking to you." It was like a bolt
out of the blue and gave the woman an electric
shock that precipitated all the previous talk to an
inevitable conclusion. It was now plain that she
was face to face with the long-looked for Messiah
of whose actual advent she had apparently heard
nothing. This was the first appearance of Jesus in
Samaria though John the Baptist had labored in
Aenon near to Salem. The time for decision had
come to this woman and she quickly made up her
mind what to do. It often happens that at critical
moments interruptions come which are sometimes
deplorable in their results. It might have been so
at this time when the disciples came back from

Sychar and found Jesus talking in public with a woman. They evidently showed their surprise to the woman, though they said nothing to Jesus about her.

So she instantly left her water pot and went hurriedly off to Sychar and had a wonderful story to tell to the people there. She is all ablaze with enthusiasm now and is not ashamed of her new faith in the Messiah. These people all knew her sinful life and she has nothing to conceal from them. So she says: "Come see a man who told me all that I have done. Is this the Messiah?" She had done so many wicked things that this fact added piquancy to her story. And she showed a woman's wit in the form of her question. She used the Greek negative (*me*) that threw doubt on the query and really expected the answer, "no." But she was psychologist enough to know that this was the way to excite the curiosity of the people of Sychar instead of starting a debate. She had not expressed a positive conviction. It was a case of too good to be true. So the people streamed out of town, were coming to Jesus in a long line. This was the first Samaritan convert and she became an evangelist of grace on the spot.

Many of the Samaritans from Sychar who came at the woman's invitation believed on Jesus as the Messiah "because of the saying of the woman bearing witness." She did not have much that she could say beyond telling her personal experience that brought the crowd to Jesus.

But these new converts begged Jesus to come

with them to Sychar and preach to them. So he
did and remained there two days. It was a short
meeting, but a powerful one. "Many more believed
because of his preaching and said to the woman:
'No longer are we believing just because of your
talk; for we ourselves have heard him, and we
know that he is truly the Saviour of the world.'"
Jew as he was, they took him as their Messiah and
Savior. They had the breadth of vision to see that
Jesus was the Savior of the whole world. It is a
remarkable outcome. This great Samaritan revival
came about in the most incidental way. The woman
who was the agent in spreading the glad news of
her own conversion was the most unlikely prospect
in the town. But, once she was converted to faith
in Christ, she wished to share her joy with others,
her friends and neighbors. She had courage and
skill to take right hold all by herself and to bring
the people to Jesus that they might see for themselves. It is pitiful what flimsy excuses we make
for our neglect and indifference. It we really took
hold right where we are, we could get people to
church and to Christ.

It was a joyful time for Jesus. He was leaving
Judea for the present because of the jealousy of
the rabbis there. He was on his way to Galilee to
get away from the opposition of the Pharisees,
which was to follow him there. But here in Samaria the soul of Jesus rejoiced at the prospect
of the harvest of the world. The conversion of this
one Samaritan woman was a prophecy of what
could come and what did come so soon at Sychar.

Jesus had no appetite for food brought by the disciples who little understood the ecstasy of Jesus who was feeding on doing the will of his Father who had sent him to do this work. They will know ere long the joy of such work, but now they do not understand the joy of Jesus. We can make Christ happy by personal evangelism. We can bring our friends to Jesus. We can start a revival in our own hearts, our own home, our own church, our own town.

CHAPTER X

SIMON MAGUS THE MERCENARY PRETENDER

THE recurrence of pious pretenders during the centuries gives poignancy and pertinency to the story of Simon Magus in Acts 8:9, 24. The very grotesqueness of this bizarre character led some scholars to doubt the historical reality of the picture in Acts. Legend has been busy with the name of this magician. In the so-called Clementine literature of the third century (the *Homilies* in Greek, the *Recognitions* in Latin) Peter is glorified and Paul is denounced. Paul is pictured under the name of Simon who holds debates with Peter in Cæsarea, Tyre, Laodicea, and Antioch. Later legend has Simon denounced by Peter in Rome. It is one of the curiosities of New Testament criticism that Baur made this legend the basis of his theory of *Tendenz* Literature in the New Testament. He denied that Simon Magus was a real character. He was merely a representation of Paul as a term of reproach in his conflict with Peter. So then Baur made Acts a book of compromise to smooth out the rivalry between Peter and Paul and without real historical value. But the Tübingen view of the New Testament has fallen by the way. It is now distinctly a back number.

It is probable that Justin Martyr, himself a native of Samaria, who wrote his *Apology* about a hundred years after the events in Acts 8, identifies Simon Magus with Simon of Gitta, six miles from Sebaste. This identification is by no means certain. The name is common enough and both are real persons. It is probable that Simon of Gitta was nearer to the time of Justin than Simon Magus of Sebaste. We know now that Justin Martyr confused a statue in Rome to the worship of *Semoni Sanco Deo Fidio,* a Sabine god, with the worship of Simon of Gitta, whom he also took to be Simon Magus, whom the Samaritans almost worshiped. Justin called him the first heresiarch, the first founder of heresy. There was a Simonian sect in Justin's day with a large following. Dante (*Inferno,* Canto XIX) cries: "Woe to thee, Simon Magus! Woe to you, his wretched followers!" There is no likelihood that Simon Magus was a full-fledged Gnostic as Justin knew the Gnostics in the second century. But he clearly held to the germs of the later Gnostic doctrines in his talk of "Power" and "Thought" much as modern theosophists do to-day. It is one incidental argument for the early date of Acts that Luke does not picture Simon in terms of the later Gnostics. He came to be regarded as the father of heresy. He was, in truth, the prototype of the later departures from the true faith. In him we see Christianity for the first time at grips with superstition and religious fraud. Such impostors were common-enough in that time. One has only to think of the Emperor

Tiberius on the Island of Capri with his flock of
Chaldaean soothsayers around him to see the prevalence of such impostors. In the Acts Luke carries
on the picture in the collision between Paul and
Elymas Barjesus in Cyprus, Paul and the Sons
of Sceva in Ephesus. The twentieth century cannot fling too many stones at the first when we recall the great vogue enjoyed by religious charlatans
to-day in all lands.

The description of Simon Magus in the Acts
gives us all our real information of this mercenary
pretender, this pious fraud, but it is enough. He
had a powerful hold in Samaria (Sebaste) and
had practiced his magical arts that astonished the
people of Samaria. They watched him ("fastened
their minds on him") because for a long time
they were astonished by his tricks. They looked
on him as a god because they could not explain
his deeds. With wide-eyed wonder the old and the
young people, in high places and in lowly homes,
gathered around him as a veritable hero. The recent death of the most famous modern wizard
ought to throw a light on this whole subject, for
he boasted that he could reproduce any tricks of
spiritualistic mediums and no one was able to solve
his gifts. But he died with his secrets unrevealed.

About A. D. 35 a false prophet gave it out that
he could find on Mt. Gerizim the sacred vessels
left there by Moses (though Moses was never
there). Such crowds followed this pretender that
Pontius Pilate sent soldiers to scatter them. It
was done with such slaughter that Pilate was sent

to Rome for trial and was banished to Switzerland.

Simon Magus reveled in the reputation that he had won in Samaria. He diligently gave it out that "he himself was some great one." He was by his own admission a personality of supreme importance. It is positively amazing how gullible people can be. Those who were under his spell kept saying: "This man is the Power of God that is called Great." So far from denying it, he rather implied by hints and chicanery that he was an emanation from God or *æon* as the Gnostics held, a common oriental doctrine. The Samaritans were grossly superstitious while Simon Magus was unprincipled. A form of conceit may have at times inclined him to belief in his own powers as divine. But whatever self-delusion he had, he was a conscious impostor. When Philip appeared with his message that Jesus was the Messiah of Jewish hope, Simon Magus was naturally interested in this preaching which presented Jesus as a rival to himself. Probably at first he scouted it all in his own mind and took the miracles wrought by Philip as humbugs like his tricks which fooled the people. But finally it was clear to him that Philip had a power that he did not possess. He was in grave peril of being supplanted by the new doctrine. Apparently there was something in this new system. So Simon decided to get in on the ground floor of the thing and find out for himself what there was in it. So he "believed" as many at the first passover of Christ's ministry "believed in his name" (John 2:23), though Jesus "did not believe

in them." So again at the feast of tabernacles
"many believed on him" (John 8:30), while Jesus
uncovered their shallow and unreliable belief. In
the case of Simon Magus he may have accepted
Jesus as an equal or even superior to himself, but
he did not take him as Savior from sin and Lord
of his life. He submitted to baptism also, though
he had not undergone the spiritual change symbolized by the ordinance. He may have regarded
baptism as a sort of magical charm or spell that
might initiate him into whatever mysteries Christianity might have. So the Mithraists had a blood-
bath (*taurobolium*) which was supposed to work a
magical change at initiation.

There is an Old Testament parallel to Simon
Magus to be found in Gehazi who made money out
of the baptism of Naaman in the Jordan (2 Kings
V). It is significant how closely Simon "clung
to Philip and beholding signs and great miracles
taking place kept on being astonished." The Greek
word means literally "stood out of himself." He
almost jumped out of his skin with jealousy when
he saw the reality of the work of Philip. Simon was
now in this Samaritan church, but he had not discovered the secret of Philip's power.

The coming of Peter and John to Samaria to
investigate the work of Philip among the Samaritans brought a new crisis to Simon Magus. They
wholly endorsed what had been done in Samaria.
One can recall that John (and James) had even
wanted to call down fire on the Samaritans for
their cold reception of Christ and his workers. But

John has learned much since then. These Samaritan Christians were not baptized again. They had already believed and were baptized, but they had not received the special gift of the Holy Spirit such as came at the great Pentecost in Jerusalem. So Peter and John prayed for the Samaritan believers that they might receive this special gift. Later such a gift came on Cornelius and his company before their baptism and also still later on some ill-informed disciples of John the Baptist who were converted and baptized and then spoke with tongues and prophesied. Evidently the Samaritan Christians spoke with tongues also for Simon Magus "saw that by the laying on of the hands of the Apostles the Holy Spirit was bestowed on them." Here at last he seemed to be getting close to what he wanted. He simply must get this new "power" that he might retain or regain his influence with the people.

He acted on the principle of the devil that every man has his price. He knew that he did himself. He came up to Peter and John and "offered them money," probably holding the coins in his palm as he said: "Give to me also this power that on whomsoever I lay my hands he may keep on receiving the Holy Spirit." It was a dastardly proposition that stirred Peter to the depths of his soul with indignation. He had seen Peter transfer power to others. This human agency appears in Acts 2:4, 33; 4:31; 10:44, but Simon thought he only had to buy it to pass it on. If he could only get this power from Peter, then there was no limit to his power and influence. He simply took Peter and John to be more accomplished sorcerers than he was, who could be induced by bribing to tell their secret to him and share their power with him.

These two Simons, Simon Peter and Simon Magus, confronted each other. Peter had his own weaknesses and cowardice had been one of them in the hour of his own denials. But he is now a rock in reality and the temptation found no lodgment in his soul. With noble majesty he replied: "Thy money perish with thee, because thou actually didst suppose that thou couldst obtain the gift of God with money." Simon is not the only one who has had the audacity to try this scheme for selfish ecclesiastical promotion, but his very name has been given to this sin and crime. "Simony" it is called to-day in England when one seeks to obtain office in the Church of England by the use of money. This treatment of sacred functions as a marketable thing is contemptible and others besides clergymen are guilty of it. One of the losses from the union of church and state is precisely this thing, but many people look to money as the means of securing spiritual privileges and prerogatives. There is surely need to-day for alertness on the part of all that they do not fall into this only too common sin. The poorest can get as close to God as the richest. An example of "Simony" occurred as early as the third century and many councils condemned it.

But Peter had still more to say to Simon Magus:

"There is no part nor lot to thee in this matter, for thy heart is not straight before God." He had said that he "believed" and had been baptized, but it was all false, "for I see that you are in the gall of bitterness and the bond of iniquity" (cf. Psalm 78:37). He had forsaken the straight way and had followed the way of Balaam, who loved the hire of wrong-doing (2 Pet. 2:15.). It was a sad outcome, but Peter had the courage to tear off the mask from this wolf in sheep's clothing and to reveal him in his true character.

Peter urges repentance and prayer: "Repent therefore of this thy wickedness if perchance the thought of thy heart will be forgiven thee." Peter clearly thinks that Simon Magus has come near to the unpardonable sin of blasphemy against the Holy Spirit. It was clear that he had never really repented or been converted. He was a charlatan and a shark, an impostor who wanted to traffic in spiritual things to his own advantage.

Simon Magus was taken aback at this sudden and unsparing exposure of his real self by Simon Peter. He said in reply: "Pray to the Lord for me that no one of these things of which you have spoken come upon me." He did not wish to pay the penalty for his great sin. Most criminals feel that way. But there is no evidence whatever that he ever repented and turned to the Lord. The root of the matter was not in him. He slunk back into his own hollow chicanery and went on trying to deceive the people. It is a tragedy that the Christian ministry is sometimes used by pretenders as a cloak to fleece the lambs. Jesus warned men against these wolves in sheep's clothing. Some of them, said Jesus, will almost deceive the very elect.

CHAPTER XI

HEROD ANTIPAS AND HERODIAS HOME WRECKERS

THE Gospels and Josephus give a vivid picture of two despicable characters in high life who serve as a warning to loose livers to-day. They are Herod Antipas and Herodias who represent the very worst elements of the time and yet who lived in the lime-light of political and social leadership.

Herod Antipas was the second son of Herod the Great and Malthace of Samaria, one of his ten wives. She was thus a Samaritan woman and only half-Jew at the most, while Herod the Great was an Idumæan. Josephus calls this Idumæan-Samaritan (only one-quarter Jew) Herod (*Antiquities,* XVIII. ii. 1) or Antipas (*Antiquities,* XVII. vii. 1). In the New Testament and in the coins he is simply termed "Herod." In the second of his father's wills he had been designated his sole successor, with the title of king, but in the last will he was to receive only Galilee and Perea with the title of tetrarch. In Mark 6:14f, and Matthew 14:9 he is called king in popular parlance. He contested this last will of Herod the Great, but Augustus sustained the will and Archelaus was given his chance in Judea (Josephus, *Antiquities,* XVII. xi. 4). Herod Antipas ruled as tetrarch from B. C.

4 to A. D. 39. When Joseph heard in Egypt that Archelaus was to get Judea, he was afraid to go to Bethlehem to live and so went back to Nazareth where Jesus spent his youth (Matthew 2:22–3).

Most of the active ministry of Jesus was spent in Galilee or Perea under the rule of this man who did not see him till the end. He was a builder of cities like his father and made Tiberias his capital, which still exists. Decapolis, a Greek region of ten cities, came in between Galilee and Perea and yet Herod Antipas managed to govern both sections with some skill. He had been educated at Rome with Archelaus and Philip and was not a man of integrity of character. Jesus warned his disciples against "the leaven of Herod" (Mark 8:15), probably his political trickery. He likewise called him "that fox" (Luke 13:31) when the Pharisees showed unusual interest in Jesus then in Perea. He informed them that he was in no sense afraid of the time-server, "for it cannot be that a prophet perish out of Jerusalem."

His brother Herod Philip, son of Herod the Great, and Mariamne (daughter of Simon of Jerusalem, the high priest), lived in Rome with his wife Herodias, daughter of Aristobulus (son of Mariamne, granddaughter of Hyrcanus II) and so a Maccabee, and niece of her own husband. On one occasion when in Rome at his brother Philip's house Antipas seduced Herodias and persuaded her to leave her husband and to come to him. It was a case of infatuation on both sides, like the affinity excuses in modern life and novels. She agreed to leave Philip, though they had a daughter, Salome, on condition that Antipas get rid of his own wife, a daughter of Aretas, king of the Nabatæans. When she heard that her husband, Antipas, had actually agreed to this dastardly proposal, she fled for refuge to her father, King Aretas, who waged war against him, A. D. 36, apparently nine years after her flight from Antipas. The severe defeat of Antipas by Aretas was interpreted by some to be a punishment by God for what he had done to John the Baptist (Josephus, *Antiquities,* XVIII. v. 2) as well as for his treatment of the daughter of Aretas. Vitellius, the Roman general, was under orders to go to the help of Antipas. The Romans did not like the pretensions of Aretas. But Vitellius had gone no further than Jerusalem when he heard of the death of the Emperor Tiberius (A. D. 37).

After the departure of his wife to her father, Aretas, somewhere about A. D. 25, Antipas married Herodias who had left her husband, Herod Philip, in Rome. It was as sorry a mess as anything that besmirches marriage to-day. Each divorced the husband or wife in order to marry. Antipas and Herodias were close kin, uncle and niece, an atrocious thing in itself from the Jewish standpoint. Women did sometimes divorce their husbands then as Salome, sister of Herod the Great, had done, and now as Herodias had done. But it was adultery in each case, as Mark 10:11 and 12 reports Jesus as saying, and in Matthew 5:32 and 19:9, remarriage of the innocent party is alone allowed. This flagrant conduct on the part of Herod Antipas and Herodias outraged the best Jewish public sentiment (Lev. 18:16; 20:21).

During the ministry of John the Baptist there was still indignant talk about it. It is possible that John was inveigled into Perea and into talk about this infamous marriage by the Pharisees who disliked him and who keenly resented his comparing them to broods of vipers (Matt. 3:7). They could easily draw him out by questions to take a stand on this marriage. But, however the issue was raised, John did not hesitate to condemn it in unmeasured terms, reproving Antipas "for Herodias his brother's wife and for all the evil things which Herod had done" (Luke 3:19). It seems that John was actually brought into the presence of Herod Antipas and Herodias, "for John said unto Herod: 'It is not lawful for thee to have thy brother's wife'" (Mark 6:18). At any rate "Herod himself had sent forth and laid hold upon John, and bound him in prison for the sake of Herodias, his brother Philip's wife; for he had married her" (Mark 6:17). This prison was at Machaerus, a powerful fortress, east of the Dead Sea (Josephus, *War*, VII. vi). It is plain in the Gospels that both Antipas and Herodias had a private grudge against John for his plain words to them. It is refreshing to find a preacher of righteousness who is not afraid to expose immorality in high places at the risk of his own life. Josephus says that Herod "feared lest the great influence that John had over the people might put it into his power and inclination to raise a rebellion" (*Antiquities,* XVIII. v. 2). But this is merely the public and political reason given by Josephus and in no way conflicts with the private anger cherished by him toward the brave prophet. Herod Antipas put John in prison and kept him in prison.

The real feeling of Herod toward John is a bit difficult to understand. Matthew 14:5 says that he wanted to put him to death, but feared the multitude who counted him as a prophet. But Mark (6:20) says that "Herod feared John, knowing that he was a righteous man and a holy, and kept him safe. And when he heard him, he was much perplexed and he heard him gladly." By combining the two statements we see that Herod really knew that John was right and was deeply impressed by his discourses in the prison. He had, however, spells of indignation against him for his plain and bold denunciation of Herodias and himself, which he apparently kept up, though a prisoner. These moods of rage were largely due to the constant prodding of Herodias, who "set herself against him (literally, had it in for him); and desired to kill him, and she could not." Herodias was a desperate woman and was determined to get vengeance on this preacher who had denounced her.

Herod had an uneasy conscience, it is plain, but Herodias watched her chance which came on the birthday of Herod when he made a supper to his lords and leaders at Machaerus. Herodias let her daughter Salome come in to dance before these dignitaries, a regular oriental licentious dance, in order to get power over Antipas when he became tipsy from the wine. So pleased was Antipas with the girl's exhibition of herself, that he gave his oath to give her what she wished, even to half of his kingdom. Probably Herodias expected this result and she was ready when Salome came out and said to her: "What shall I ask?" The answer was at hand, "The head of John the Baptist." "The king was exceeding sorry, but for the sake of his oaths, and of them that sat at meat, he would not reject her" (Mark 6:26). So the head of John the Baptist was brought into the feast to Herodias on a charger. The inference of the grewsome story (Mark 6:19–29; Matt. 14:6–12) is that Herodias gloated over her victim and Salome exulted in her sensual triumph, while Antipas in his muddled mind from drink and debauchery, sought to justify his brutality by respect for his oath in the presence of his guests. This was no road-house or bagnio, but the palace and fortress of the ruler of Galilee and Perea when his birthday feast was in progress. Wine, lewd dancing, murder. It is a modern combination and as old as human history. Herodias had sunk so low that she flung her own daughter into this drunken crowd to carry out her will against John the Baptist. The only noble picture here is that of John, who lost his head for his courage, but who towers still above them all. One thinks of Elijah before Ahab and Jezebel. Herodias was as relentless as Jezebel, but John did not run away, could not in fact.

It is plain that Herod Antipas was deeply grieved

over this outcome when he recovered from his drunken spree. The third tour of Galilee by Jesus, when he sent the Apostles out by twos, created a tremendous sensation. Herod had never seen Jesus, but he had seen John and still saw him at night as the head on a charger came slipping towards him in the dark. So he said unto his servants about Jesus: "This is John the Baptist; he is risen from the dead; and therefore do these powers work in him" (Matt. 14:2). He asked the people what they made of it all and the answers perplexed him still more (Luke 9:7). Some said it was Elijah, others agreed with Herod that it was John the Baptist come to life. But Herod argued: "John I be' eaded; but who is this about whom I hear such things?" (Luke 9:9). If he could only see him, but Jesus kept out of the way of this sly old "fox" who had had John beheaded. When he did see Jesus at his trial, Jesus kept absolute silence and wrought no miracles for his curiosity. Pilate had made friends by this courtesy, but he still had Jesus on his hands.

Both Herod Antipas and Herodias disappear from the New Testament story. Josephus (*Antiquities*, XVIII. vii. 2) gives the sad sequel which shows how powerful was the hold of Herodias on Antipas. When the young scapegrace, Herod Agrippa II, boon companion of Caius Caligula, the Emperor, won a crown, it was too much for Herodias. He had once been a mere beggar and unable to pay his spendthrift debts. So Herodias prodded Herod Antipas against his judgment to go to Rome and to beg of Caligula the title of King instead of

Tetrarch. But young Agrippa took advantage of this opportunity to reveal to Caligula the military supplies collected by Herod Antipas as if against Caligula. The result was that Antipas lost A. D. 39 the tetrarchy of Galilee and Perea, which went to young Agrippa while Antipas was sent in banishment to Lyons in Gaul. Caligula excused Herodias, who was really the cause of it all, but she accompanied her husband and proudly took her medicine with what grace she could. One wastes no sympathy upon the fate of this couple of home-wreckers. The lurid light of their wicked lives flares up beside the steady flame of John the Baptist and of Jesus our Lord.

CHAPTER XII

THE OPEN-EYED CHAMPION OF JESUS

ONE wishes that one knew the name of the fine spirit so brilliantly sketched in John 9:1–38. For some reason the Fourth Gospel does not give his name. But it is quite worth while to study him carefully even if we do not know his name. It is difficult to think that he is a legendary character as some modern scholars think. It is far simpler to accept the historicity of the narrative than to believe in the creative genius of the author. The whole story hangs together with wonderful verisimilitude and has pith and point for us to-day when some are timid about the claims of Jesus to deity.

The narrative opens with the puzzle of the disciples over the theological problem of the responsibility for the blindness of the unfortunate man (John 9:1–5), whether, since he was born blind, the sin was that of his parents or of the man himself. There is such a thing as disease caused by the sin of one's parents, a lamentable fact. How to prevent the birth of children by mental defectives and by hopelessly diseased parents is a real problem to-day. Some of the states in America have rigid laws on the subject. In the case of the lame man he had brought disease on himself by his own sin

(John 5:14). But the result (consecutive use of *hina* in 9:2) in the case of the man born blind was not his fault or that of his parents. Jesus affirms that God had a purpose in the man's tragedy. There is a comfort in this thought for many of us with our many limitations. God can and often does over-rule them for his glory and for working his own will. The phrase "the works of God" leads Jesus to link us with himself. The correct text in 9:4 is "We must work the works of him who sent me." There is dignity in this high association with Jesus in the works of God. There is power in it also. Linked with Christ, the Light of the world, we can shed light on others and use the power of God in Christ. So Jesus gave the disciples a profound philosophy of Christian work that should cheer all to-day who are pushing on the program of Christ for the redemption of the world.

The discussion over, Jesus voluntarily proceeded to heal the blind man who apparently had not asked or expected healing. Jesus was passing along and saw the man sitting at his usual place and begging alms as he had been doing all his life. The disciples had called the attention of Jesus to the man and much of good came out of their theological specula-tion, though they themselves apparently had no hope that Jesus would cure the man born blind (9:32). One cannot believe that Jesus made use of the clay and the spittle because there was any value in it, though some of the ancients did attach heal-ing virtue to the spittle. The power to heal rested in Jesus Christ who only occasionally used any intermediate agencies. Sometimes he employed the touch, but often it was a mere word. The use of spittle and clay would make the man willing to obey Jesus and go to the Pool of Siloam. But why was he sent to the water at all? Perhaps this act of obedience had some influence on the man's attitude. It was objective and may have counted for something in the man's own psychology. Coöperating with nature and helping the powers of nature often restores health. But here nature was completely defeated by this case of blindness. It was a simple thing that Jesus commanded. "He went off therefore and washed himself and came seeing." The impossible had happened and he was seeing the wonderful world for the first time. He did not know the name of the wonderful man who had healed him, but he knew that his eyes were opened however ignorant he might be of the method employed. Many patients to-day bear like witness to the skill and prowess of physicians and surgeons who have saved their lives.

The man had been a beggar all his life and so went back to his trade, but with wide open eyes (9:8–12). He had his regular stand and was apparently well known to those who passed him there. They had never seen him with his eyes open before. However, some men are fakirs and pose as blind men with blind days, so that a dispute arose among them concerning his identity. Some asked: "Is not this the fellow who used to sit and beg?" Others were positive and said: "This is he." Still others regarded it as a case of similarity or mistaken identity. "Not a bit of it, but he is just like him." So the matter stood till the man could bear it no longer. He had to speak: "I am the man." But this solution only increased their curiosity: "How then were your eyes opened?" It was a natural question, if he was not a fraud. He did not himself know how, the thing had been done. He could only tell the bare facts which he did. He only knew him as "the man called Jesus." But the inquirers were not satisfied: "Where is he?" They wanted to question Jesus about it. But the man could only say: "I do not know."

So they appealed to the Pharisees as responsible theological guides who ought to be able to solve all difficulties (9:13–16). This is the chief use that some people have for preachers and teachers. It is to settle theological disputes and untie hard knots. The Pharisees looked wise and solemn in their inquiry and brought out the fact that the thing was done by Jesus on the Sabbath day. But this item at once divided these doctors of the law. Some bluntly concluded: "This man (Jesus) is not from God, because he does not keep the Sabbath" (their ideas of the Sabbath as had been expressed before, John 5:18). But others of the Pharisees went further and asked: "How is a sinful man able to do such things?" It was a hard nut to crack. No wonder that a schism arose among the Pharisees on the point. They were not able to throw any light on the problem.

The Pharisees then turn to the man himself for help in their dilemma (9:17): "What do you say about him, since he opened your eyes?" It was a helpless and pitiful appeal by the theologians. All that he could say was: "He is a prophet." He did not really know any more.

The hostile Jews turn to the man's parents to see if there was not some slip in the thing somewhere, because they did not really believe that the man actually was born blind (9:18–23). This appeal was also a confession of failure on the part of the Jewish leaders. They were trying to save their faces, as pastmasters of wisdom. They really ask three questions in one: "Is this your son, who you say was born blind? How then does he now see?" It was adroit, but the parents knew more about Jesus than their son and also more of the animosity of the Jews whom they feared, because they had already plotted to turn out of the synagogue those who confessed Jesus as Messiah. They did not wish to run that risk. So the parents answered that he is their son and was born blind. They could certify to that, but they declined to say who had opened his eyes and how and passed that problem over to the son: "Ask him. he is of age, he will speak for himself." It was a skillful turn that completely discomfited the rabbis.

Once again they turn to the once-blind man, their only alternative in their theological tangle over the facts (9:24–34). To admit the facts would be to admit the claims of Jesus as Messiah. This time they take the turn of proposing that, if the fact is admitted, Jesus gets no credit for it: "Give glory to God. We know this man is a sinner." This was a distinct retreat from the position that a sinner could not do such a deed and, if it was done, it proved that Jesus was from God (9:16). They had to do something and they stand upon the other foot and claim their theological omniscience in spite of their proved incompetence. By this time the once-blind man's sense of humor is aroused. He knows little about Jesus save what he did to him, but he uses raillery and sarcasm as he lays bare the hopeless inconsistencies of these wiseacres. The man was quick in his pungent repartee: "Whether he is a sinner I do not know; one thing I do know, that though once blind, I now see." It was a homethrust and brushed aside all the pettifogging subterfuges of the Pharisees. They weakly ask again: "What did he do to you? How did he open your eyes?" The man's answer cut to the very quick: "I told you already and you did not listen. Why do you want to hear it again? Do you also wish to become his disciples?" This dig was too much, so that they reviled him with being the disciple of Jesus, which was not yet true. Sermons and hymns have misinterpreted the man's words about the opening of his eyes. The Pharisees claimed to be the disciples of Moses to whom God had spoken: "But this fellow we do not know whence he is." The man quickly saw the opening and waded right in: "Why herein is the wonder that you do not know whence he is and yet he opened my eyes." There is no answer to this sarcasm. He reminds them of their dictum that God does not hear sinners and yet he had opened his eyes: "If this man were not from God, he could

not do anything." He turned their own words to
their own confusion. The end comes to a tension
like this with withering scorn from the Pharisees:
"You were begotten, all of you, in sins and yet you
are trying to teach us." The ignorant upstart was
actually rebuking the learned professional ex-
pounders of the law! It was the limit and was not
to be endured. So they cast him out of the synagogue for his uppishness in getting the best of the
rabbis and exposing their theological quibbles before the public. The ounce of fact in this man's experience had put to rout a whole windbag of
reactionary and traditional theologizing.

The sequel is most interesting (9:35–40). Jesus
heard what the Pharisees had done to the man for
his valiant opposition to them. So he hunted him
up and said to him: "Do you believe on the Son
of man?" That was a piece of theology beyond his
knowledge. Se he merely says: "And who is he, sir,
that I may believe on him?" Jesus pointedly says:
"You have both seen him and he is the one who is
talking with you." The moment of decision for the
man had come. He was ready by the experience
that he had had. He surrendered on the spot: "I
believe, Lord." He would believe any claim made
by Jesus. So he worshiped him as Messiah and
Savior. God uses all his dealings with us to focus
them all on the great moment of crisis. Jesus had
won the open-eyed champion, this outcast from the
synagogue, this able and alert contender of the now
new faith. Jesus had lost the Pharisees who posed
as guides and lights. Their spiritual eyes were more

blind than ever, though they could still see with their physical eyes. But this once-blind man had his eyes open to see the wondrous world and the eyes of his heart were now open to see the glory of Jesus. It mattered little now what the Pharisees thought about him or did to him. He had seen the light of the knowledge of the glory of God in the face of Jesus Christ.

CHAPTER XIII

GAMALIEL THE THEOLOGICAL OPPORTUNIST

SCHOLARS are unable to agree on the spirit and
motives of Gamaliel I in his championship of Peter
and the other apostles who were brought again before the Sanhedrin for disobedience and for the
charge that they were responsible for the blood of
Jesus (Acts 5:28). Peter boldly affirmed that they
must obey God rather than man (5:29) and repeated his charge and reaffirmed the fact of the
resurrection of Jesus of which he and the other
apostles were witnesses. The Sanhedrin were cut
to the heart as if a saw had sawn them in two and
wanted to kill them on the spot though they no
longer had the power to put to death. They could
only do so illegally by mob law as they later did
in the case of Stephen. It was a real crisis that confronted the Sanhedrin, composed, as it was, of
both Pharisees and Sadducees, though the Presi-
dent of the Sanhedrin until after the destruction
of Jerusalem was a Sadducee (the chief priest)
and not a Pharisaic rabbi. After the destruction of
the temple the Sadducees and priests lost their influence. Whatever was done had to be done quickly,
if Peter and the apostles were not to be stoned as
Stephen was later. The attacks made against Peter,

John and the rest had so far been made by the Sadducees on the ground that they proclaimed in Jesus the resurrection from the dead (Acts 4:2–5: 17). Meanwhile the Pharisees were apparently quiescent until Stephen stirred them into hostility. Then the Sadducees were bent on a policy of destruction. What were the Pharisees to do at this crisis? It is at this juncture that Gamaliel steps forth as their spokesman.

Gamaliel (Reward of God) was the grandson of Hillel, the rival of Shammai and founder of the more liberal of the two theological schools of the Pharisees in Jerusalem. Furneaux (*The Acts,* p. 79) suggests that "Gamaliel may have been one of the doctors in the midst of whom the boy Jesus had sat, hearing and asking questions (Lu. 2:47)." At any rate we know that he had great influence in the Sanhedrin as the leader of the Pharisaic party. He was the first of the seven Jewish doctors of the law to be called *Rabban* like *Rabboni* applied to Jesus by Mary Magdelene (John 20:16). Once when Gamaliel was absent from the Sanhedrin, their decision to appoint a leap-year was to be valid only if Gamaliel agreed (Mishna, *Edajoth* vii:7). He had a grandson named Gamaliel II while he was himself later termed Gamaliel the Elder (*ha-zākēn*). He was a man of scholarly tastes as shown by his studies in Greek literature and by his advice to his students to follow his example in the study of Greek writers. The narrower rabbis thought that the study of Greek literature was as bad as Egyptian thaumaturgy. His more liberal outlook on life is shown by his teaching that the Jews should greet the heathen with "Peace be with you" even on a heathen feast day. He also taught that poor Gentiles should have the same right to glean the harvest fields as poor Jews. So also he championed the cause of wives against unprincipled husbands and of widows against greedy children. In fact the Mishna says (*Sota* ix:15) that "with the death of Gamaliel the reverence for the law ceased and purity and abstinence died away." It is plain also that Paul was proud of the fact that he had sat at the feet of Galamiel while a student in Jerusalem (Acts 22:3). It is a great experience for a brilliant student to have a great personality for a teacher. One thinks of Aristotle as the teacher of Alexander the Great. It is small wonder that young Saul cut forward in Judaism beyond his fellow students (Gal. 1:14.). It is plain that Gamaliel was the outstanding Pharisee of his day in the Sanhedrin as he was later considered the glory of the law. Annas and Caiaphas and John and Alexander were the leaders of the Sadducees in the attacks upon the Apostles (Acts 4:5 and 6). Against Jesus at first the Pharisees took the lead and only later the Sadducees joined them. Now the Sadducees were the aggressors while the Pharisees were reluctant to line up with the Sadducees where the doctrine of the resurrection was the issue.

But now Gamaliel came to the fore. What was his real attitude in this crisis, this "doctor of the law held in honor by all the people?" He first desired that the apostles be put out for a brief space that the Sanhedrin might discuss the problem without the embarrassment of their presence. Precisely this precaution had been taken once before (Acts 4:15). Then Gamaliel proceeded to give his interpretation of the situation in the nature of a *caveat* to the Sadducees who were bent on blood: "Ye men of Israel, take heed to yourselves in the case of these men as to what you are about to do." The members of the Sanhedrin were on trial, as well as the apostles. In this warning Gamaliel was undoubtedly right. That is always true in every emergency. But Gamaliel does not pointedly say that the apostles were innocent of any wrongdoing and should therefore be set free. He rather appeals to the self-interest of the Sadducees who might be running greater risks than they understood. In proof of his warning Gamaliel cites two historical examples of men who made great pretensions and who had come to naught by the natural course of events. The first is that of Theudas. Now Josephus (*Antiquities* xx. 5:1) tells of Theudas, a false prophet, who won a large following. He promised to divide the river Jordan as Joshua had done. But Cuspius Fadus, the Roman Procurator, sent a squadron of horse who slew many and took prisoners also and scattered the rest. Theudas himself was beheaded. So the episode came to naught. But this incident in Josephus occurred A. D. 46, ten years or more after the speech of Gamaliel. The event in Luke would have to be thirty years before that in Josephus. Hence a chronological historical difficulty arises with various solutions that are

offered. The easiest one is to say that either Luke
or Josephus has made a blunder in the date. The
blame used to be placed on Luke on the ground that
Josephus is more reliable as a historian. But Luke's
credibility has received strong reënforcement by
the new discoveries in the papyri and the inscrip-
tions, and Josephus has many errors in his writings. Another solution is that both are correct and
refer to different men. Josephus tells of four men
named Simon within forty years and three named
Judas within ten years who were instigators of rebellion. This can be said to those who consider it
improbable that two men of the same name within
thirty years should make false claims and meet a
like fate. Besides, the name Theudas is abbreviated
and may come from Theodosius, Theodorus, Theo-
dotus, etc. As matters stand now one will credit
Luke or Josephus according to his prejudices and
predilections. There is no trouble about the case of
Judas the Galilean (also Gaulonite) except that
the first failures of Judas the Galilean suits the
early date for Gamaliel's speech. Later the cause
of Judas the Galilean rallied again and made still
more trouble. So thus the two instances given by
Gamaliel are pertinent to his point. Theudas gave
himself out as a man of importance ("somebody")
and gathered four hundred followers, but he was
slain and his party dissolved and came to nothing.
Judas the Galilean in this early stage belonged to
the time of the enrollment (census), the second
one under Augustus, A. D. 6. This puts the date of
Theudas in Luke still earlier, for Luke says that

Judas came "after this one" (Theudas). Judas himself perished and his followers were scattered, even though in later years some of them did rally again. So much for the historical illustrations.

Now for the application, "now as to the present situation," Gamaliel draws his own conclusion along the line of his advice: "Stand off from and leave them alone." The Bezan text adds "and defile not your hands." But Gamaliel argues the case further: "Because if this counsel or this work be from men (a condition of the third class with the subjunctive mode, undetermined, but with probability of being determined), it will be overthrown; but if it is from God (a first-class condition with the indicative, assuming it to be true), you will not be able to overthrow them (the Bezan text adds, 'Neither ye nor kings nor despots. Refrain therefore from these men'), lest perchance ye be found even fighting against God." It was a powerful message, shrewd and convincing, that carried conviction for the moment. The Pharisees were in the majority in the Sanhedrin and they yielded assent to his doctrine of letting things go for the present. So the apostles were called in and beaten for having disobeyed the previous command to stop preaching Jesus and were told again not to speak in the name of Jesus and were set free.

But what were the real motives of Gamaliel in scoring this victory over the Sadducees for such it was? Some men even say that Gamaliel had become a convert to Christianity, but was afraid to show his colors even now, a secret disciple like

Nicodemus and Joseph of Arimathea, who had like them been really opposed to the crucifixion of Christ. But there is no real evidence for this interpretation. And the Talmud affirms that Gamaliel died a Jew. Some, like Wendt, deny that Gamaliel made this speech and consider it the invention of Luke, just as Baur holds that the peace-loving Gamaliel could not have been the teacher of the fanatical young Saul who came to relish the slaughter of the saints. One needs common sense in the interpretation of history and the avoidance of fanciful and whimsical difficulties. It is common enough for pupils to go beyond the master in extremes. It is to be noted also that, in the case of Stephen, Gamaliel did not lift his hand to stop the lynching, for the Pharisees, not the Sadducees, were attacking Stephen.

It is true that Gamaliel used the language of one who knew the power of God as the decisive factor in human affairs. As a broad generalization his point is true that it does not pay to fight against God. As Furneaux well says, immediate success is no criterion of the truth, and in the beginning of things the right often lies with the minority. But in the end God's power is felt. Some present Gamaliel as a teacher of tolerance, a humane, and liberal-minded man. But he may have feared to antagonize the growing power of the Christians in Jerusalem and to have had what Milligan calls "a prudential dread of violent measures." Others still regard Gamaliel as a mere time-server without real convictions and unwilling to take a positive stand against the apostles or against the reactionaries among the Pharisees as well as the Sadducees. Probably that view gives too low a conception of this really able man. But it is difficult not to feel that he really desired a temporizing policy as more likely to succeed against the apostles than violent oppression. So he took the attitude of a cool and wise deliberation and "advocated an opportunist policy" as Rackham holds. The fight before Stephen's day was between the apostles and the Sadducees on the doctrine of the resurrection. His attitude need not be called cynical, but it was that of the ordinary politician (Ewald, Knowling). He had good rabbinical backing also for his interpretation of Providence. Neander holds that Gamaliel was too wise a man to stir a fanatical movement, such as he considered Christianity, into a violent flame. Knowling thinks that the principle of Gamaliel enunciated in his speech shows "his abhorrence of wrangling and over-scrupulosity" and "a proof of his adherence to traditionalism." Like other great rabbis he had his saying that was passed on: "Procure thyself a teacher, avoid being in doubt; and do not accustom thyself to give tithes by guess." The advice is good, but it is that of a thorough Pharisee. On the point of being in doubt he probably would say, as Davy Crockett used to say, that one must be sure that he is right and then go ahead. The path did not seem clear to him about the punishment of the apostles and so he urged caution.

There are times, of course, when the general principle of letting things drift is wise. It is easy enough to take dogmatic positions on doubtful points. That does not help matters at all. On the other hand a policy of undue timidity and fear robs one of courage and power. Gamaliel failed to understand Christianity because of the grip of Pharisaism on his mind and life. He disliked the Sadducees intensely and was glad of the chance to score a point against them. He was a theological opportunist and was unwilling to take a decided stand for the gospel or against it. He was in favor of drifting. In the end he was still a confirmed Pharisee. He did not follow his brilliant pupil Saul whom he probably looked on as his probable successor. What he thought of Saul when he turned to Christ we can only guess.

CHAPTER XIV

FELIX THE GRAFTER

LUKE gives a fairly clear picture of Felix in Acts 23 and 24. Josephus (*Antiquities,* Book XX, Chapter 8; *War,* Book II, Chapter 13) gives a sketch of Felix that is quite in harmony with that in Acts. He tells of the numerous robber bands that infested Palestine and that gave a vast deal of trouble. Felix slew a great many of them. Josephus may be allowed his customary exaggeration, but a basis of fact must lie behind his statement: "Felix took Eleazar the arch-robber, and many that were with him, alive, when they had ravaged the country for twenty years together, and sent them to Rome; but as to the number of robbers whom he caused to be crucified, and of those who were caught among them, and whom he brought to punishment, they were a multitude not to be enumerated." Felix came to be regarded as a terror to the lawless robber bands, though he was not above using them for his own purposes in order to slay the high priest Jonathan. As a result the robbers grew bolder than ever for they felt sure of the connivance of Felix the Roman Procurator. Josephus moralizes upon the situation thus: "And this seems to me to have been the reason why God, out of his hatred of these men's wickedness, rejected our city; and as for the

136

temple, he no longer considered it sufficiently pure
for him to inhabit therein, but he brought the
Romans upon us, and threw a fire upon the city to
purge it; and brought upon us, our wives, and
children, slavery, as desirous to make us wiser by
our calamities." It is interesting to place beside
this philosophy of woe the doom of Jerusalem as
foretold by Jesus with the reasons for it. At any
rate the disorders under Felix were not suppressed,
but broke out afresh in a new place.

Felix himself is pictured as more hurtful than
all the robbers. Tacitus is scornful of him as one
"who used the powers of a king with the disposition
of a slave" (*Hist.* V. 9). The state of Palestine
grew constantly worse. At one time thirty thousand
fanatics followed "the Egyptian" mentioned by
Claudius Lysias in Acts 21:38. His cruelty stim-
ulated the Zealots to form fighting bands called
Sicarii (Assassins) who helped bring on the War
with Rome. Felix, according to Tacitus (*Ann.* xii.
54), "deemed that he might perpetrate any ill-deeds
with impunity." It is small wonder that his cruel-
ties ended in disaster. Though a man of low origin
he was allowed both military and civil power
(Suetonius, *Claud.* 28). His final and fatal misstep
was at Cæsarea when in a disturbance between the
Jews and the Syrians he was investigated and "he
had certainly been brought to punishment, unless
Nero had yielded to the importunate solicitations
of his brother Pallas" (Josephus, *Antiquities* XX.
viii. 9). He was recalled as a result of his complic-
ity in the civil war there.

He was a freedman, like his brother Pallas, the rather infamous favorite of Claudius. Tacitus calls him "Antonius Felix." The Latin adjective *felix* is seen in our English "felicitous." He was appointed by Claudius to be Procurator of Judea in succession to Cumanus, probably A. D. 53, though that is not certain. Tacitus says that he had married a granddaughter of Antony and Cleopatra whom he calls Drusilla, probably an error in the name. Suetonius mentions another princess as his wife also. But in the Acts Drusilla is the mistress of Felix. She left her husband, Azisus, the King of Emesa, for this liaison with Felix. Felix is pictured in far darker colors in Josephus, Tacitus, and Suetonius than in Luke, but his chicanery is plain in the Acts. He had a cynical disregard for justice, an open contempt for morality, a frank greed for money quite plain in his conduct towards Paul. These traits are modern enough for any student of present day history.

Claudius Lysias was glad to be rid of the puzzling case of Paul about whom he could learn nothing definite from the mob or the Sanhedrin. His letter to Felix makes the false claim that he had rescued Paul from the mob, "having learned that he was a Roman" (Acts 23:27) in order to cover up the fact that he had been about to scourge a Roman citizen (Acts 22:25). It is worth while to follow the reaction of Felix to Paul.

It began suspiciously enough. When Paul was presented to him, he said: "I will hear thee fully, when thine accusers also are come" (Acts 23:35).

Lysias had directed that these "accusers" make their accusations against Paul. It took them five days to come down to Cæsarea and Ananias brought a Roman lawyer or pleader, "an orator, one Tertullus" (Acts 24:1), who "informed the governor against him" in regular style. It is interesting to observe the skillful flattery employed by the Roman orator, as he begins his plea against Paul: "Seeing that by thee we enjoy much peace," a statement belied by all that the historians tell us of the riots and banditry. Tertullus proceeds: "and that by thy forethought reforms are coming to this nation," or "evils are being corrected for this nation." Such unvarnished flattery could only provoke a smile, but it would sound well to Felix even though he knew that it was untrue. "We accept it in all ways and in all places, most excellent Felix, with all thankfulness." Public officers and politicians in particular are quite open to fulsome praise. There are some preachers who are not above listening to it. Lysias had said that he found against Paul only "questions of their law, but to have nothing laid to his charge worthy of death." From the official standpoint, therefore, Felix could be quite disposed to give Paul a fair hearing. The charges that Tertullus brought against Paul were that (1) he was a "pestilent fellow," Paul the pest in a word, (2) "a mover of insurrection among the Jews throughout the world," (3) "a ringleader of the sect of the Nazarenes," (4) and, in particular, a man "who moreover assayed to profane the temple." This bill of particulars seemed specious enough and Tertul-

lus complimented Felix in the charge, affirming
that these things were so." The case seemed made
out by the accusers.

So Felix beckoned to Paul to speak in his own
defense (Acts 24:10–21). He had to win a hearing
by courtesy without fawning flattery. He confines
himself to saying that Felix has been for many
years a judge unto this nation and so he ought to
be able to judge his case properly. Paul therefore
makes his defense cheerfully. It is only twelve days
since he went up to Jerusalem and so the events
preceding his arrest are all recent. He pointedly
denies all the charges save one: "Neither in the
temple did they find one disputing with any man
or stirring up a crowd, nor in the synagogues nor
in a city." As a matter of fact, when the uproar
came he was engaged in observing the rites of the
temple worship. "Neither can they prove to thee
the things whereof they now accuse me." They had
furnished no proof and Paul was well within his
rights in demanding it. Mere denunciation did not
constitute proof.

But Paul had one confession to make. He did be-
long to "the sect of the Nazarenes." If that was a
crime, then he was guilty. But Gallio, proconsul of
Achaia, had decided that Christianity was a form
of Judaism and so a *religio licita*. We do not know
whether Paul reminded Felix of this decision or
not, but Felix most likely was familiar with it.
"But this I confess unto thee, that after the Way
which they call a sect, so serve I the God of our
fathers." Paul definitely agrees with the opinion

of Gallio and affirms to Felix that Christianity is
merely his form of Judaism. He believed the Law
and the prophets and had a hope of the resurrection
of the just and the unjust. He had kept a good conscience in his conduct toward God and men. It was
a most skillful defense. If he had stopped at this
point, Felix would have had difficulty in holding
him a prisoner. But Paul proceeded to tell the purpose of his recent visit to Jerusalem, "to bring alms
to my nation, and offerings." It is pretty clear that
this allusion to money aroused the cupidity of Felix
who saw a chance of a larger bribe to be offered by
Paul or his friends for his freedom. Paul proceeded
to give the occasion of his arrest, due to "certain
Jews from Asia, who ought to have been here before
thee, and to make accusation, if they had aught
against thee." Here Paul made a home-thrust.
These Jews from Asia made the false charge that
Paul was defiling the temple at the very moment
when he was honoring it and observing its forms
of worship. These Asiatic Jews roused the mob to
fury and then vanished, never to be heard of more.
But it will take Paul over five years to get out of
this tangled skein of false charges. But Paul turns
to the Sanhedrin, his present accusers, who are
making charges against him now before Felix. "Or
else let these men themselves say what wrong-doing
they found when I stood before the council, except
it be for this one voice, that I cried standing among
them, Touching the resurrection of the dead I am
called in question before you this day." There was
no denying that Paul had told the facts as they oc-

curred, including the onset of the Pharisees and the Sadducees on each other because Paul affirmed that he was a Pharisee still on the point of the resurrection.

The case was now before Felix and he should have set Paul free on the evidence before him. But Luke adds a remark quite in keeping with what we know of Felix: "But Felix, having more exact knowledge concerning the Way, deferred them." The meaning is probably that he knew of Gallio's decision concerning the equality of Christianity and approved it. Hence he could not condemn Paul as the Sanhedrin desired. Why did he not set him free? He feared the Jews and so left Paul a prisoner after two years, "desiring to gain favor with the Jews." He was the Roman ruler of these Jewish leaders who could make damaging charges against him as they did when he was recalled at the end of the two years when Festus succeeded him. Felix gave his judicial decision a political twist with an eye on his own interest.

But this is not all. He said, to be sure, that he would determine Paul's case after Lysias came down and he could talk the matter over with him. That sounded specious, but it was mere camouflage. What he really hoped for was money. Bribery was the quickest and the usual way to get a favorable decision from this Roman provincial judge. It is probable that Drusilla, a Jewess, and the mistress of Felix, was responsible for the coming of Paul before them for a sermon, not for trial.

She may have had some curiosity to hear him "concerning the faith of Christ Jesus" (Acts 24:24). But the effect was wholly unexpected to both Felix and Drusilla. "And as he reasoned of righteousness, and self-control, and the judgment to come, Felix was terrified." Felix is now on trial before his conscience as he listened to Paul who threw a powerful light upon his own life of evil. The time had come for Felix to settle his own account with God, but he put it off, this procrastinator, with the polite excuse: "Go thy way for this time; and when I have a convenient season, I will call thee unto me." Felix was deeply moved, but he was a grafter at heart and this master passion won the day. "He hoped withal that money would be given him of Paul: wherefore also he sent for him the oftener, and communed with him." He was never terrified again. He stifled his conscience with the hope of money. He kept sending for Paul and let him talk with the hope that Paul would offer money for his liberty. He knew, as Lysias did, that Paul was guilty of no crime. But he would not set him free. He was afraid of the Jews and he wanted money. These two reasons overcame his evident fondness for Paul and suppressed his terrified conscience and postponed indefinitely his personal interest in the faith in Christ Jesus. One could wish that Felix stood alone among the Roman governors who listened to their fears more than to their sense of justice. But the figure of Pilate rises before us. And Festus is not a whit better. Judges ought to be above partisanship, personal interest, and graft. If that were true always, conviction for crime would come with more speed and with more frequency.

CHAPTER XV

SIMON THE CRITIC OF CHRIST

(Luke 7:36–50)

THERE are few passages in Luke's wonderful Gospel more thoroughly characteristic of the author's style and spirit. Stanton (*Gospels as Historical Documents*, vii. p. 229) feels sure that here Luke is not quoting a literary document, but is telling the story in his own words. As is often the case, Luke gives no date and no place for the incident, though it does serve as a striking illustration of the sneers of the Pharisees about Christ as a glutton and a wine-bibber, a friend of publicans and sinners (Luke 7:34) and the conclusion holds true that wisdom is justified of her children (7:35).

The name Simon is very common. There are about twenty in Josephus and ten (or eleven) in the New Testament. There is no reason whatever for identifying this Pharisee with the Simon who was a leper and who gave a feast to Jesus (Mark 14:3–9; Matthew 26:6–13; John 12:2–8). It may be said also that there is no ground for confounding this sinful woman with Mary Magdalene of Luke 8:1–3 and least of all with Mary of Bethany who is so clearly pictured by Luke himself (10:39–

145

42). Ragg (*The Gospel according to St. Luke* p. 97) feels rather helpless over the curious confusion of artists on this subject: "In any case we may be sure that for *history* this unnamed sinner, and Mary Magdalene, and Mary of Bethany are three separate persons; though for *Art* they will probably remain one." That is only true in the sense that the ancient paintings cannot be now altered, but they undoubtedly slander both Mary Magdalene and Mary of Bethany.

But we are concerned here with the picture of Simon the Critic of Christ. Criticism of Jesus was inevitable then as it is now. Our age is one of untrammeled criticism and sifting of all data and ideas about Christ. One cannot wish it otherwise. Certainly no one wishes any fact about Jesus to be concealed or overlooked or forgotten. He could not be hid when upon earth and desiring seclusion. One does not wish Christ to be hid now. Jesus condemned captious criticism in severe terms. One does not become a scholar by reason of his gift at criticizing or picking flaws. One is not necessarily right because he is able to make sharp and specious criticism. After the messengers had started back to John the Baptist in prison Jesus gave a scathing indictment of the Pharisaic critics of the time who could not be pleased about either John or Jesus (Luke 7:24–35). They found fault with John because of his dress and his food and his unlikeness to people of the time. They found fault with Jesus because he was too much like the people of the age. The Pharisees assumed the critical attitude toward Jesus as they had the right to do. Only they had their eyes blinded by prejudice so that they could not see the light. They were unable to tell the truth when they saw it. These men who posed as the exponents of truth shut the door of truth, flung away the key, and would not let those enter into the house of knowledge who wanted to do so. They became the past-masters of obscurantism and the synonym for hypocrisy in all ages.

This Simon who invited Jesus to his house for dinner was a Pharisee and illustrates the wrong kind of criticism of Christ in a really wonderful way. He was evidently kindly disposed towards Jesus. There is nothing to indicate that he had any sinister motive in inviting Jesus to dine with him. It may (Plummer) have been a really courageous act on his part to give Jesus this invitation since the Pharisees were generally hostile. Luke mentions two other later instances where Pharisees invited Jesus to meals (Luke 11:27-54; 14:1-35). In each of the three instances the thing turned out badly. In Luke 11 the Pharisee criticized Christ for not bathing (probably dipping the hands and feet in water on entrance) before the breakfast, a criticism that led to three woes to the Pharisees and three to the lawyers. In Luke 14 the Pharisees themselves had come with hostile intentions and were on the lookout for flaws. Ragg terms "Luke's the Gospel of Hospitality." That is true, but the Pharisaic atmosphere was not very congenial to Christ. Probably this Pharisaic host had an element of self-importance in inviting Jesus as a sort of

social lion and he may even have desired to know
Jesus better in order to make up his mind about
him (Easton).

It is clear, of course, that the woman of the town
had not been invited by this particular and punc-
tilious Pharisee. She was a well-known character
who had evidently accepted Christ as her Savior
(note verse 50, "Thy faith has saved thee") and
wished to show her gratitude to him for her rescue
from sin. She knew that public opinion still regarded her as a harlot in spite of the change of
heart and life. In the orient even now uninvited
guests can enter the banquet hall and stand around,
but it called for courage for this woman to enter
the Pharisee's house. The guests reclined at table,
having dropped their sandals as they entered. This
woman came in on purpose because she had learned
that Jesus was to dine that day at this Pharisee's
house (verse 37). So she was an intruder as Mary
of Bethany was not when she anointed Jesus. This
woman had the box of ointment and slipped fur-
tively behind, but she was evidently overcome with
emotion and burst into tears that fell on the feet
of Jesus as she stood weeping. Then she felt that
she must wipe the tears away and unloosed her
long hair for that purpose. The Jews looked on
loosened hair in public as a shameful thing, but
she made this sacrifice (Plummer), knowing what
people would think. And then she kissed His feet
repeatedly and kept pouring out (imperfect tense)
the ointment till it was gone. She had not acted as
she had planned and the emotional excitement led

to the tears, the wiping with her hair, the kissing the feet.

Meanwhile Simon, the sedate Pharisee, had watched the performance with growing amazement that his distinguished guest should allow such a scene in his house without a word of protest and of displeasure at the woman's unseemly conduct. His indignation grew apace and finally he began to draw conclusions of a thoroughgoing nature concerning the claims of Jesus to be the Messiah. Perhaps the Pharisees were right after all in their wholesale rejection of this Galilean who violated the conventions. Perhaps he had more affinity with publicans and sinners than people generally supposed. Even to-day there are not wanting critics who identify this woman with Mary Magdalene and assert that she was the mistress of Jesus, horrible insinuations we rightly feel. But there is a whole group of critics to-day who argue that Jesus was a paranoiac with definite psychic abnormalities. So hostile criticism of Jesus has always existed and always will. Jesus challenged the fullest investigation. He asked the disciples what men thought of him and then what *they* themselves thought of him. In itself criticism simply means sifting and that process is necessary in making all right decisions.

What was the trouble with this Pharisee when "he said in himself" what he did about Jesus? He drew the conclusion about the character and claims of Christ from a false interpretation of this one incident. He said in his heart: "This fellow, if he

were a prophet, would know who and what sort the
woman is who is clinging to him, because she is a
sinner." There is a sneer in the contemptuous use
of the pronoun. The condition belongs to the second
class which states the thing as untrue (determined
as unfulfilled). A Greek conditional sentence puts
the thing according to the conception of the user,
not according to the actual facts. In this instance
Jesus is the prophet and does know the character
of the woman. But Simon puts it as he sees it. The
conclusion drawn so positively by Simon is that
Jesus is ignorant of the character of the woman
and therefore is not a prophet (least of all, *the*
prophet, as some manuscripts have it). If he were
the Messiah, he would know better. Even if he were
a prophet, he would not be so ignorant. He was
shocked (Ragg) along with the others to see Jesus
"submitting to these defiling caresses." There is no
finer illustration anywhere of the folly of posing as
omniscient under the influence of prejudice that
flies off the handle at small provocation. Simon
ridicules Jesus in his heart because he allows no
other motive for the conduct of Jesus than ignorance. Simon is incapable of comprehending the
love, pity, and forgiveness of Christ as the explanation of his conduct. Simon is not the first or the
last critic of Christ who has such a narrow grasp
of the facts that he draws a wholly erroneous conclusion. It is one of the monumental follies of
scholarship that a specialist is necessarily correct.
We need specialists in every line of learning and
of business. But no class of men show more nar-

rowness than some specialists who are unable to
see anything beyond the one item under observation. Diagnosis is the first step in therapeutics.
Doctors do not always agree in that and they dis-
agree often in the treatment of the disease. But
dogmatism about disease is no worse than dogmatism in theology when one is in possession of only
one fact. The only safety lies in criticizing the
critic of Christ.

This Jesus proceeds to do. Jesus not only knows
the character of this woman, her present repentance as well as her past sin, but he reads the
thoughts of Simon like a book. With Socratic irony
(Godet) Jesus lays bare Simon's inmost doubts
with the surgeon's scalpel. Probably his very face
revealed to Jesus the thoughts of his heart, but
Jesus knew what was in man without a spoken
word. Calling his critic and host by name Jesus
says: "Simon, I have something to say to thee."
Simon was probably still a bit contemptuous and
shocked. Easton thinks that what Jesus did may
be misunderstood as "a gentle correction of a natural error." It is to me far from gentle, but Simon
could only say: "Teacher, speak," with all outward
politeness and courtesy.

The reply of Jesus takes the form of a parable, a
pungent and powerful one, The Parable of the Two
Debtors. In this instance Jesus not only told the
inimitable little story, but he made direct application in the most unmistakable manner. It was a
moment of tension. The unfortunate woman was
standing at the feet of Jesus. The attention of

the guests was alert. Simon himself was on the *qui vive*. The story (verses 41 and 42) is crisp and cutting. The creditor *forgave* both the debtors. That was the point that Simon had overlooked in his wrong inference. Simon is put on the defensive by the pointed question of Jesus in a way that he cannot evade as to which of the debtors will love more. His reply is inevitable even if his air is that of supercilious indifference (Plummer). Ragg thinks that he was merely polite, but not really interested when he said: "I suppose." But at any rate he saw the point and admitted it, which is not always true of those who listen to stories. The moral of the story was self-evident and the Pharisee admitted it and Jesus commended him for doing so: "You have judged rightly." But Jesus did not stop with the mere answer to a conundrum. He turned to the woman and spoke to Simon in a way to make the contrast as sharp as possible. Jesus pointed out three items wherein Simon had failed in common courtesy to Jesus as his invited guest. He had provided no water for His feet, no kiss of greeting, no oil for the head. The woman had wet His feet with her tears and wiped them with her hair, she had kissed His feet, and she had anointed His feet with ointment. The sarcasm of Jesus was positively biting. But Jesus not only exposed the narrow criticism of Simon in the presence of all the guests, but he also further justified His conduct towards the woman in allowing her to show her grateful love in her own exceptional way. This statement of Jesus has been much misunderstood. Roman Cath-

olic commentators take verse 47 to mean that her
many sins have been forgiven because of her much
love, the doctrine of *contritio caritate formata,*
and the pictures of the Magdalene grew out of it.
The language of verse 47 is capable of that meaning if it stood by itself, but verse 48 flatly contradicts it: "He to whom little is forgiven loves little."
This is the point of the parable and of Christ's justification of the conduct of the woman and of his
treatment of her. Her much love is proof of the
great forgiveness, not the ground or reason of the
forgiveness. Her sins were many and have been
forgiven. Hence her love is great. This is the clear
meaning of Jesus in his wonderful interpretation
of the Parable of the Two Debtors as a final reply
to Simon the Critic. Simon was left overwhelmed
as all shallow critics of Christ will be some day
when they stand in the full glare of all the facts.

But Jesus has a further word to the penitent
woman: "Thy sins stand forgiven" (perfect passive
indicative, a state of completion). The critical sneer
of Simon cannot change this essential fact. Thank
God for that. In the welter of carping criticism of
Christ all about us he stands calm and victorious.
The guests at the banquet are now heard from.
They had seen and heard all that had transpired,
but now they had troubles of their own. Jesus now
actually assumed the right to forgive sins, a divine
prerogative as they understood it. And yet they
dared not speak out aloud what they were thinking
within themselves: "Who is this who even forgives
sins?" But Jesus had in reality answered their

thoughts by what he had said. He does not stop to answer their puzzled minds. We sometimes wonder why God leaves us with so much perplexity. He means us to use our minds if we can and get the good out of perplexity. Life is a matter largely of balancing probabilities and making the right choice. So Jesus has a final word for the woman: "Go in peace." We are not told what happened to the meal after this. That is a small matter, important as such a function seems at the moment.

CHAPTER XVI

MARTHA AND MARY OR TEMPERAMENT IN RELIGION

THE Bethany family included Martha, Mary and Lazarus. The names are common enough, but these were very unusual persons. They were all unmarried and lived together in a home of evident comfort if not affluence. The great number of prominent Jews who came out to comfort the sisters upon the death of Lazarus (John 11:19, 31) shows that the family was one of prominence in social life. The great cost of Mary's offering proves that she had considerable ready money. Martha apparently was the head of the household if we may judge from Luke 10:38 where Martha possibly a widow (Easton), acts as hostess. The glory of this family is that they provided a home for Jesus during his later Jerusalem ministry. He had withdrawn from Galilee because of the hostility of the populace. It was a time when Jesus said that the foxes had holes and the birds had nests, but the son of Man had not where to lay his head. But there was always one place near Jerusalem, the very seat of the ecclesiastic opposition to Jesus, where he found a welcome. There are always some people who have the courage

to take a stand in the open for Jesus and for all
that he means for men. There came loss of prestige
to this family after the raising of Lazarus for the
rulers conspired to put him to death as well as
Jesus because of the interest in Jesus created by
this miracle.

But the two sisters are the chief figures in the
family and their pictures are drawn by Luke and
by John. They have all the marks of reality, a striking "undesigned coincidence" (Ragg), because,
though John and Luke differ in method and style,
yet each draws these sisters with characteristic in-
dividuality. Evidently characters so true to the
life in each book were drawn from actual person-
ages. They appear in three remarkable scenes, once
as hostesses in the home (Luke 10:38–42), once
when great grief broke their hearts (John 11:17–
44), once as guests in the home of a friend (Mark
14:3–9, Matthew 26:6–13, John 12:2–8).

Each acts in perfect accord with herself in each
instance and each is sharply distingushed from
the other. The keen differences of conduct are
largely due to variations in temperament which are
deep and permanent. Lightfoot (*Biblical Essays,*
pg. 38) has a fine word concerning the way Luke
and John have noted the distinction between Mary
and Martha: "But these characteristics of the two
sisters are brought out in a very subtle way. In St.
Luke the contrast is summed up, as it were in one
definite incident; in St. John it is developed gradually in the course of a continuous narrative. In
St. Luke the contrast is direct and trenchant, a

contrast (one might almost say) of light and darkness. But in St. John the characters are shaded off, as it were, into one another." It is not necessary to find types of creed or of doctrine in these two noble women. They do admirably illustrate the different reactions found in women and men to all religious truth. They both felt the charm and the appeal of Christ, but they responded in different ways. There is personality in religion as in all else. Many of the tragedies and sorrows of the ages have been due to unwise and impossible efforts to regulate each other often in more or less unimportant matters. People have different eyes and do not see alike when they look at the same object. People have different minds and cannot think alike about the same things. This does not mean that one view is as good as another. Jesus Christ is the same yesterday, to-day and forever. But each one has his own angle of vision and is entitled to the experience that he has.

Mary and Martha did not always understand one another's attitude toward Jesus. There is a phrase often used about unhappy marriages, incompatibility of temperament, that does not justify divorce, but throws some light on family jars. Some people seem not to know how to live together without explosions, whether in family, church, school or state. Sometimes it is a matter of nerves that improves with better health. Overstrain explains much of the unpleasantness of life. A vacation has the great merit of change of environment and outlook and thereafter the common tasks seem less onerous. Much of life is a study in adaptation to one's environment. Worry wears out the nerves more than work and makes work difficult.

In the first incident (Luke 10:38–42) Martha acted as hostess and welcomed Jesus to her house as the margin has it in Westcott and Hort's text and as the article really means even without the pronoun. That is her rôle throughout, while Mary appears rather as the adoring disciple who sat (right down beside and facing) at the feet of Jesus and listened in rapture (imperfect tense) to his wondrous talk. But Luke has one little word ("also") that is commonly overlooked. Weiss and Easton take it to refer to Mary's eagerness while Plummer is uncertain what the precise idea is, though certainly not "even." The most natural way of taking it is that Martha as well as Mary loved to sit at the feet of Jesus, but gradually the household duties engrossed her more while Mary followed her bent and devoted herself more to the delights of listening to Jesus talk. Each followed her own inclination and each justified herself in doing mainly the one thing because of the conduct of the other. Mary's continual sitting at the feet of Jesus led to Martha's monotonous devotion to the drudgery of household duties till it became a habit with her that began to show on her face and on her nerves. She was literally "drawn around" (imperfect tense as the verb picturesquely says, "distracted") because of the much serving. The inevitable explosion came suddenly, as is usually the case. Martha stopped her work, stepped up to

Jesus and burst out with what seemed like a rebuke to him for having allowed Mary to act as she
had been doing. Martha said: "Do you not care
that my sister had been leaving me alone to go on
serving?" Her temper and petulance were plain.
She went on: "Bid her therefore that she take hold
(ingressive aorist subjunctive) along with me" (a
double compound verb that occurs also in Romans
8:26 about the help of the Holy Spirit, and one
common in the vernacular *Koine* of the time).
Martha was plainly tired of doing all the work
while Mary did nothing but listen and talk. It was
a most embarrassing moment in the life of this de-
lightful family where Jesus was most welcome and
felt most at home. At such a moment most of us
are wise in preferring silence. But Jesus had been
directly appealed to and even directly blamed so
that there was no way of escape. So the Lord replied to Martha's outburst briefly, but pungently:
"Martha, Martha, you are anxious and bustling
about many things." The repetition of the name
was a gentle chiding, perhaps with a smile (Ragg).
The Syriac Sinaitic manuscript omits the chiding
entirely, but it is probably genuine. Her anxiety
was natural, but was overdone and had led to the
explosive disturbance that she had just made. The
external agitation was due to the mental distraction (Plummer). Jesus goes on, but the text is uncertain: "There is need of few things (instead of
the many dishes planned by Martha, kindly but
mistaken hospitality seen often in elaborate
'spreads' at table) or one" (with a double meaning,

as Plummer shows, even one is enough for a meal, and this one is illustrated in a spiritual way by what Mary has done). It is possible that the oldest text was "one" or "few" which were both combined into "few or one." But the one thing needful directly refers to the one dish on which a meal can be made in place of the great variety contemplated by Martha. But the next clause gives the full justification of Mary by Jesus and carries the figure of the one dish into the spiritual realm: "For Mary chose the good portion which will not be taken away from her." Jesus here definitely declines to do what Martha asked. He will not forbid Mary's sitting at his feet in order that he may have more to eat. Martha's distracting anxiety was the result of affection (Plummer), but all the same between the two extremes Jesus preferred the conduct of Mary to that of Martha. Jesus did not condemn the service that Martha had rendered, but only her finding fault with Mary and her undue excited state of mind. She had definitely stepped beyond her prerogative in trying to make Mary conform to her own habits of life. It is a curiosity of modern criticism when the Tübingen school deny the historical character of the narrative and take Martha to represent Judaic Christianity and Mary Pauline Christianity or Martha the impulsive Peter and Mary the philosophic Paul (see Plummer). Dante caught the conception of the two sisters more nearly when he said: "Do as you are doing, but do not fret about it: Mary also is doing the right thing." Martha is thus a type of the active, Mary of the contemplative life. Christ here preaches the simple life.

In John 11 the two sisters again are true to life. Luke had not named the village as John does, but John calls Bethany the village of Mary and Martha as if they were the chief characters of the town. The sickness and death of Lazarus cast a shadow over this home and Jesus was away apparently a journey of two days (John 11:6, 17) in Perea. It seemed almost heartless to the agonized sisters that Jesus did not come at once when he received the message that Lazarus was at the point of death. They did not know what Jesus told the disciples that he remained away on purpose (John 11:6) and let Lazarus die "that the son of God might be glorified" thereby (John 11:4). One is permitted to cherish the hope that in the midst of like sorrows the Son of God may be glorified in ways that we do not understand. The two sisters did not doubt the love of Jesus for Lazarus and for themselves nor his power to prevent the death of their brother. Evidently they had talked the problem over with each other because each of them said separately to Jesus: "Lord, if thou hadst been here, my brother would not have died" (John 11:21, 32). It was to them unthinkable that Jesus would let Lazarus die if He were present. But, now that he had been dead these four days, it was not so certain what He would do. We do not know what the sisters knew concerning the raising of the daughter of Jairus and the son of the widow of Nain. The practical Martha went right out to see Jesus as soon as she learned that he had come (11:20). She even suggested to Jesus the raising of Lazarus from the dead by an exhibition of the most marvelous faith: "And even now I know that whatsoever thou shalt ask of God, God will give it thee." What was Jesus to do with this challenge of Martha to his love and his power? It was not a time for mere argument or dialectical fencing and yet it was necessary to prove Martha's faith and mental attitude. So Jesus said to her: "Thy brother will rise again." But this promise of the general resurrection hope did not satisfy Martha's present needs. So she replied: "I know that he will arise at the resurrection on the last day." Jesus now explained his meaning with a marvelous claim to Martha, the power to give eternal life to him: "I am the resurrection and the life," words that astound us to-day with their amazing implications. Jesus had a way of saying the most profound things in an incidental way to individuals as to Nicodemus and to the Samaritan woman at the well. These words fully justified Martha's hope, but Jesus proceeded with a double sense of life and death: "He that believeth in me even if he die (physical death) shall live (spiritual life), and no one who believes in me shall ever die (spiritual life)." It was still not clear what Jesus meant to do for Martha. But he suddenly put her faith to the severest possible test: "Believest thou this?" or "Is this your belief?" What had Jesus meant to claim to Martha? The power to give eternal life to every one who believes on him beyond a doubt. Had he also claimed the power to raise Lazarus from

the dead here and now? Not in so many words, but
he had implied it by saying: "I am the resurrection
and the life." And Jesus could not mean to mock
the hope of Martha. She falls back upon the confession of her faith in which she has rested for long,
the best that any of us can do in a great crisis:
"Yea, Lord, I have believed (state of completion,
perfect tense) that thou art the Messiah, the Son
of God, who was to come into the world" (John
11:27). This settled conviction explains why she
had said what she did (11:22). Simon had made a
great confession on Mount Hermon (Matt. 16ff.),
but no one ever made such a confesssion under more
trying conditions than did Martha. If Jesus meant
to raise Lazarus, he was evidently putting Martha
to a severe test beforehand and she fully realized
it. But she rose to the occasion in a magnificent
fashion. We need to add this strong side of her
faith and character to the nervous petulance ex-
hibited in Luke 10:38–42. This is permanent with
her, that was temporary. We must not allow the
natural revulsion of Martha by the tomb of Lazarus (John 11:39f.) to obscure her really great
faith. That was an instinctive recoil under the obvious environment. Jesus gently rebuked that mo-
mentary doubt with the reminder of his promise
to her that she should see the glory of God. Martha,
like most of us, had her moods of confidence and of
depression, but she rose to great heights of faith
in the presence of death. The picture of Mary is
drawn with equal vividness, and shows her characteristic traits. Martha told her that the Teacher

had come and was calling for her. So she quickly arose and went on out to see Jesus. All that Mary could say as she fell at the feet of Jesus was the lament already made by Martha (John 11:32). She was weeping without further words. What can Jesus say to Mary? He could argue with Martha's robust faith, but he could not with Mary. He treats each according to her temperament. The hostile Jews were there also and their presence called for self-control if he was to comfort Mary. But the very effort at self-mastery in such an atmosphere made Jesus burst into tears (ingressive aorist). After all what else can one do with a weeping woman but weep with her? We do not have to say that Mary was hysterical and should not have given way to her grief or that her grief was greater than that of Martha or that Jesus loved Mary more than he did Martha. Sympathy is fellow-suffering, entering into one's mood and taking a stand with one. Martha's practical nature sought a solution for her sorrow and Jesus met her on that plane. Mary's heart was all broken and bleeding. Her hurt was too deep for words, even words from Jesus. Jesus gave her His tears, real tears of human love and sympathy. But then He went on to the grave of Lazarus and raised him from the dead. That was the answer to Martha's query and the confirmation of her faith. That act stopped the flow of Mary's tears. That act led many of the Jews to believe on Jesus and led also to His own crucifixion (John 11:45-53).

The last time that we see Martha and Mary is

at the feast of Simon the former leper in gratitude
to Jesus (Mark 14:3-9, Matthew 26:6-13, John
12:2-8). This was at Bethany near Jerusalem on
Tuesday evening of Passion Week according to the
Synoptic Gospels. It was a remarkable company
including Jesus and the twelve apostles and the
Bethany sisters and Lazarus. It has been held by
some that Martha was the wife of Simon because
she "served" on the occasion. But that is unneces-
sary and wholly unlikely in view of Martha's own
separate home in Bethany. She here is merely true
to her own practical nature as already seen on the
other occasions. It is Mary who plays the important
rôle at this feast. Her act was premeditated and
prearranged. The whole room was filled with the
odor of the ointment poured on the head and the
feet of Jesus. It was Judas Iscariot (John 12:4)
who made violent protest against this "waste" of
money that might have been used for the poor, a
protest supported by the other disciples after it
was made (Matt. 26:8) as "they murmured against
her" (Matt. 14:5). It was a most embarrassing
moment for Mary. She had poured out her very
heart's love in this act of devotion with thoughts
full of the death of the Master of which he had
spoken so often and of which the apostles seemed to
have no proper appreciation. And now she has had
this public rebuke from the preachers who should
have understood her. What if Jesus shared the
same feeling? But she had not long to wait. Jesus
sharply rebuked Judas and the rest and defended
Mary for showing her love in her own way. "She

hath done what she could." These words have gone with the story of the gospel through the ages as Christ's memorial for Mary's deed of love (Mark 14:9). She had anointed Christ beforehand for his burial while the disciples had utterly failed to understand his words about his death. Here Mary rises to the heights with her temperament of mystical insight as Martha stood firm in the hour of despair and of the death of Lazarus. Later the disciples came to understand their own shortsightedness and to see that Judas was all wrong because a thief in fact (John 12:6) and had misled them by his concealed stinginess in opposition to Mary's generosity and nobility of sentiment.

The supreme lesson for modern men and women in the lives of Martha and Mary is precisely that of toleration, forbearance, liberty in matters of personal idiosyncrasy and outlook. The two sisters loved Jesus with equal sincerity and devotion, but they showed their love in very different ways. It is not going too far to say that denominations have arisen on less important differences than existed between Martha and Mary. Compulsory uniformity on all points is impossible in the family, in the church, in the state. It is a distinctly modern problem to learn when to be firm, when to be tolerant. Law is necessary in essential things if we are to have stability in society, but love must carry on for the rest. They say that no two leaves are precisely alike and yet it is not difficult to tell a maple leaf from that of the oak or the elm. Temperament in religion gives the variety of life and the joy of in-

dependence. We must never forget that Jesus loved
Martha and that he loved Mary, that he treated
each according to her temperament, and that he did
not attempt to make either of them like the other.

CHAPTER XVII

ANANIAS AND SAPPHIRA OR THE FIRST ANANIAS CLUB

(Acts 5:1–11)

FEW things in the Acts have caught the popular imagination like the story of Ananias and Sapphira. The couple had lovely names Ananias (to whom Jehovah has been gracious), Sapphira (either a sapphire or the Aramaic word for beautiful). But names play a very small part in one's actual life. It was another Ananias in Damascus who was charged with the duty of opening the eyes of Saul who was stopping at the home of one Judas. Undoubtedly Ananias and Sapphira before the incident in Acts 5 bore a good reputation in the Jerusalem church.

It is a bit remarkable (Rackham) how large a part the greed for gain played in the book of Acts. The sin of Achan and of Gehazi reappears here in the life of Ananias and Sapphira as we see it also in Simon Magus, Elynas, the masters of the poor girl in Philippi, Demetrius of Ephesus, the chicanery of Felix. Certainly the love of money is a root of all kinds of evil.

Luke does not hesitate to tell the unvarnished

facts about this sin in the early church in Jerusalem. He lets the facts speak for themselves and makes no effort to gloss it over with any pious platitudes or excuses. The incident stands out in sharp contrast to the noble deed of Joseph Barnabas whose generosity undoubtedly was the occasion for the evil act of Ananias and Sapphira. It is plain that the disciples of this early period were not immune to the darts of the devil. Rackham wrongly uses Luke's fidelity in recording the facts about Ananias and Sapphira as a protest against the effort "to found new and 'pure' churches," though he admits that "against this experience of the kingdom of God spiritually minded men have risen in all ages." It is true that in the Acts we see in the life of the disciples themselves first hypocrisy (V), then murmuring (VI), then dissension and contention (XV). But the leaders like Peter and Paul did not commend the practice of evil in the churches. Certainly it is small consolation to know that the tares do grow among the wheat, for the field is the world as Jesus taught. The final separation comes only at death and the judgment. The good and the evil live together in the world. This is no argument against church discipline or cleansing, but it is one against pessimism. We often speak of the good old times, but forget that evils existed then as well as now. No halo of glory can cover up the selfish greed and ambitious pride observable in the tragic careers of Ananias and Sapphira over money and church money at that.

It is clear that the hearty praise given by the

church to Joseph Barnabas excited Ananias and
Sapphira to follow his example. Barnabas was a
man of considerable wealth and he voluntarily sold
his piece of property and laid the money at the feet
of the apostles (Acts 4:37). It is small wonder
that he was called the Son of Consolation for this
timely liberality. The communism practised by the
Christians at Jerusalem was voluntary and was
used only as need required. It was in no sense compulsory and does not seem to have been practised
elsewhere. But human nature changes little in its
essential features through the ages.

Ananias and Sapphira felt that their social
standing entitled them to as much praise as Barnabas had received. They talked the matter over
and decided to sell their property and keep back
part of it and to give the other part as if it was the
whole price of the property sold. It was duplicity,
but they thought it would not be known. Then they
proceeded to put the plan into execution like the
little boy who wanted to keep his cake and eat it
too. They wanted all the credit and applause that
had been bestowed upon Barnabas without the
deprivation of absolutely all this property. So Ananias brought the money (part of it) and laid it
ostentatiously at the feet of the apostles as Barnabas had done and waited for the commendation
that Barnabas had received. It was thus a deliberate offense, his wife knowing all that he was doing. Satan had entered his heart and had obscured
the real nature of his sin. It was not merely pur-
loining, bad as that is. It was lying, acting a lie.

He was not doing the truth (I John 1:6). He was doing a lie (Rev. 22:15). He was trying to serve God and mammon like Deacon Skinflint who asked the grocer boy to come on to prayers if he had put sand in the sugar and rocks in the coffee. Here was the same type of hypocrisy in some in the Jerusalem church that Jesus had so strongly condemned in the Pharisees, the pious pretense that was more concerned with the outward show than the inward reality.

It was a shock to Ananias when Simon Peter suddenly exposed his hollow pretense to the whole church. The Holy Spirit was unwilling for this pious fraud to go through and revealed it to Peter, who spoke out with courage and power. Ananias had lied to the Holy Spirit in keeping back part of the price of the property. Peter argued the matter with him, though it was too late. He did not have to sell it nor did he have to give it after it was sold. This point proves that it was not compulsory or legal communism. It was certainly proper for Ananias to give half of his property which is far more than most modern Christians do. The sin lay, not in giving part, but in giving part as if it were all and expecting credit for giving all. Peter is amazed that Ananias could have conceived such a base falsehood, a lie not merely to men (bad as that is) but a lie to God. Satan had put it into the heart of Ananias, but that suggestion of the Devil in no sense absolved Ananias of his responsibility for the sin.

One can easily imagine how Ananias quailed be-

fore this terrible exposure of the secret ambition
of his heart. It is not said that Peter smote him
with death. Paul called down blindness on Elymas
Barjesus as Peter condemned Simon Magus. But
without any sentence from Peter, Ananias suddenly
fell down and gave up the ghost. He fell as he was
listening to the words of Peter. The physical cause
of his death is not clear. On physiological grounds
it is not hard to conceive that the sudden revulsion
of emotion burst a blood vessel and caused apo-
plexy as he was listening to Peter's denunciation.
But, natural as all this may be, the sudden death
was the judgment of God for the wickedness of
Ananias.

The effect upon the people was great and in-
stantaneous. The people were full of fear and it
affected the whole church (first use of the word
church in the critical text of Acts) and all the
people paused and pondered before they rushed
heedlessly into the membership of a body like this
where one was expected to walk so straight a line.

The burial of Ananias within three hours seems
undue haste to us, but in Jerusalem the interval
between death and burial was brief (Numbers 19:
11, Deut. 21:23). Furneaux considers it inconceiva-
able that a man of substance like Ananias could
be put into the tomb so quickly and without the
knowledge of his wife. But sometimes the body
was placed in a temporary tomb or vault before
final burial. We know too little about ancient cus-
toms to call it cruel and heartless or incredible.

The younger men stand out in contrast to the elders, very much like active pall bearers to-day or the ushers in some churches. It is not certain that already there was a definite body of church workers called the younger men by way of anticipation of the deacons. Then young men did the honors of the burial. They placed the limbs together, wrapped the body round with some robe and decently bore it out and buried it.

But the incident was not over. Without knowing how matters had gone with Ananias, Sapphira, (his wife,) came in after an interval of some three hours. She may (Noesgen) have come in at the next hour of prayer. But at once she subjected to a direct query by Peter: "Did you sell the land for so much?" He probably named the price as that of the money laid at his feet by Ananias. She was thus given the opportunity to tell the truth about it and to retract the lying agreement with her husband about it. She had her chance to come clean without knowing the fate of Ananias. But she persisted in the sin and spoke plainly the lie that Ananias had acted by deed. She stuck to the nefarious compact and Peter instantly foretold her fate. But he first expressed his amazement at the depth of depravity that led her and her husband to agree together to tempt the Spirit of the Lord. Probably they had not realized that they were really doing this thing. Usually sin blurs the mental and spiritual perceptions so that the worse appears the better reason. To them the end justified the means in this case. They felt that they were entitled to as much prestige as Joseph Barnabas had achieved.

Certainly the solemn prediction that "the feet of those who buried thy husband are at the door and they will bear thee out" was a shock equal to that received by Ananias. Her immediate death was the judgment of God upon her for her share in the common sin as was the sudden death of Ananias. The same young men, though a different word is employed, that had buried Ananias came in and found her dead and bore her out and buried her beside her husband.

It was a tragic dénouement to the sinful conduct that had promised them so much pleasure and profit. If one is disposed to question the love and justice of God for this quick retribution for secret wrongdoing, he can gain some light by reflecting upon the evil consequences in American life to-day of the slow and uncertain processes in our legal procedure when technicalities often give loopholes for the escape of the guilty and for the consequent spread of crime. This was the first social sin in the life of the Jerusalem church of which we know. The sin was primarily against God. The exposure was by the Holy Spirit to Simon Peter. The local church had no experience to guide them. This sin cut to the very vitals of the church life and made a mockery of all that was true in Christianity. When one considers all these things, the severe judgment of the Holy Spirit through Simon Peter is more intelligible to us.

The effect upon the whole church was most salutary. A great and wholesome fear came upon the whole community and they all saw that hypocrisy could not pass muster in the kingdom of God. The new church had its justification for existing as an effort to carry on the ideals and standards of Jesus Christ who had denounced so vigorously the hypocritical Pharisees. But hypocritical disciples of Jesus were far worse for the very reason that they made higher claims to purity of life. They had the example of Jesus before them and the promise of the Holy Spirit to cheer and help and hold them to the highest.

Another result was that this incident gave pause to all the outsiders who heard these things. It was already becoming with some a popular thing to become disciples of Jesus. If it meant death for slips like that made by Ananias and Sapphira, it was a serious and solemn thing to join such an organization as the Jerusalem church. One had best search his own heart carefully before he stumbled into a thing that might have such tragic consequences. This was all to the good and a wholesome restraint came that sifted out the superficial timeservers who did not have the root of the matter in them. The appeal was all the stronger to the courageous who all the more believed in the Lord Jesus and took an open stand for him (Acts 5:14). That is always the case in times of testing and Christ calls the high-minded souls who are willing to take risks for him. The appeal is made to the heroic so that in all the Christian centuries as at the first multitudes of young men and young women of the very highest types have gladly laid their lives at the feet of Jesus for service wherever he needed them most.

It is a curious bit of history that the very name of Ananias has been used for what we call an Ananias Club, a bunch of real liars, or a group so denominated by their opponents. But he deserved this fate for his name because he did get his wife Sapphira to agree to the despicable plot for selfish promotion in the church life by lying even to the Holy Spirit.

CHAPTER XVIII

LAZARUS THE SILENT WITNESS OF THE SECRETS OF DEATH

THERE was never a keener interest in the future life than there is to-day. Thomas A. Edison has actually been carrying on a scientific investigation to see if he can find evidence of a survival after death. Because he has not been able to find material proof of such survival he doubts its reality, a very unscientific conclusion and one that refuses to recognize any differences between matter and spirit. The thin wall between matter and spirit should make one cautious. The very electrons and ether offer a warning.

On the other hand a scientist like Sir Oliver Lodge claims that he has had communications with his son Raymond in the other world. He holds to this view with full faith in the claims of Christ and Christianity. But Sir Conan Doyle puts spiritualism in the place of Christianity and is a protagonist for knowledge to be derived from spiritualistic mediums concerning the future life. They both bear witness to the perennial interest in the life beyond the grave, however bizarre their ideas appear to us. It is certainly curious, to go no further, that such spiritualistic revelations can be

177

had only in the dark and with many proven instances of trickery and fraud.

Far back in Job's time the Lord said to him:
"Have the gates of death been revealed unto thee?
Or hast thou seen the gates of the shadow of
death?" (Job 38:17). Job did not know what was
beyond the grave. The Jewish conception of Sheol,
or the grave, was that it was darkness beyond the
gates of the shadow of death. The very image
used in Matthew 16:18 by Jesus appears in Job
38:17 and in Psalm 89:48 except that the Greek
word Hades takes the place of Sheol. The Greeks
called the unseen world Hades.

But people through all the ages have longed for
one to come back from the grave and tell what
they have seen on the other side. In the Parable
of the Rich Man and Lazarus (the other Lazarus,
not he of the Bethany family) the Rich Man who
is now in Hades and in torment begs Abraham to
send Lazarus to the house of his father and to
warn his five brothers that they may not come into
the place of torment (Luke 16:27 and 28). It was
a natural wish, but Abraham replies: "They have
Moses and the prophets; let them hear them." We
have still more. We have Jesus and the witness
of the apostles. The Rich Man continued his pleading along the line of modern spiritualism: "Nay,
Father Abraham, but if one from the dead go to
them, they will repent." That sounds like a specious plea, but all history is against it. Abraham
answered: "If they do not hear Moses and the

prophets, not even will they be persuaded if one rise from the dead."

The supreme illustration of this fact is the case of Jesus himself. His resurrection from the dead was a necessity to fulfill his own prediction that he would rise from the dead on the third day after his crucifixion. We all observe how difficult it was for Jesus to convince his own disciples that he had really risen from the grave, vital as that fact is to real Christianity. And Jesus did not appear to any of those who did not already believe in him except in the case of Saul of Tarsus, who was already kicking against the goad. And to-day many people profess that they would believe in Jesus as a great prophet and teacher of ethics if they did not have to believe in his supernatural birth and resurrection from the grave, a spineless belief that leaves Jesus making false claims about himself.

But the Gospel of John gives the tremendous miracle of the Raising of Lazarus from the grave after he had been dead four days. There is no more difficulty in believing this miracle than the other raisings from the dead. Jesus claimed to have the power of life and death, to be himself the resurrection and the life. But the admission of the historical character of John 11 which narrates this wondrous event carries with it the consideration of the attitude of the people towards Lazarus, who had been raised from the dead in such a public manner before crowds of prominent Jews from Jerusalem. Many believed on Jesus because of it. Others went to the Sanhedrin and told them of their faltering faith in Judaism and their leaning toward Christ. The Sanhedrin in desperation called a meeting and said: "If we leave him (Jesus) alone thus, all men will believe on him and will take away both our place and the nation's." The raising of Lazarus had the immediate effect of making the Sanhedrin decide to put Jesus to death. So Jesus left the vicinity of Jerusalem.

But when he returned some weeks later at the fatal passover Lazarus is the object of excited interest to the visitors from afar who all hear of the tremendous event. A great multitude came out to Bethany not merely to see Jesus who is again the guest of the Bethany family, but "to see Lazarus whom he had raised from the dead" (John 12:9). Who can blame this curiosity on the part of crowds at the passover? A well authenticated case like that to-day would make a stir that would throw even Lindbergh into the shade. The Sanhedrin were enraged afresh and determined to kill both Lazarus and Jesus (John 12:10). With both of them dead, they argued, Lazarus would stay dead this second time. Because of Lazarus as a live specimen of Christ's supernatural power "many of the Jews were going and believing on Jesus" (John 12:11). Once again Lazarus has become a thorn in the side of the Sanhedrin.

The only other appearance of Lazarus in the narrative is at the feast in Bethany given by Simon, the one time leper, in honor of Jesus. He was simply one of the guests on this occasion (John 12:2). But there is not a word given in John's Gospel of anything said by Lazarus about the life beyond the grave. There was the keenest curiosity to see a man who had really come back from the grave. But not a word from the other side. The Rich Man had hoped that the messenger sent to his brothers might bear witness to them about his own sad state. But the testimony of Lazarus is only the silent witness of one who declined to be garrulous about trivial nonentities such as fill up the talk of mediums. Lazarus did not need to say anything to show that it was he who was back in human life. That was a manifest fact to all. But he had not a word to say, so far as we know, concerning what people are so anxious to know. There is dignity in this silence that puts to shame the modern efforts to prove the existence of the other life. The raising of Lazarus proved the essential fact. Here he was again as all could see.

There is one who does speak clear words concerning the future life and that is Jesus. Before his death he was conscious of his preëxistence with the Father. He has told us the really essential things concerning heaven and hell. If one will run through the Gospels to see, he may be surprised to find how much Jesus has said about the future life. He has lifted the veil for us on all really vital matters, but he has not satisfied idle curiosity in any way. It is a reflection on Christ for one to credit table-rappings and such things more than the clear and sure word of Jesus Christ who came to us from the bosom of the Father and who has gone back to the Father and who will take us to be with him in the Father's house. He did not tell the disciples all that they wished to know, but more than they at first fully comprehended and then he gave them and us the Holy Spirit to be our Guide and Teacher.

Lazarus has been credited by some scholars with the authorship of the Fourth Gospel. I do not myself believe it as the Apostle John wrote the book in my opinion. But even so, if Lazarus did write it, his silence is all the more remarkable. He left it to Jesus in any case to be the speaker to us about the life beyond the grave.

THE END

A Study of JOB

A Study of

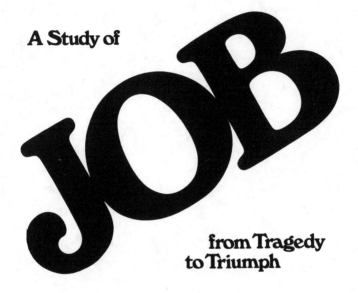

JOB

from Tragedy
to Triumph

H. L. Ellison

ZONDERVAN
PUBLISHING HOUSE OF THE ZONDERVAN CORPORATION
GRAND RAPIDS, MICHIGAN 49506

To my Friends
ISAAC and LYDIA FEINSTEIN
who have shown me,
one in death,
the other in life,
how to suffer to the glory of
God

CONTENTS

PREFACE

I UNDERTOOK the obligation to furnish a series of studies on the Book of Job to *The Hebrew Christian Quarterly* something more than three years ago. I had hardly started my task, when a period of suffering and distress broke over me, which profoundly affected my understanding of the book and the scale of my treatment of it. These studies have now been thoroughly revised and considerably expanded.

There are few books of the Bible more difficult to write on than Job. One may, on the one hand, give one's interpretation of the thought but entirely lose touch with the actual text in so doing. On the other hand one may so occupy oneself with the difficulties of the language that the spiritual message and the poetry become swamped under textual and linguistic comments. However much my exposition may have dressed itself in modern clothes, I have always tried to see to it that it does not stray far from the text; since poetry is as much understood by the heart as by the brain, I have not troubled overmuch about minor difficulties in the R.V. —the A.V. is generally only then mentioned, when there was need to warn against its rendering—when I thought that the general meaning was clear.

The main writings on *Job* I have leaned on will be found by referring to the list of abbreviations. My thanks are due to Messrs. Burns & Oates for their gracious permission to quote Monsignor Ronald Knox's translation of 12: 13–25 as well as of odd verses elsewhere. The text printed at the beginning of chapters or sections is that of the R.V., with the substitution of the marginal renderings, when these are generally accepted as superior.

My hope is that just as Job's anguish brought me comfort in the days of my distress, so this book will make the triumph of Job more real and a greater blessing to others who pass through distress.

H. L. ELLISON.

LIST OF ABBREVIATIONS

This work uses standard abbreviations for the names of the books of the Bible as well as many in common use. Only the following need mention.

a (b, c)	refers to the first (second or third) part of the verse mentioned.
ad loc.	at the appropriate place.
A.V.	The Authorised or King James' Version of 1611.
Davidson	Davidson & Lanchester: *The Book of Job*—Cambridge Bible for Schools and Colleges, edition of 1918.
f.	and the following verse.
ff.	and the following two verses.
I.C.C.	Driver & Gray: *The Book of Job*—International Critical Commentary (1921).
Job	The Book of Job in contrast to the man.
Koehler	Koehler & Baumgartner: *Lexicon in Veteris Testamenti Liberos*.
Knox	Bible translation by Monsignor Knox; O.T. in 1949.
mg.	margin.
Moffatt	Bible translation by James Moffatt; O.T. in 1924.
Peake	Peake: *Job*—The Century Bible (1905).
R.S.V.	Revised Standard Version; O.T. in 1952.
R.V.	Revised Version; O.T. in 1885.
Stevenson	Stevenson: *The Poem of Job*—The Schweich Lectures for 1943.
Strahan	Strahan: *The Book of Job* (1914).
tx.	text.

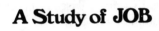

A Study of JOB

THE STRUCTURE OF JOB

A.   Prologue in Heaven and on Earth, chs. 1, 2
B.   Job's Complaint, ch. 3
C.   Job's Friends, chs. 4–27

    1. First Cycle of Discussion, chs. 4–14
      (*a*) Eliphaz, chs. 4, 5
      (*b*) Job replies, chs. 6, 7
      (*c*) Bildad, ch. 8
      (*d*) Job replies, chs. 9, 10
      (*e*) Zophar, ch. 11
      (*f*) Job replies, chs. 12–14
    2. Second Cycle of Discussion, chs. 15–21
      (*a*) Eliphaz, ch. 15
      (*b*) Job replies, chs. 16, 17
      (*c*) Bildad, ch. 18
      (*d*) Job replies, ch. 19
      (*e*) Zophar, ch. 20
      (*f*) Job replies, ch. 21
    3. Third Cycle of Discussion, chs. 22–27
      (*a*) Eliphaz, ch. 22
      (*b*) Job replies, chs. 23, 24
      (*c*) Bildad, ch. 25
      (*d*) Job replies, chs. 26, 27*

D.   Interlude: In Praise of Wisdom, ch. 28
E.   Job's Summing Up, chs. 29–31

    1. The Past, ch. 29
    2. The Present, ch. 30
    3. The Future, ch. 31
F.   Elihu's Interruption, chs. 32–37

    1. Introduction, ch. 32
    2. First Answer, ch. 33
    3. Second Answer, ch. 34
    4. Third Answer, chs. 35–37
G.   God's Reply, chs. 38–42: 6
H.   Epilogue on Earth, ch. 42: 7–17

* But see pages 21 and 87 f.

THE BOOK OF JOB

M ANY who have never read *Job* have caught something of its spirit as they have listened to the Burial Service of *The Book of Common Prayer*. Three times *Job* is quoted:

The Lord gave, and the Lord hath taken away; blessed be the Name of the Lord (1: 21),

and,

Man that is born of a woman hath but a short time to live, and is full of misery. He cometh up, and is cut down, like a flower; he fleeth as it were a shadow, and never continueth in one stay (14: 1f);

there is also the triumphant note taken up as well in Handel's *Messiah*,

I know that my Redeemer liveth, and that he shall stand at the latter day upon the earth. And though after my skin worms destroy this body, yet in my flesh shall I see God: whom I shall see for myself, and my eyes shall behold, and not another (19: 25ff).

Great writers and theologians have hailed it as a poetic masterpiece. Carlyle's words may serve as an example*:

I call it, apart from all theories about it, one of the grandest things ever written with pen. One feels, indeed, as if it were not Hebrew; such a noble universality, different from noble patriotism or noble sectarianism, reigns in it. A noble Book; all men's Book! It is our first, oldest statement of the never-ending Problem—man's destiny, and God's way with him here in this earth. And all in such free flowing outlines; grand in its sincerity, in its simplicity; in its epic melody, and repose of reconcilement . . . Sublime sorrow, sublime reconciliation; oldest choral music as of the heart of mankind;—so soft, and

* *On Heroes and Hero-Worship*, p. 49 in Centenary Edition.

great; as the summer midnight, as the world with its seas and stars! There is nothing written, I think, in the Bible or out of it, of equal literary merit.

A catena of similar opinions may be found in Strahan, p. 28f.

For maturer men and women who are familiar with the Bible there are few Old Testament stories that exercise a stronger and more perennial attraction than that of Job. This is not because of the poetry of the book, though unfortunate is the man who has not felt the music and poetic power of some of its chapters. It is not even because of the effect made on him by the book as a whole, for the number of those who have intelligently read the whole book is small. It is rather that when life loses the first simplicities of youth we increasingly feel its mysteries, that of suffering being perhaps its greatest. As the Lord leads us in strange paths of pain and loss, or when our eyes are opened to glimpse something of the anguish around us, we feel that even if we cannot understand all in the book of Job, it does indicate an answer to these problems.

There are two main reasons for the lack of detailed knowledge and understanding of *Job* among Bible students. The former derives from the fact that it is poetry of the highest order. Tennyson could say that it was "the greatest poem of ancient or modern times." The effort of mind and heart needed, if we are to enter into the depths of great poetry, is not one that most associate with the study of the Bible. The second is the inadequacy of the Authorised Version. Davidson, no mean or biased critic, says (p. lxxviii), "Of the English Versions the A.V. appears at its worst in this book. It is frequently obscure and several times it misses the meaning entirely . . . The R.V. has done much to make the book intelligible to English readers."

Though this present attempt to grasp and display the message of *Job* is based on the R.V., no more modern rendering has been despised, whether taken from a translation of the Bible or from a commentary, if it has brought out the meaning more clearly. The R.S.V. has proved especially helpful.

We may perhaps add a third and more subtle reason for our difficulty in understanding and appreciating *Job*. From Greece our civilization has learnt to think in general terms and abstract conceptions. The world of the Old Testament thought, as does the Western child today, in concrete terms and of particular cases.

We talk vaguely of the problem of suffering; the Old Testament deals with Job's 'Why?' We feel that to reach the truth we must strip a problem of its 'accidentals'; the Old Testament presents Job as a figure in the round, detailing apparently all the accidentals of his life. Closer study shows that it is wiser and more subtle than that. All that is needed to make Job a real man for the writer's generation is retained; that which would make him an alien to the reader is normally passed over, but for all that the "accidentals" are an essential part of the book.

Unfortunately, however, there is an immeasurably greater gulf between us and the writer's generation than there was between them and Job. We are in danger of being so occupied with the exotic details of life and thought in the land of Uz, details which still live on there, that we fail to realize how modern Job and his questionings, his friends and their obtuseness are. That is why so much in this exposition is devoted to stripping the characters of their Eastern garments, that they may speak to us in the language of today.

CHAPTER II

THE MODERN SCHOLAR LOOKS AT JOB

THE scholar has been attracted to *Job* just as the ordinary man has been, for the problem it handles spares no rank or class, nor can learning free us from suffering. He has, however, found additional attractions in the book, when he has looked on it merely as a literary product. Very many of the questions he has raised and discussed have no bearing on the purpose of this book and may be completely ignored. Others, however, vitally affect our understanding of *Job* and must be briefly considered.

AUTHORSHIP AND DATE

There is no agreement on the date when *Job* was written, and no convincing suggestion as to its authorship has ever been made. While it is true that the "official" Talmudic tradition (*Baba Bathra* 14b, *seq.*) attributes it to Moses, the discussion that follows it shows that it is no more than a pious pronouncement of no authority, for the rabbis place the book, or the lifetime of Job, at varying times between Isaac and Joseph to Cyrus and Ahasuerus. Virtually the only arguments that can be advanced in favour of Mosaic authorship are a general sense of fitness, and the use in common of certain rarer words in *Job* and the Pentateuch. In fact the differences of vocabulary are more striking than the similarities, and subjective arguments can be made to prove almost anything.

Both the *International Standard Bible Encyclopedia* and Young in his *Introduction to the Old Testament* reject a Mosaic authorship, and it seems clear that we should bow to the Holy Spirit's silence and accept the book as anonymous. As regards the date of the book we would do well to take up a similar position. Young adopts the view of Delitzsch that it was written in the time of Solomon, but the evidence can equally well be interpreted as supporting a later date. The simple fact is that nothing depends either on the date of composition or on the authorship.

The suggestion that the book must be early because the law of Moses, the Exodus, etc., are not mentioned has no validity, because the characters in it are not Israelites, and it is no chance that in the actual speeches the name Jehovah is found only once (12: 9), and here seven manuscripts, undoubtedly rightly, have God instead. The background is, in fact, kept deliberately as general and as vague as possible, so that the problem of Job may be seen in all its mystery, unobscured by any purely temporal considerations.

HISTORY OR PARABLE?

It will come as a surprise to many that there have been Jewish rabbis who denied the historicity of Job. The Talmud (*Baba Bathra* 15a) tells us of one in the third century A.D. who stated, " Job did not exist and was not created; he is a parable." While the view was obviously a minority one, Maimonides, the greatest Jewish scholar of the early middle ages, could say (*Moreh Nebuchim* iii. 22), "Its basis is a fiction, conceived for the purpose of explaining the different opinions which people held on Divine Providence." While we do not agree with this, we believe that, at least in its earlier formulation, it was intended to express a truth which most today tacitly accept.

Ezek. 14: 14, 20 is sufficient evidence for the historical existence of Job. If I am correct in earlier statements* as to the identity of the Daniel here mentioned by Ezekiel, he is referring to three men from an early date in human history. It is also clear that the story of Job circulated widely in forms differing materially from that in the Bible—a summary will be found in Stevenson, pp. 76–86—but, in spite of the opinion of Theodore, Bishop of Mopsuestia (392–428), I see no reason for preferring any of the popular versions to the form of the story in the Bible.

Though the story will have come down the centuries to the writer of the book, its heart (chs. 3–42: 6) will represent his re-writing of it under the Spirit's guidance. The difficulties of style and language prevented the translators of the A.V. from doing justice to the magnificence of the poetic language, and though the R.V. is much superior, it still leaves much to be desired. As a result we often fail to realize that we cannot be reading a verbatim report: we have a poetic transformation of the original prose narrative before us.

* *Men Spake from God*, p. 142; *Ezekiel: The Man and His Message*, p. 59.

Against this there has been urged the ability of the Arab to break out in spontaneous poetic utterance, when under great emotional stress.   If it were only Job who speaks in poetry, we might give considerable weight to this fact, but all the characters do, and all the time at that.

This is not to suggest that *Job* is a mere invention based on an old story, or that the author has so transformed his hero that he would not have recognized himself.   We have the same magic of the Spirit's transforming power as in the Psalms.   There the joys and sorrows of men, David and others, are taken and so transformed that they have become expressive of the experiences of all men of God, so that the Psalter is the hymn book of Synagogue and Church alike.   In the same way the sufferings and strivings of Job and the sophistications of his friends have been touched with a gold that makes them speak to all generations in all lands.

When modern Jewish scholars claim that Job is a parable of Israel and its sufferings, there is more than a little truth in it.   Though Job is an individual and a historical character, he is also the representative sufferer.   So too, when we pass from the individual to the national, the Jew stands before us in a representative character.   Jewry, knowing the hand of God to be over it, but suffering as no other people, without knowing why, shows true spiritual insight, when it sees the parallel between itself and Job.

Job and Wisdom Literature

Our unknown author did more than turn the prose of suffering into deathless verse and universalize it; he definitely set it in the framework of what is now known as "wisdom literature"; on this point conservative and liberal are of one mind.   It links up with Proverbs and Ecclesiastes.

In an age in which the possibilities of book learning were few, those who had it were known as the Wise and were highly honoured in the community.   In Jer. 18: 18, we find them standing beside the priest and the prophet.   As Rylaarsdam says of them "The role of the sages and the public estimate of them were very similar in all lands.   They were the schoolmasters and the court counsellors."*   Since God wills to be served by all

* *Revelation in Jewish Wisdom Literature*, p. 9.

portions of a man, we have the wisdom of the Wise represented in the Old Testament.

In Proverbs we see the Wise, Solomon and others, seeking to understand the working out of God's providence among men. Apart from Agur (ch. 30), they are convinced that where the fear of the Lord is there also will be an understanding of His works. They saw in man's experiences such uniformities that the Wise, if they were humble, could lay down the general methods of God's workings. Note that there is no claim to prophetic inspiration in Proverbs.

In Qohelet (Ecclesiastes) the writer, placing himself in the position of Solomon in his old age, a disappointed backslider whose unequalled wisdom had failed to make him wise in the things of God, questions the unqualified optimism of Proverbs. He shows that however great the wisdom it will fail to make sense of God's actions, if it once becomes purely self-centred.

Job, on the other hand, is a direct challenge to the whole concept of Proverbs. As we shall see in our study, one of its main conclusions is that man cannot always understand the ways of God, and God does not always will to reveal them to men. Job is finally satisfied not by having his questions answered but by a revelation of the incomparable majesty of God.

There is no real contradiction between the three wisdom books. The picture given in Proverbs holds good for the vast majority of cases. The case of Job is obviously intended to be exceptional, but we cannot dictate to God whether we are to have exceptions or not. God may at any time upset our carefully made plans and show that His actions cannot be contained within the narrow span of human understanding. Qohelet then reminds us that all our wisdom is nothing worth unless it is linked with true godliness; otherwise the purposes of God will always remain enigmatic even to the wisest. So the three books form a spiritual unity, and we may never forget the message of the other two as we study *Job*.

Earlier I said that our author had deliberately set *Job* in the framework of what is now known as "wisdom literature". This was not meant to imply that it is in any way typical of wisdom literature, as Proverbs is. Pfeiffer writes very well:*

"If our poet ranks with the greatest writers of mankind, as can hardly be doubted, his creative genius did not of necessity rely on earlier models for the general structure of his work and

---

* *Introduction to the Old Testament*, p. 683f.

for the working out of its details.   Admitting at the outset that there is no close parallel to his poem, in form and substance, we may regard it as one of the most original works in the poetry of mankind.   So original in fact that it does not fit into any of the standard categories devised by literary criticism.   All general classifications fail to do justice to the overflowing abundance of its forms, moods, and thoughts; it is not exclusively lyric, . . . nor epic, . . . nor dramatic, . . . nor didactic or reflective, . . . unless the poem is cut down to fit a particular category. . . . Even the more comprehensive characterizations . . . fail to do justice to the scope of the work."

We must bear in mind also that whatever the rank and social position of Job and his friends, they are introduced to us as belonging to the Wise.   The one exception is Elihu.   Entirely consistently with this their discussions are, so far as Job will allow them to be, the discussions of the Wise, in which we see the world mirrored not always as it is but as it ideally should be. The anguished realism of Job first angers them and then silences them, but if Job is more realistic than they, it is because he has learnt from bitter experience.

The Integrity of the Book

The question whether the prose framework of *Job*, as we now have it, is by the same author as the verse that forms the heart of the book, or whether it is older, is normally a mere literary question, and as such may be ignored.   But there are cases like that of Stevenson in his recent penetrating study of the book, where the separation is made in order that the poetic part may be given an interpretation contrary to that permitted by the prose introduction.   We grant without hesitation, that by this process much of the difficulty of the book is removed, but this is an outstanding example of how the Bible must not be handled and interpreted.   No really cogent reason for the separation is given; indeed the whole suggestion is in itself most improbable.   Apart from this we are under obligation to let the Word speak to us in its wholeness, not to cut it down and cut it up until it suits our perception.

Most modern commentaries wish to delete longer or shorter parts of the book as later insertions.   The reasons given are almost invariably subjective, and they are normally palpably weak or of minor importance. The only two cases noted in this book are ch. 28, the Praise of Wisdom, and the speeches of Elihu (chs. 32–37). It has seemed wisest to defer discussion of these passages until they are reached in the normal order of events, cf. pp. 89 and 103. It is only as we have been studying *Job* through all its development of thought that we shall be in an adequate position to judge whether these passages do or do not fit into its warp and woof.

It has been very strongly urged that in places the text has been dislocated. Our increasing knowledge of ancient manuscripts shows us how easily this might have happened. The most obvious example is 31: 38ff. There can be no doubt that 31: 35ff represent the climax and conclusion of Job's words—as they stand, the closing verses of the chapter present an intolerable anticlimax. It is easier, however, to recognize the dislocation than to say at what point in the chapter the misplaced verses originally stood.

The other passage that concerns us is chs. 25–27. As our text stands, Bildad gives a half-hearted reply in ch. 25, and when Job answers in ch. 26, Zophar shrugs his shoulders and leaves Job to wind up in ch. 27. If it stood by itself, there would be no real difficulty in the fact that in 26: 5–14, Job out-Bildads Bildad in his description of God's greatness and transcendence, but in 27: 13–23, we find Job repeating his friends' views on the fate of the wicked in even stronger terms than they had used, although in 27: 5, 6, 12, he had just reaffirmed his unshakable dissent. This is patently absurd and a contradiction of the book as a whole. None of the many attempts to re-arrange the text is wholly convincing, and the trouble may be in part due to loss of a section owing to the breaking of the papyrus roll. In the treatment of the text in ch. VII no attempt at rearrangement has been made.

The Poetry of the Book of Job

When we try to discover what determines whether a passage of literature is to be considered prose or poetry, we find that there are two factors involved. One, undoubtedly the more important, is the language used. This is so generally recognized, that there is no need to deal with it here. Long before the technical principles of Hebrew poetry became known to Western readers, the beauty of the language of *Job*, even in translation, had brought universal conviction that here was poetry of the highest order.

The other factor that distinguishes poetry from prose is that the former uses certain technical devices which create the sense of compactness and regularity. These have varied from period to period and language to language.

Almost the first thing that strikes a child about the poetry, or it might be better to say verse, that it meets is the rhymes. These are completely lacking in Biblical poetry, though they may be found in mediaeval or modern Hebrew poetic writings. It is true that Stevenson claims (p. 60), "Rhyme is used very sparingly, but it is not to be ignored where it occurs." This is unlikely; the few examples are probably accidental or possibly special cases of assonance. Alliteration in the formal sense in which it is normally used in English is not found either, but assonance, the repetition of similar sounds, is quite frequent in *Job*, far more so than is normal in Hebrew poetry.

The second feature in most of our poetry that strikes even the casual reader is the regular rhythm we call metre. This undoubtedly existed as a major factor in Hebrew poetry, but for various reasons we are not able to be certain of its details today. There seems little doubt, however, that more metrical freedom was allowed than in most English poetry.

To these technical devices Hebrew adds parallelism, which is unknown in classical or modern European poetry. It may be briefly explained by saying that each metrical unit was divided into two, occasionally three or even four, approximately equal sections. Normally this metrical unit, except in the prophets, coincides with the traditional verse divisions. The thought in the first section is then in some way continued or balanced in the following section, or sections.* The printing adopted in the R.V. and more modern versions, except Knox, makes this parallelism clear.

The outstanding importance of this parallelism has been that it has permitted translators to give the sense of rhythm and balance in Hebrew poetry without having to struggle to reproduce its metres and assonances. A word of warning has to be given to the reader. He must always be prepared to take the metrical unit as a whole in his interpretation instead of concentrating on the smaller sections. These are consciously incomplete.

* A more formal treatment of the subject is given in my *Men Spake from God*; reference can also be made to any good Bible dictionary.

CHAPTER III

THE PROLOGUE

THERE was a man in the land of Uz, whose name was Job; and that man was perfect and upright, and one that feared God, and eschewed evil. ²And there were born unto him seven sons and three daughters. ³His substance also was seven thousand sheep, and three thousand camels, and five hundred yoke of oxen, and five hundred she-asses, and a very great household; so that this man was the greatest of all the children of the east. ⁴And his sons went and held a feast in the house of each one upon his day; and they sent and called for their three sisters to eat and to drink with them. ⁵And it was so, when the days of their feasting were gone about, that Job sent and sanctified them, and rose up early in the morning, and offered burnt offerings according to the number of them all: for Job said, It may be that my sons have sinned, and renounced God in their hearts. Thus did Job continually.

6. Now there was a day when the sons of God came to present themselves before the LORD, and Satan came also among them. ⁷And the LORD said unto Satan, Whence comest thou? Then Satan answered the LORD, and said, From going to and fro in the earth, and from walking up and down in it. ⁸And the LORD said unto Satan, Hast thou considered my servant Job? for there is none like him in the earth, a perfect and an upright man, one that feareth God, and escheweth evil. ⁹Then Satan answered the LORD, and said, Doth Job fear God for nought? ¹⁰Hast not thou made an hedge about him, and about his house, and about all that he hath, on every side? thou hast blessed the work of his hands, and his substance is increased in the land. ¹¹But put forth thine hand now, and touch all that he hath, and he will renounce thee to thy face. ¹²And the LORD said unto Satan, Behold, all that he hath is in thy power; only upon himself put not forth thine hand. So Satan went forth from the presence of the LORD.

13. And it fell on a day when his sons and his daughters were eating and drinking wine in their eldest brother's house, ¹⁴that there came a messenger unto Job, and said, The oxen were plowing, and the asses feeding beside them: ¹⁵and the Sabeans fell *upon them*, and took them away; yea, they have slain the servants with the edge of the sword; and I only am escaped alone to tell thee. ¹⁶While he was yet speaking, there came also another, and said, The fire of God is fallen from heaven, and hath burned up the sheep, and the servants, and consumed them; and I only am escaped alone to tell thee. ¹⁷While he was yet speaking, there came also another, and said, The Chaldeans made three bands, and fell upon the camels, and have taken them away, yea, and slain the servants with the edge of the sword; and I only am escaped alone to tell thee. ¹⁸While he was yet speaking, there came also another, and said, Thy sons and thy daughters were eating and drinking wine in their eldest brother's house: ¹⁹and, behold, there came a great wind from the

wilderness, and smote the four corners of the house, and it fell upon the young men, and they are dead; and I only am escaped alone to tell thee. 20. Then Job arose, and rent his mantle, and shaved his head, and fell down upon the ground, and worshipped; ²¹and he said, Naked came I out of my mother's womb, and naked shall I return thither: the LORD gave, and the LORD hath taken away; blessed be the name of the LORD. ²²In all this Job sinned not, nor charged God with foolishness.

2. Again there was a day when the sons of God came to present themselves before the LORD, and Satan came also among them to present himself before the LORD. ²And the LORD said unto Satan, From whence comest thou? And Satan answered the LORD, and said, From going to and fro in the earth, and from walking up and down in it. ³And the LORD said unto Satan, Hast thou considered my servant Job? for there is none like him in the earth, a perfect and an upright man, one that feareth God, and escheweth evil: and he still holdeth fast his integrity, although thou movedst me against him, to destroy him without cause. ⁴And Satan answered the LORD, and said, Skin for skin, yea, all that a man hath will he give for his life. ⁵But put forth thine hand now, and touch his bone and his flesh, and he will renounce thee to thy face. ⁶And the LORD said unto Satan, Behold, he is in thine hand; only spare his life. ⁷So Satan went forth from the presence of the LORD, and smote Job with sore boils from the sole of his foot unto his crown. ⁸And he took him a potsherd to scrape himself withal; and he sat among the ashes. ⁹Then said his wife unto him, Dost thou still hold fast thine integrity? renounce God, and die. ¹⁰But he said unto her, Thou speakest as one of the foolish women speaketh. What? shall we receive good at the hand of God, and shall we not receive evil? In all this did not Job sin with his lips.

In Heaven

HOWEVER familiar the opening scene of Job may be, there seem to be few who take it seriously. Most Christian depictions of Satan are entirely incompatible with what we are here told. We see Satan coming into the presence of God, and though it is not expressly stated, it is a fair inference that it was his duty so to do. What particular role he plays in the sovereign purposes of God is not made clear, though he goes up and down the world seeking whom he may accuse. But the vital point is that he is a servant of God, albeit an unwilling one. When in rabbinic tradition the personal name Sammael is given him with the office of angel of death, it is, of course, pure fancy, but the underlying principle is true.

The attitude of the liberal scholar tends to be that here we have a relatively primitive and outmoded conception of the Accuser (the meaning of Satan, which is a title, not a proper name). The more conservative scholar is apt to think that he need take only New Testament passages into consideration.

We must first of all remember that we cannot dismiss this picture as merely the expression of an old popular legend. Zech. 3: 1f and I Chron. 21: 1, the other two passages in the Old Testament where Satan is mentioned by name, express an identical outlook, as do Judges 9: 23, I Sam. 16: 14, 18: 10, 19: 9, I Kings 22: 19–23.

We must further bear in mind that the New Testament writers were familiar with the teaching of the Old and based themselves upon it. Even where they carried it further, they were affirming its truth. If then from the New Testament we have inferred views about the role and power of Satan which are in contradiction to the picture in *Job*, it means that by ignoring the Old Testament we have misunderstood the New.

It is not unfair to say that the vast majority of Christians either fly in the face of revelation and experience and deny the existence of Satan, or attribute to him such wide-reaching power and authority as to become virtual dualists in their religion. The teaching of Scripture is clear that nothing exists without God's will and permission. All power and authority are derived from Him. Whatever the position and power of Satan, he is God's creation, his power is derived from God, and willingly or unwillingly he is working out God's purposes. This is clearly seen in his conversation with God about Job.

It is usual to explain Job's sufferings by the malignity of Satan, but this is obviously false. Satan cannot even mention Job, for he has no accusation against him, until God invites him to do so (1: 8, 2: 3). Equally he has no power over Job or his possessions until God gives it him. So it is clear that, while God uses Satan's malignity, the origin of Job's sufferings goes back to God Himself, and no explanation of God's action is ever offered.

The fact that Satan is a fallen angel and in rebellion against God does not give to him any power at all except such as God chooses to give him. He is not sovereign in a rival kingdom, but a rebel to whom God gives as much rope as will glorify His own name.

Satan's fundamentally subservient role in the whole story is born out by his non-mention in the epilogue. Having carried out his task in stripping Job of wealth and health and in rousing Job's fellow-townsmen against him, he can be dismissed as of no further interest in the development of the story.

On Earth

The ease and speed with which all Job's wealth and happiness vanished once Satan was allowed to touch them should be to us not merely a reminder that the angel of the Lord encamps around those who fear Him, and delivers them, but also that it is God who rules in the affairs of men, and that He mercifully restrains the power of evil. We should be so concerned with the power of God, that the power entrusted to Satan will seem very small in comparison.

The pious Christian might have seen the hand of Satan in his loss and have prayed that he might be restrained. Probably more wisely, Job recognized the sovereignty of God. We are told that he did not charge God "with foolishness" (1: 22), but this is hardly an adequate translation, while "with wrong" (R.S.V.) is too strong. The Hebrew means "insipidity" or "unseemliness" (Koehler). It means that he did not consider that God had acted out of character; the I.C.C. is correct with "unworthiness."

There can be no certainty as to the nature of the disease with which Job was smitten. It may have been elephantiasis, a form of leprosy, or one of various oriental diseases proposed by doctors familiar with the Near East, or even smallpox, as recently suggested by Dr. Rendle Short.* It was not so much the pain of the disease that prostrated Job; it is referred to comparatively little in the speeches, and Stevenson, pp. 34ff, shows that in fact it may not be mentioned at all in them. It was that it had made him unclean, an outcast who found his resting place on the rubbish-mound outside the town gate. Though it is not stated in as many words, it is clear that Job's choice of the dung-hill (*the ashes*, 2: 8) outside the gate is not an expression of his despair, but it had been forced upon him because he had been thrust out by his fellow-townsmen.

Wetzstein writes in Delitzsch's *The Book of Job* about the dung-hills of the Hauran villages, now called *mezbele*:

> "The dung . . . is carried in baskets in a dry state to that place outside the village, and there generally it is burnt once a month. . . . If a place has been inhabited for centuries, the *mezbele* attains a height far greater than that of the place itself. The rains of winter reduce the layers of ashes to a compact

---

* *The Bible and Modern Medicine*, p. 53f.

mass, and gradually convert the *mezbele* into a solid hill of earth. . . . There lies the outcast who, smitten by loathsome disease, is no longer admitted to the dwellings of men. . . . There lie the dogs of the village, gnawing perhaps some fallen carcase, such as is often thrown there."

For Job's contemporaries, as for the inhabitants of the Near East in general and for Israel in particular for many centuries to come, a man's prosperity or adversity, his health or sickness, were regarded as the verdict of heaven on his conduct. Job himself believed this, and this belief lies in one form or another behind all the arguments of his friends. The sting of this spiritual pain, of the belief that he was cast off by God, hurt far more than any physical suffering. But there was more to it than this. To be shut out of the fellowship of one's community was much worse. So great was the feeling of "corporate personality" that it was not till the spiritual victory of Jeremiah that men could realize that a man might be in fellowship with God even if he were cut off from his community. This explains the advice of Job's wife (2: 9). For her Job is as good as dead already, for he is not only ill, but cut off from God. For him to curse God and so bring swift and merciful relief in God's blasting death-stroke could not worsen his relationship to God. We can see the inner reality of Job's faith in that he does not allow his outward circumstances to overwhelm the inner witness of the Spirit within him. Though he cannot understand the reasons for his sufferings, he does not believe that God has cast him out. It should be noted that *in all this did not Job sin with his lips* does not imply in Hebrew, as it might well be construed in English, that Job sinned in his unspoken thoughts.

11. Now when Job's three friends heard of all this evil that was come upon him, they came every one from his own place; Eliphaz the Temanite, and Bildad the Shuhite, and Zophar the Naamathite: and they made an appointment together to come to bemoan him and to comfort him. 12And when they lifted up their eyes afar off, and knew him not, they lifted up their voice, and wept; and they rent every one his mantle, and sprinkled dust upon their heads toward heaven. 13So they sat down with him upon the ground seven days and seven nights, and none spake a word unto him: for they saw that his grief was very great.

We should not minimize the friendship of the three who came a long distance to comfort him. Although men of wealth and worth, they were not ashamed to associate with the outcast on the rubbish-mound. But fundamentally they had accepted without question the verdict of the men of his own town. The seven days and nights they sat with him (2:13) are the period of mourning for the dead (cf. Gen. 50:10, I Sam. 31:13). In the name of friendship they tried to hide their convictions about Job, until he drove them to speak openly, but all their efforts at comfort were vitiated by their fundamental presupposition. Nothing ties us more readily than inherited superstitions.

CHAPTER IV

MY GOD! WHY?

A FTER this opened Job his mouth,
and cursed his day. ²And Job
answered and said:
³Let the day perish wherein I was
born,
and the night which said,
There is a man child conceived.
⁴Let that day be darkness;
let not God inquire after it from
above,
neither let the light shine upon
it.
⁵Let darkness and the shadow of
death claim it for their own;
let a cloud dwell upon it;
let all that maketh black the day
terrify it.
⁶As for that night, let thick darkness seize upon it:
let it not rejoice among the days of
the year;
let it not come into the number of
the months.
⁷Lo, let that night be barren;
let no joyful voice come therein.
⁸Let them curse it that curse the
day,
who are skilful to rouse up leviathan.
⁹Let the stars of the twilight thereof
be dark:
let it look for light, but have none;
neither let it behold the eyelids of
the morning:
¹⁰because it shut not up the doors of
my *mother's* womb,
nor hid trouble from mine eyes.
¹¹Why died I not from the womb?
why did I not give up the ghost
when I came out of the belly?
¹²Why did the knees receive me?
or why the breasts, that I should
suck?
¹³For now should I have lien down
and been quiet;

I should have slept; then had I
been at rest:
¹⁴with kings and counsellors of the
earth, which built up waste places
for themselves;
¹⁵or with princes that had gold,
who filled their houses with silver:
¹⁶or as an hidden untimely birth
I had not been;
as infants which never saw light.
¹⁷There the wicked cease from
troubling;
and there the weary be at rest.
¹⁸There the prisoners are at ease
together;
they hear not the voice of the task-
master.
¹⁹The small and great are there;
and the servant is free from his
master.
²⁰Wherefore is light given to him
that is in misery,
and life unto the bitter in soul;
²¹which long for death, but it
cometh not;
and dig for it more than for hid
treasures;
²²which rejoice exceedingly,
and are glad, when they can find
the grave?
²³*Why is light given* to man whose
way is hid,
and whom God hath hedged
in?
²⁴For my sighing cometh like my
meat,
and my roarings are poured out
like water.
²⁵For the thing which I fear cometh
upon me,
and that which I am afraid of
cometh unto me.
²⁶I am not at ease, neither am I
quiet, neither have I rest;
but trouble cometh.

As his friends sat there day after day, full of sympathy but unable to comfort—for what words of comfort can one speak to the sinner?—Job realized that it was not only the wicked of his own town and the fickle mob that had turned their backs on him, but also the wisest and best among his own friends. It may well be that Eliphaz, Bildad and Zophar were rising to leave, their period of mourning ended, when Job broke out into one of the most moving passages of the Bible.

As literature Job 3 is magnificent; so much so that it sweeps us along by its very vehemence and keeps our minds from asking what it all means.

He cursed the day of his birth (v. 1, R.S.V.). It is, alas, no rare experience to meet the man who has enjoyed health, riches and honour, who in middle life has lost all three and who longs for death. But it is most rare for such a one to say, at least with any conviction, unless indeed his conscience is already making him feel the flames of Hell, "I wish I had never been born." He has lived, and for most of the time living was good; even the final suffering cannot rob the earlier years of their sweetness. But it is precisely this that Job is saying with such vehemence. It is true the chapter ends (vv. 20–26) with the wish that he were dead, but this is subsidiary to the main thought.

There is only one strictly comparable passage in the Bible, viz. Jer. 20: 7–18). Not only is there an obvious literary resemblance between Jer. 20: 14–18 and Job 3: 3–10, however it is to be explained, but I believe a striking spiritual similarity between the two men can be demonstrated as well.

As a young man Jeremiah had followed the call of God to be a prophet. He could have reasonably expected recognition and honour, at least from the better elements among his people, and the joy of fellowship with God in his own heart. He found himself rejected by all and had apparently lost his relationship with God. I believe that in a very much simpler way this was true of Job as well. It is to be noticed that in this tremendous outburst Job does not refer to his material loss and physical affliction at all, unless it is by implication. It is only our knowledge of the circumstances that tempts us so to understand v. 24:

For my sighing comes as my bread,
  and my groanings are poured out like water (R.S.V.).

There is some element of doubt in vv. 25f. as to the best translation, but there can be little doubt that the translators of the A.V. were misled by preconceived theory. The R.S.V., which is substantially the same as the R.V., seems to give the meaning:

> For the thing that I fear comes upon me,
>   and what I dread befalls me.
> I am not at ease, nor am I quiet;
>   I have no rest; but trouble comes.

This is surely looking to something quite other than his physical afflictions.

Let us take a closer look at Job himself. Throughout the book he is presented, as are his friends, as a member of the highly respected class of the Wise. He was obviously brought up in the strict orthodoxy of the time, for which it was beyond dispute that prosperity was the result and reward of godfearing goodness, and disaster and suffering of wrongdoing. He is portrayed to us as *tam* (1: 1, 8, 2: 3). The meaning of the word is "completeness" rather than "perfection." All sides of his life and character were harmoniously developed. The R.S.V. and Moffatt in rendering "blameless," are probably as near as we can get to the thought of the Hebrew. The whole orthodoxy of the time proclaimed that this man should prosper, and in fact for many years he did. Then disaster, absolute and horrible, swept over him. Since Job never claims sinlessness, he might have welcomed some normal trouble as the acceptable chastisement of God. But with the afflictions that are his there is only one logical course for him to follow. He must agree with the unanimous voice of the world and of his friends and accept that he is the chief of sinners.

Here is Job's problem. If his theology is correct, he is the chief of sinners, but he *knows* he is not. But if he listens to the testimony of his own heart, then his theology, on which he has built up his whole life, must be wrong. The fact that his concepts of God and man are rudimentary compared to the highly developed ones of Christian dogmatics does not mean that we are not entitled to use the word theology, when speaking of him. This thought is more agonizing even than the thought that he may be the chief of sinners. So he finds that the firm moorings of his life have vanished; that the ship of his life is adrift on the dark ocean, without chart, without light, being carried he knows not where.

He turns to his friends for sympathy, advice and comfort, but dogmatic orthodoxy has ever been without heart or understanding. It cannot conceive of religion as a vitally free fellowship with God, but insists on confining it to the Procrustean bed of man's limited understanding of the omnipotence and all-wisdom and love of God. But though they have no understanding for the plight of their friend, it is the three who really help Job back to peace, for they so increase his anguish that they drive him back to God. It is noticeable that in virtually all of Job's answers to his friends, while he first reacts to what has just been said, he then turns from his friends to God. Much that he says in his anguish is false and exaggerated, and some of it is virtually blasphemous, but what matters is that he turns to God.

CHAPTER V

THE DEBATE BEGINS

Eliphaz the Temanite (Chs. 4, 5)

Then answered Eliphaz the
Temanite, and said,
²If one assay to commune with
thee, wilt thou be grieved?
but who can withold himself from
speaking?
³Behold, thou hast instructed many,
and thou hast strengthened the
weak hands.
⁴Thy words have upholden him
that was falling,
and thou hast confirmed the bow-
ing knees.
⁵But now it is come unto thee, and
thou faintest;
it toucheth thee, and thou art
troubled.
⁶Is not thy fear *of God* thy confidence,
and thy hope the integrity of thy
ways?
⁷Remember, I pray thee, who *ever*
perished, being innocent?
or where were the upright cut off?
⁸According as I have seen, they
that plow iniquity,
and sow mischief, reap the same.
⁹By the breath of God they perish,
and by the blast of his anger are
they consumed.
¹⁰The roaring of the lion, and the
voice of the fierce lion,
and the teeth of the young lions,
are broken.
¹¹The old lion perisheth for lack of
prey,
and the whelps of the lioness are
scattered abroad.
¹²Now a thing was secretly brought
to me,
and mine ear received a whisper
thereof.

¹³In thoughts from the visions of
the night,
when deep sleep falleth on men,
¹⁴fear came upon me, and trembling,
which made all my bones to shake.
¹⁵Then a breath passed over my
face;
the hair of my flesh stood up.
¹⁶It stood still, but I could not discern the appearance thereof;
a form was before mine eyes:
and I heard a still voice,
¹⁷Shall mortal man be just before
God?
shall a man be pure before his
Maker?
¹⁸Behold, he putteth no trust in his
servants;
and his angels he chargeth with
folly:
¹⁹how much more them that dwell
in houses of clay,
whose foundation is in the dust,
which are crushed like the moth!
²⁰Betwixt morning and evening they
are destroyed:
they perish for ever without any
regarding it.
²¹Is not their tent-cord plucked up
within them?
they die, and that without wisdom.

5. Call now; is there any that will
answer thee?
and to which of the holy ones wilt
thou turn?
²For vexation killeth the foolish
man,
and jealousy slayeth the silly one.
³I have seen the foolish taking root:
but suddenly I cursed his habitation.

⁴His children are far from safety,
and they are crushed in the gate,
neither is there any to deliver
them.
⁵Whose harvest the hungry eateth
up,
and taketh it even out of the
thorns,
and the snare gapeth for their
substance.
⁶For affliction cometh not forth of
the dust,
neither doth trouble spring out of
the ground;
⁷but man is born unto trouble,
as the sparks fly upward.
⁸But as for me, I would seek unto
God,
and unto God would I commit my
cause:
⁹which doeth great things and unsearchable;
marvellous things without number:
¹⁰who giveth rain upon the earth,
and sendeth waters upon the fields:
¹¹so that he setteth up on high those
that be low;
and those which mourn are exalted
to safety.
¹²He frustrateth the devices of the
crafty,
so that their hands can perform
nothing of worth.
¹³He taketh the wise in their own
craftiness:
and the counsel of the froward is
carried headlong.
¹⁴They meet with darkness in the
daytime,
and grope at noonday as in the
night.
¹⁵But he saveth from the sword of
their mouth,
even the needy from the hand of
the mighty.

¹⁶So the poor hath hope,
and iniquity stoppeth her mouth.
¹⁷Behold, happy is the man whom
God correcteth:
therefore despise not thou the
chastening of the Almighty.
¹⁸For he maketh sore, and bindeth
up;
he woundeth, and his hands make
whole.
¹⁹He shall deliver thee in six
troubles;
yea, in seven there shall no evil
touch thee.
²⁰In famine he shall redeem thee
from death;
and in war from the power of the
sword.
²¹Thou shalt be hid from the scourge
of the tongue;
neither shalt thou be afraid of
destruction when it cometh.
²²At destruction and dearth thou
shalt laugh;
neither shalt thou be afraid of the
beasts of the earth.
²³For thou shalt be in league with
the stones of the field;
and the beasts of the field shall be
at peace with thee.
²⁴And thou shalt know that thy
tent is in peace;
and thou shalt visit thy fold, and
shalt miss nothing.
²⁵Thou shalt know also that thy seed
shall be great,
and thine offspring as the grass of
the earth.
²⁶Thou shalt come to thy grave in a
full age,
like as a shock of corn cometh in in
its season.
²⁷Lo this, we have searched it, so it is;
hear it, and know thou it for thy
good.

O F Job's three friends Eliphaz is by far the most attractive.
He is an obvious gentleman, sympathetic and courteous.
While he will not compromise with his convictions, he does
his best not to obtrude them too crudely until Job virtually forces
him to. Then, for such is the character of an Eliphaz, he goes
much farther than the others (ch. 22). However anachronistic it

may be, I always see him, not in the robes of an eastern gentleman, but in frock coat, striped trousers and top hat, the revered vicar's warden or senior deacon of a wealthy and fashionable church.

Orthodoxy is in itself a very precious thing. It becomes hard, cruel and narrow when it becomes the expression of something other than a continuous living fellowship with the God of truth.

For Eliphaz his religious life revolved around a revelation that God had given him in a dream (4: 12–21):

A spirit glided past my face;
the hair of my face stood up.
It stood still,
but I could not discern its appearance.
A form was before my eyes;
there was silence, then I heard a voice:
"Can mortal man be righteous before God?
Can a man be pure before his Maker?" (R.S.V.)

His dream left Eliphaz with a profound realization of the sinfulness of man, and it coloured his whole outlook on life from then on. But, as is so often the case with religious experiences, it became something complete in itself, something by which men could be measured and judged. There is absolutely nothing in all that Eliphaz says that suggests that it ever brought him to see that he was the chief of sinners, or that it drew him nearer God.

A religion without personal experience to which testimony can be borne is a poor thing, but there is a very real danger that where there is experience it may be equated with religion. When this happens, the victim of this delusion comes to think that there is little more to be reached, and that his experience is an infallible yard-stick by which he may measure the religion of others. We see this attitude all around us today; there are even denominations that make certain experiences the test of conversion or spirituality.

Eliphaz has much that is beautiful and true to say:

Who ever perished, being innocent?
or where were the upright cut off?
According as I have seen, they that plough iniquity,
and sow trouble, reap the same. . . .
But man is born unto trouble,
as the sparks fly upward. . . .
Behold, happy is the man whom God reproveth:
therefore despise not thou the chastening of the Almighty. . . .

He shall deliver thee in six troubles;
yea, in seven there shall no evil touch thee.

But behind all this truth and solicitude Job feels himself being poured into the mould of Eliphaz' experience. He may be too kind to pass judgment on his friend, but his whole bearing proclaims what the judgment would be, if it were spoken.

We have much to learn from Eliphaz. A gospel without experience will seldom warm the hearts of men, but an experience preached as the gospel will repel all but those cut in our pattern, while an experience that becomes the yard-stick of truth will turn itself into falsehood.

JOB'S REPLY TO ELIPHAZ (CH. 6)

THEN Job answered and said,
²Oh that my vexation were but weighed,
and my calamity laid in the balances together!
³For now it would be heavier than the sand of the seas:
therefore have my words been rash.
⁴For the arrows of the Almighty are within me,
the poison whereof my spirit drinketh up:
the terrors of God do set themselves in array against me.
⁵Doth the wild ass bray when he hath grass?
or loweth the ox over his fodder?
⁶Can that which hath no savour be eaten without salt?
or is there any taste in the white of an egg?
⁷My soul refuseth to touch *them*;
they are as loathsome meat to me.
⁸Oh that I might have my request;
and that God would grant the thing that I long for!
⁹Even that it would please God to crush me;
that he would let loose his hand, and cut me off!
¹⁰Then should I yet have comfort;
yea, I would exult in pain that spareth not:
for I have not denied the words of the Holy One.

¹¹What is my strength, that I should wait?
and what is mine end, that I should be patient?
¹²Is my strength the strength of stones?
or is my flesh of brass?
¹³Is it not that I have no help in me,
and that effectual working is driven quite from me?
¹⁴To him that is ready to faint kindness *should be shewed* from his friend;
even to him that forsaketh the fear of the Almighty.
¹⁵My brethren have dealt deceitfully as a brook,
as the channel of brooks that pass away;
¹⁶which are black by reason of the ice, *and* wherein the snow hideth itself:
¹⁷what time they wax warm, they vanish:
when it is hot, they are consumed out of their place.
¹⁸The caravans *that travel* by the way of them turn aside;
they go up into the waste, and perish.
¹⁹The caravans of Tema looked,
the companies of Sheba waited for them.
²⁰They were ashamed because they had hoped;

they came thither, and were confounded.

21For now ye are nothing;
ye see a terror, and are afraid.

22Did I say, Give unto me?
or, Offer a present for me of your substance?

23or, Deliver me from the adversary's hand?
or, Redeem me from the hand of the oppressors?

24Teach me, and I will hold my peace:
and cause me to understand wherein I have erred.

25How forcible are words of uprightness!
but what doth your arguing reprove?

26Do ye imagine to reprove words?
seeing that the speeches of one that is desperate are as wind.

27Yea, ye would cast *lots* upon the fatherless,
and make merchandise of your friend.

28Now therefore be pleased to look upon me;
for surely I shall not lie to your face.

29Return, I pray you, let there be no injustice;
yea, return again, my cause is righteous.

30Is there injustice on my tongue?
cannot my taste discern mischievous things?

ONE word spoken by Eliphaz had pricked Job—*ka'as* (5: 2, 6: 2). *Ka'as*, which appears with far too wide a range of renderings in the A.V., is our natural reaction of vexation, impatience, grief and even anger, when faced with injustice and offence. Only a fool will show it when rightly rebuked (Prov. 12: 15f), and only a fool will react this way when chastened by God. (5: 2). The R.V., R.S.V. and I.C.C. render "vexation," while Knox prefers "impatience," but entirely misses the point in Job's answer by using "provocation" in 6: 2; Moffatt's "passion" is misleading. Eliphaz was in fact very unfair, for Job had shown exemplary behaviour when calamity had fallen on him (1: 20f.; 2: 10).

Faced with this determination on the part of his friends not to take him as he is, but as a vindication of their principles, Job reacts with his first vigorous rebuke. He pleads that calamity as great as his may reasonably be allowed an outlet. In our estimate of Job we must never forget his frank avowal that his words have been rash (6: 3, R.V.) or wild (Moffatt). They have been torn from him by anguish and are not the calm reflection of theological reasoning.

We have an interesting confirmation in 6: 6, that Job's sufferings were primarily spiritual. He compares them to tasteless unsalted food and to the *slime of the purslane* (R.S.V., I.C.C.). This would be a strange comparison if he were thinking of violent pain that left him without a moment's ease, but we can see the force of it, if he is thinking of mental suffering that makes him shudder whenever he allows the thoughts to invade his mind, as he shudders when faced with such food. Sooner than live with them he would die (6: 8f); the sense becomes clear when we realize that the *pain that spareth not* (6: 10, R.V.) is the last pain of death.

Many have found difficulty in *For I have not denied the words of the Holy One* (6: 10). It is argued with justice that Job consistently speaks of Sheol, the abode of the dead, as a place where all the dead are equal (3: 13–18), etc., hence it would make no difference to him after death whether he had kept the words of God or not. But Job is typical of so many truly godly men. He had been able to accept the popular view of rewards and punishments without much thought, but when it was challenged by experience he was prepared to abandon orthodoxy to feel after God. Similarly, while he shared in the then orthodox view of Sheol, in the moment of crisis his knowledge of God told him that there must be something beyond orthodoxy, and that at the last God could not be indifferent to the life lived by man. This is his first step that is to lead him to that ray of light that for a moment pierced beyond the grave (19: 25ff.).

The gist of Eliphaz' advice was that Job should submit himself to God and wait trustfully: Job's scornful answer is that he will be dead long before his friend's hope can be fulfilled (6: 11–14). We are reminded of James' angry sarcasm in his Epistle (2: 15f.). The three friends are then compared to one of the wadies of Transjordan "bringing down great floods of dark and troubled waters in spring," when they are least needed; but in the hour of need in the summer heat it is dry. All Job had asked of his friends was understanding and sympathy, not money (6: 22) or valiant deeds (6: 23). Ironically enough, but entirely consistently with human nature, he would probably have received the latter had he asked for them. True sympathy and understanding are always costlier than charity.

THE MISERY OF LIFE (CH. 7)

Is there not a time of service to
    man upon earth?
    and are not his days like the days
    of an hireling?
²As a servant that earnestly desir-
    eth the shadow,
    and as an hireling that looketh for
    his wages:
³so am I made to possess months of
    vanity,
    and wearisome nights are appoin-
    ted to me.
⁴When I lie down, I say,
    When shall I arise? but the night
    is long;
    and I am full of tossings to and

fro unto the dawning of the day.

⁵My flesh is clothed with worms and clods of dust;
my skin closeth up and breaketh out afresh.

⁶My days are swifter than a weaver's shuttle,
and are spent without hope.

⁷Oh remember that my life is wind: mine eye shall no more see good.

⁸The eye of him that seeth me shall behold me no more:
thine eyes shall be upon me, but I shall not be.

⁹As the cloud is consumed and vanisheth away,
so he that goeth down to Sheol shall come up no more.

¹⁰He shall return no more to his house,
neither shall his place know him any more.

¹¹Therefore I will not refrain my mouth;
I will speak in the anguish of my spirit;
I will complain in the bitterness of my soul.

¹²Am I a sea, or a sea-monster, that thou settest a watch over me?

¹³When I say, My bed shall comfort me,
my couch shall ease my complaint;

¹⁴then thou scarest me with dreams, and terrifiest me through visions:

¹⁵so that my soul chooseth strangling,
and death rather than *these* my bones.

¹⁶I loathe *my life*; I would not live alway:
let me alone; for my days are vanity.

¹⁷What is man, that thou shouldest magnify him,
and that thou shouldest set thine heart upon him,

¹⁸and that thou shouldest visit him every morning,
and try him every moment?

¹⁹How long wilt thou not look away from me,
nor let me alone till I swallow down my spittle?

²⁰If I have sinned, what do I unto thee, O thou watcher of men?
why hast thou set me as a mark for thee,
so that I am a burden to myself?

²¹And why dost thou not pardon my transgression,
and take away mine iniquity?
For now shall I lie down in the dust;
and thou shalt seek me diligently, but I shall not be.

IT was probably the look of troubled or cold incomprehension on his friends' faces that made Job look away from them to God. *Remember* (7: 7) is in the singular, and is addressed to God, not to Job's friends; there is no need to doubt that this holds good for the whole chapter.

As we trace our way through the book we find that Job's sufferings bring him not only to a truer knowledge of God but also to a more living knowledge of his fellow men. As he turned from the puzzled incomprehension of his friends, he suddenly realized with a start that it was not only he whom they failed to understand, and that his lot was far from being unique. It was all very well for Eliphaz to fold his hands over his plump belly and say sententiously, *Man is born unto trouble, as the sparks fly upward.* It was true enough, but it meant all too little to him.

But when Job breaks out, *Is there not hard labour for man upon earth? and are not his days like the days of an hireling?* (7: 1), for a moment we are introduced to the solidarity of suffering. But it is only in Christ that the solidarity of suffering can become really constructive. For Job it only increased his burden, for now he saw it as only an aggravation of misery ample in itself.

Remarkably enough, Job's increased vision of suffering did not shake his trust in God. With a touching naïvety he says, *Thine eyes shall be upon me, but I shall not be* (7: 8). It is quite understandable that the rabbis should be upset by a man like Choni the Circle-drawer,* of whom Simeon ben Shetach said that he behaved petulantly before God as a son behaves before his father. But both in public and in private prayer there is a strange lack of willingness among many Christians to be completely frank with their heavenly Father. This is one of the greatest lessons we can learn from Jeremiah and Job. They never hesitated to open their hearts to God, even though men might call their words blasphemy. Here Job suggests that God has in some strange aberration forgotten His normal behaviour and that when the mood is over He will look for Job to be kind to him again, but it will then be too late, for he will be among the dead.

There follow some of Job's bitterest words (7: 11–21), which he must have regretted with all his heart, after God had revealed Himself to him. Job has been led to reject the orthodoxy in which he had been reared and which Eliphaz has been repeating to him, but so far he cannot grasp that God may be doing something entirely alien to man's beliefs about Him. It is a weakness of ours to assume, when in real or pretended humility we acknowledge that we do not understand God's working in any particular circumstance, that we are dealing merely with an uncommon variant of the normal. Man hates to say that he does not understand what God's intentions may be. That is why our comfort and advice so often miss the mark with those who suffer. So Job assumes that his sufferings must have some relation to his sins. He tells God, using popular mythological language, that after all he has never been, like the powers of Chaos, a rebel against Him, nor has his sin, whatever it may have been, injured the majesty

* Among the stories told of him is that in a time of great drought he drew a circle in the dust and told God that he was not going to step outside it until God gave rain. When a downpour followed, he told God that they did not want a flood but suitable rain for the fields. In this too he was heard.

of the Almighty. Once again, in v. 21, he takes up the thought of v. 8, and says that when God changes His mind it will be too late, for he will be gone.

Bildad the Shuhite (Ch. 8)

THEN answered Bildad the Shuhite, and said,

²How long wilt thou speak these things?
and *how long* shall the words of thy mouth be *like* a mighty wind?

³Doth God pervert judgement?
or doth the Almighty pervert justice?

⁴If thy children sinned against him,
and he delivered them into the hand of their transgression:

⁵if thou wouldest seek diligently unto God,
and make thy supplication to the Almighty;

⁶if thou wert pure and upright;
surely now he would awake for thee,
and make the habitation of thy righteousness prosperous.

⁷And though thy beginning was small,
yet thy latter end should greatly increase.

⁸For inquire, I pray thee, of the former age,
and apply thyself to that which their fathers have searched out:

⁹(for we are but of yesterday, and know nothing,
because our days upon earth are a shadow:)

¹⁰shall not they teach thee, and tell thee,
and utter words out of their heart?

¹¹Can the papyrus grow up without mire?
can the reed-grass grow without water?

¹²Whilst it is yet in its greenness, *and* not cut down,
it withereth before any *other* herb.

¹³So are the paths of all that forget God;
and the hope of the godless man shall perish:

¹⁴whose confidence shall be cut off,
and whose trust is a spider's web.

¹⁵He shall lean upon his house, but it shall not stand:
he shall hold fast thereby, but it shall not endure.

¹⁶He is green before the sun,
and his shoots go forth over his garden.

¹⁷His roots are wrapped about the heap,
he beholdeth the place of stones.

¹⁸If he be destroyed from his place,
then it shall deny him, *saying*, I have not seen thee.

¹⁹Behold, this is the joy of his way,
and out of the earth shall others spring.

²⁰Behold, God will not cast away a perfect man,
neither will he uphold the evil-doers.

²¹He will yet fill thy mouth with laughter,
and thy lips with shouting.

²²They that hate thee shall be clothed with shame;
and the tent of the wicked shall be no more.

BILDAD is in many ways the most dogmatic of the three friends. He is not as downright brutal as Zophar, but he is more pitiless. He is the only one to refer to the fate of Job's children:

If your children have sinned against Him,
He has delivered them into the power of their transgression (8: 4),

where the "if" is of course a polite "because." Left to himself
he would probably have been a humble and likeable man, but he
had constituted himself a champion of the orthodoxy of the past.
If he had lived at a later period, he would willingly have burnt
Job's body in the hope of saving his soul.

His position is made clear in 8: 8ff.:

> For inquire, I pray you, of bygone ages,
>   and consider what the fathers have found;
> for we are but of yesterday, and know nothing,
>   for our days on earth are a shadow.
> Will they not teach you, and tell you,
>   and utter words out of their understanding? (R.S.V.)

Bildad is a pillar of the Church and a champion of orthodoxy.
We can ill do without him and he has a rare gift of recognizing the
first insidious inroads of false doctrine. Just because he has no
axe to grind, because he is the faithful depository of the wisdom
and experience of the past, he is often a valued and revered
teacher. But for all that he is apt to be the Church's worst friend
in the hour of change and of crisis. Above all, when men are sore
tried and distressed, and the landmarks of life are hidden, it is
seldom to Bildad that they turn.

I cannot think of Bildad without contrasting him with John
Robinson at Delfshaven in 1620, as he speaks to the members of
his church leaving for the new world:

> "I charge you before God and His blessed angels, that you
> follow me no farther than you have seen me follow the Lord
> Jesus Christ. If God reveals anything to you by any other
> instruments of His, be as ready to receive it as you were to
> receive any truth by my ministry, for I am verily persuaded the
> Lord hath more truth yet to break forth out of His holy word.
> For my part, I cannot sufficiently bewail the condition of those
> reformed churches which are come to a period in religion, and
> will go, at present, no farther than the instruments of their
> reformation. The Lutherans cannot be drawn to go beyond
> what Luther saw; whatever part of His will our God has
> revealed to Calvin, they will rather die than embrace it; and
> the Calvanists, you see, stick fast where they were left by that
> great man of God, who yet saw not all things. . . ."

Entirely consistently with his inherited theology, Bildad can only see life as it conforms to the pattern set for it. Characteristically, where Eliphaz had spoken of the foolish and had seen all men with their share of suffering, Bildad speaks of the perfect—*tam*, cf. 1: 1 and p. 31—and the evil-doers (8: 20), and the wicked (8: 22). These last, the *resha'im*, are to recur repeatedly from this time on. We would do well to notice that it is not sinners in general who are intended. A study of the passages where they are mentioned will show that they are rich and mighty men, such as Job was before his calamity, who, however, flaunt their wickedness in the sight of God and man. The problem of the wicked in Job is not concerned with the secret sinner or the small man ground down in life, but with those for whom there is no excuse in their sinning.

It would seem at first reading that Bildad was merely shocked at the wildness of Job's words and that he was really convinced of his essential innocence (8: 20f.). When, however, he says,

> Will the papyrus rise up proudly without mire?
> Will the reed-grass grow without water? (8: 11, I.C.C.)

he seems to be suggesting that there is no smoke without fire. His real feelings are suddenly revealed at the very end, when he says, *And the tent of the wicked shall be no more* (8: 22b); we cannot doubt that he is thinking of Job's loss of all things. Though he is holding open the door of repentance to Job, he leaves no doubt that he considers him one of the wicked on whom the well-merited judgments of God have fallen.

JOB'S REPLY TO BILDAD (CH. 9: 1–24)

THEN Job answered and said, ²Of a truth I know that it is so: but how can man be just with God? ³If one should desire to contend with him, he could not answer him one of a thousand. ⁴*He is* wise in heart, and mighty in strength: who hath hardened himself against him, and prospered? ⁵Which removeth the mountains, and they know it not, when he overturneth them in his anger.

⁶Which shaketh the earth out of her place, and the pillars thereof tremble. ⁷Which commandeth the sun, and it riseth not; and sealeth up the stars. ⁸Which alone stretcheth out the heavens, and treadeth upon the waves of the sea. ⁹Which maketh the Bear, Orion, and the Pleiades, and the chambers of the south. ¹⁰Which doeth great things past finding out;

yea, marvellous things without number.

¹¹Lo, he goeth by me, and I see him not:

he passeth on also, but I perceive him not.

¹²Behold, he seizeth *the prey*, who can hinder him?

who will say unto him, What doest thou?

¹³God will not withdraw his anger;

the helpers of Rahab did stoop under him.

¹⁴How much less shall I answer him, and choose out my words *to reason* with him?

¹⁵Whom, though I were righteous, yet would I not answer;

I would make supplication to mine adversary.

¹⁶If I had called, and he had answered me;

yet would I not believe that he hearkened unto my voice.

¹⁷For he breaketh me with a tempest,

and multiplieth my wounds without cause.

¹⁸He will not suffer me to take my breath,

but filleth me with bitterness.

¹⁹If *we speak* of the strength of the mighty, lo, *he is there!*

and if of judgement, who will appoint me a time?

²⁰Though I be righteous, mine own mouth shall condemn me:

though I be perfect, he shall prove me perverse.

²¹I am perfect; I regard not myself;

I despise my life.

²²It is all one; therefore I say,

He destroyeth the perfect and the wicked.

²³If the scourge slay suddenly,

he will mock at the calamity of the innocent.

²⁴The earth is given into the hand of the wicked:

he covereth the faces of the judges thereof;

if *it be* not *he*, who then is it?

JOB knew Bildad from of old, and doubtless he anticipated all he had to say as soon as he opened his mouth. So there are no wild reproaches in his answer.

I pointed out in ch. II that we are dealing with wisdom literature, with men striving by their wisdom to discover the ways of God. The everlasting power and divinity of God are revealed to us in God's creation (Rom. 1: 20), but the moral character of God is only truly recognizable in the sphere of redemptive revelation—and Job and his friends were not even within the covenant of Sinai, still less the new covenant. We should never forget that man's conscience is very far from being an infallible guide to God's moral demands on men. Its purpose is rather to insist that God does make such demands.

Job accepts Bildad's insistence on the justice of God (8: 3), but sets it in a new setting. When Eliphaz said, *Can mortal man be righteous before God?* (4: 17), he was thinking of the sinfulness of man. Job takes up the thought (9: 2), but makes it mean that man is not in the position to establish his right before God, for God always has the *power* to prove him wrong. There are in the law of Moses certain apparently arbitrary commandments which have been the despair of commentators. The only reasonable interpretation to be placed on them is that they are a revelation of a sovereign power that has the right to impose arbitrary commands. Certainly in the experience of the saints there are happenings which cannot be explained by finite man, though doubtless we shall understand them in eternity. Job tells his friends that—apart from revelation—there is no evidence of God's moral government in the affairs of this world.

He then strangely anticipates God's own revelation to him, and on the basis of God's all-might challenges the possibility of knowing God's ways;

Lo, He goeth by me, and I see Him not:
He passeth on also, but I perceive Him not (9: 11)

is a challenge to the whole concept that God's ways are essentially understandable. What to his friends is even worse, he flatly denies their whole interpretation of life:

The earth is given into the hand of the wicked:
He covereth the faces of the judges thereof;
if it be not He, who then is it? (9: 24).

We shall see that the major part of their later discussion revolves around this statement by Job.

But how is it that men living in the same land, brought up together, can come to such diametrically opposed views of society? Life around us is so rich and manifold that if we are to understand any of its manifestations we must learn to choose those phenomena that are significant and virtually to ignore the rest. That is what the scientist is doing all the time. But few of us are trained scientists or observers. We normally see what we want to see, and overlook or minimize that which does not suit our theories. The teaching of the Wise was based on carefully selected facts. When Job had to suffer, his eyes were opened to the suffering around him; when he felt the smart of injustice, he saw for the first time clearly the prevalence of injustice around him. We know that Job's friends were wrong; we must not jump to the conclusion that Job was right. They and he alike are giving us partial views of reality, but, for all that, Job tends to see more of the essentials than they do. Each in his own way, Job's friends see the world through the spectacles of their respective theories. Job has no theory; he is an explorer of new realms.

Even though his observation is distorted by passion and suffering, it still remains nearer the truth than the picture which has to conform to preconceived ideas.

We do well to remember this. God's estimate of man and his life is not the sinner's, and the world is seldom willing to welcome the proclamation of human sin. It is seldom, however, that the man caught up in a system sees the world as it is revealed to us in the Scriptures. The more authoritarian the system, the more distorted its view of the world and of man. The captives of the system, especially our ·Bildads, sincerely reverence God's revelation and wish to know His will and do it. For all that they insist that revelation and will must conform to their understanding and tradition, and so they fail to grasp either.

THE POTTER AND THE CLAY (CHS. 9: 25–10: 22)

23 Now my days are swifter than a runner:
they flee away, they see no good.
26 They are passed away as the ships of reed:
as the eagle that swoopeth on the prey.
27 If I say, I will forget my complaint, I will put off my *sad* countenance, and be of good cheer:
28 I am afraid of all my sorrows, I know that thou wilt not hold me innocent.
29 I shall be condemned;
why then do I labour in vain?
30 If I wash myself with snow, and cleanse my hands with lye;
31 yet wilt thou plunge me in the ditch,
and mine own clothes shall abhor me.
32 For he is not a man, as I am, that I should answer him,
that we should come together in judgement.
33 There is no umpire betwixt us, that might lay his hand upon us both.
34 Let him take his rod away from me,
and let not his terror make me afraid:

35 then would I speak, and not fear him; for I am not so in myself.

10. My soul is weary of my life;
I will give free course to my complaint;
I will speak in the bitterness of my soul.
2 I will say unto God, Do not condemn me;
shew me wherefore thou contendest with me.
3 Is it good unto thee that thou shouldest oppress,
that thou shouldest despise the work of thine hands,
and shine upon the counsel of the wicked?
4 Hast thou eyes of flesh, or seest thou as man seeth?
5 Are thy days as the days of man, or thy years as man's days,
6 that thou inquirest after mine iniquity,
and searchest after my sin,
7 although thou knowest that I am not wicked;
and there is none that can deliver out of thine hand?
8 Thine hands have framed me and fashioned me
together round about; yet thou dost destroy me.

⁹Remember, I beseech thee, that thou hast fashioned me as clay; and wilt thou bring me into dust again?

¹⁰Hast thou not poured me out as milk,
and curdled me like cheese?

¹¹Thou hast clothed me with skin and flesh,
and knit me together with bones and sinews.

¹²Thou hast granted me life and favour,
and thy visitation hath preserved my spirit.

¹³Yet these things thou didst hide in thine heart;
I know that this *is* with thee:

¹⁴if I sin, then thou markest me,
and thou wilt not acquit me from mine iniquity.

¹⁵If I be wicked, woe unto me;
and if I be righteous, yet shall I not lift up my head;
being filled with ignominy and looking upon mine affliction.

¹⁶And if *my head* exalt itself, thou huntest me as a lion:
and again thou shewest thyself marvellous upon me.

¹⁷Thou renewest thy witnesses against me,
and increasest thine indignation upon me,
changes and warfare are with me.

¹⁸Wherefore then hast thou brought me forth out of the womb?
I had given up the ghost, and no eye had seen me.

¹⁹I should have been as though I had not been;
I should have been carried from the womb to the grave.

²⁰Are not my days few? cease then, and let me alone, that I may take comfort a little,

²¹Before I go whence I shall not return,
to the land of darkness and of the shadow of death;

²²A land of thick darkness, as darkness *itself*;
of the shadow of death, without any order,
and where the light is as darkness.

JOB had not proclaimed the power of God to his friends as a mere abstract principle. The time was soon to come when the knowledge of the all-might of God, not as grasped by his own intellect but as revealed by God Himself, would bring peace to the wounded soul of Job. But that was not yet. At the moment he was overwhelmed; shut in on every side by a power he neither knew nor understood, he refused to abandon his belief that it was merciful and loving, and yet he could see no signs of mercy and love. He longed to come before His judgment seat and reason his case before Him, and yet he knew he could never prove his case. So when he had thrown down his challenge to Bildad (9: 24), he turned to speak to God. In this section Job no longer speaks about God, but to Him; indeed we may question how far his friends were even intended to hear him.

There are few more affecting passages in Scripture. Here is a broken man, who has lost all. Racked with pain and troubled in heart, he yet refuses to listen either to his fellow townsfolk or to his friends. He knows himself a sinner, yet he cannot believe that God has cast him off. He longs for a daysman, an umpire, between him and His God, but not to Job was there given a vision of the Mediator who was to come. So he turns in trembling hope to his Creator, but all he can ask for is a few days of brightness before he goes *to the land of darkness and of the shadow of death* (10: 21).

ZOPHAR THE NAAMATHITE (CH. 11)

THEN answered Zophar the Naamathite, and said,

²Should not the multitude of words be answered?
and should a man full of talk be justified?

³Should thy boastings make men hold their peace?
and when thou mockest, shall no man make thee ashamed?

⁴For thou sayest, My doctrine is pure,
and I am clean in thine eyes.

⁵But Oh that God would speak,
and open his lips against thee;

⁶and that he would shew thee the secrets of wisdom,
that it is manifold in effectual working!
Know therefore that God remitteth unto thee of thine iniquity.

⁷Canst thou find out the deep things of God?
canst thou find out the Almighty unto perfection?

⁸It is high as heaven; what canst thou do?
deeper than Sheol; what canst thou know?

⁹The measure thereof is longer than the earth,
and broader than the sea.

¹⁰If he pass through, and shut up,
and call unto judgement, then who can hinder him?

¹¹For he knoweth vain men:
he seeth iniquity also, even though he consider it not.

¹²But an empty man will get understanding,
when a wild ass's colt is born a man.

¹³If thou set thine heart aright,
and stretch out thine hands toward him;

¹⁴if iniquity be in thine hand, put it far away,
and let not unrighteousness dwell in thy tents;

¹⁵surely then shalt thou lift up thy face without spot;
yea, thou shalt be stedfast, and shalt not fear:

¹⁶for thou shalt forget thy misery;
thou shalt remember it as waters that are passed away:

¹⁷and *thy* life shall be clearer than the noonday;
though there be darkness, it shall be as the morning.

¹⁸And thou shalt be secure, because there is hope;
yea, thou shalt search *about thee*,
and shalt take thy rest in safety.

¹⁹Also thou shalt lie down, and none shall make thee afraid;
yea, many shall make suit unto thee.

²⁰But the eyes of the wicked shall fail,
and they shall have no way to flee,
and their hope shall be the giving up of the ghost.

WHETHER or not Job intended his words to God to be heard and taken in by his friends, they drove Zophar to fury, and he could hardly refrain from interrupting. As soon as Job had finished, he brushed all to one side as just "words." He is the typical man of common sense, for whom life holds few problems, and who is suspicious of him who finds them, and still more of him who discusses them.

It is not that he is not a God-fearing man, but simply that the mysteries of God do not concern him, for they are too high:

Canst thou find out the deep things of God?
   Canst thou find out the Almighty unto perfection?
It is high as heaven; what canst thou do?
   deeper than Sheol; what canst thou know? (11: 7f).

For him Job's "Why?" is Job's greatest sin, the supreme proof that he had not even begun to walk in the paths of Wisdom:

An empty man will get understanding,
   when a wild ass's colt is born a man (11: 12).

All Job has to do is to set his heart aright and pray and put away iniquity (11: 13f.) and all will be perfectly all right.

All of us are familiar with Zophar. He is the man who is perpetually demanding the simple Gospel, by which he does not mean the greatest mystery of God's love expressed so that a child can understand it, but God's love stripped of all mystery. He looks on every doubt as being in itself sin, and every difficulty as the sign of an evil heart of unbelief. The neurotic and the mentally ill receive short shrift at his hands, and he generally has some authority, not over profound, appeal to whom settles every controversy. He is uneasy the moment intellectual discussion begins, and he finds the late Professor Joad's famous opening gambit, "It all depends on what you mean by . . .", a sign of intellectual dishonesty. To suggest to him that a verse of Scripture may bear a different sense than does its plain meaning in the Authorised Version is the cloven hoof of modernism, while to appeal to the Greek and the Hebrew is mere sophistry.

The Church needs its Zophars. They are a salutary check upon us when we grow too abstract, too clever, too intellectual, when we feed the flock on wind and speculation. Their shrewd common sense will often show a committee the obvious, and they often strip the veil of make-believe from man's heart. But for all that, God have mercy on Job when he falls into Zophar's hands!

Eliphaz is too gentlemanly to be over-harsh with Job, until Job rouses him to theological fury. Bildad is too humble to want to sit as judge on Job himself; he would rather that the voices of the past should judge. But Zophar does not hesitate: *Know therefore that God remitteth unto thee of thine iniquity* (11: 6), i.e. compared with what Job's sin deserves his calamities are very forgiveness itself.

Job's Reply to Zophar (Chs. 12: 1–13: 19)

THEN Job answered and said,
²No doubt but ye are the people,
and wisdom shall die with you.
³But I have understanding as well as you;
I am not inferior to you:
yea, who knoweth not such things as these?
⁴I am as one that is a laughing-stock to his neighbour,
a *man* that called upon God, and he answered him:
the just, the perfect man is a laughing-stock.
⁵In the thought of him that is at ease there is contempt for misfortune;
it is ready for them whose foot slippeth.
⁶The tents of robbers prosper,
and they that provoke God are secure;
that bring *their* God in their hand.
⁷But ask now the beasts, and they shall teach thee;
and the fowls of the air, and they shall tell thee:
⁸or speak to the earth, and it shall teach thee;
and the fishes of the sea shall declare unto thee.
⁹Who knoweth not by all these,
that the hand of the Lord hath wrought this?
¹⁰In whose hand is the soul of every living thing,
and the breath of all mankind.
¹¹Doth not the ear try words,
even as the palate tasteth its meat?
¹²With aged men is wisdom,
and in length of days understanding.
¹³With him is wisdom and might;
he hath counsel and understanding.

¹⁴Behold, he breaketh down, and it cannot be built again;
he shutteth up a man, and there can be no opening.
¹⁵Behold, he withholdeth the waters, and they dry up;
again, he sendeth them out, and they overturn the earth.
¹⁶With him is strength and sound wisdom;
the deceived and the deceiver are his.
¹⁷He leadeth counsellors away spoiled,
and judges maketh he fools.
¹⁸He looseth the bond of kings,
and bindeth their loins with a girdle.
¹⁹He leadeth priests away spoiled,
and overthroweth the mighty.
²⁰He removeth the speech of the trusty,
and taketh away the understanding of the elders.
²¹He poureth contempt upon princes,
and looseth the belt of the strong.
²²He discovereth deep things out of darkness,
and bringeth out to light the shadow of death.
²³He increaseth the nations, and destroyeth them:
he spreadeth the nations abroad, and bringeth them in.
²⁴He taketh away the heart of the chiefs of the people of the earth,
and causeth them to wander in a wilderness where there is no way.
²⁵They grope in the dark without light,
and he maketh them to stagger like a drunken man.

13. Lo mine eye hath seen all *this*, mine ear hath heard and understood it.

2What ye know, *the same* do I know also:
I am not inferior unto you.
3Surely I would speak to the Almighty,
and I desire to reason with God.
4But ye are forgers of lies,
ye are all physicians of no value.
5Oh that ye would altogether hold your peace!
and it should be your wisdom.
6Hear now my reasoning,
and hearken to the pleadings of my lips.
7Will ye speak unrighteously for God,
and talk deceitfully for him?
8Will ye respect his person?
will ye contend for God?
9Is it good that he should search you out?
or as one deceiveth a man, will ye deceive him?
10He will surely reprove you,
if ye do secretly respect persons.
11Shall not his excellency make you afraid,
and his dread fall upon you?
12Your memorable sayings *are* proverbs of ashes,
your defences *are* defences of clay.
13Hold your peace, let me alone, that I may speak,
and let come on me what will.
14Wherefore should I take my flesh in my teeth,
and put my life in mine hand?
15Though he slay me, yet will I wait for him:
nevertheless I will maintain my ways before him.
16This also shall be my salvation;
that a godless man shall not come before him.
17Hear diligently my speech,
and let my declaration be in your ears.
18Behold now, I have ordered my cause;
I know that I shall be justified.
19Who is he that will contend with me?
for now shall I hold my peace and give up the ghost.

FACED with Bildad's appeal to the past, Job must have felt helpless trying to answer a man who would not think for himself. Faced with Zophar's brutal common sense that made all revolve around his own understanding, he felt hopeless, and for a moment he broke out in bitter sarcasm: *No doubt but ye are the people* [i.e. all the wisdom of the world is found in you, and so] *wisdom shall die with you* (12: 2). Sarcasm has its place in the Christian's armoury, for sometimes it is the only way to deflate the proud complacency of the self-satisfied. But Job's barb is too weak to puncture the hide of these champions of orthodoxy. He would have needed a harpoon at the least: as it is he only pricks and angers them.

A new thought now begins to emerge. The fact that his friends failed to understand him, were unable to comfort him, and even condemned him for imagined sin, were painful but bearable. But now has come Zophar's bitter jibe about the ass's colt (11: 12, R.V. mg.). Job sees his position among the Wise denied, attributed doubtless to his skill in learning the right answers by rote; his asking of awkward questions is considered merely a sign of stupidity. Job's friends have been caught in the trap that always lies hidden for the defenders of orthodoxy, however the term be defined, *viz.* the belief that failure to agree with the dominant majority must be due to intellectual, moral or spiritual faults. With their falling into this trap the discussion tends to move from Job and his personal sufferings (though these remain in the fore-front) to the wider problem of whether the experience and specula-tion of the Wise enable them to dogmatize on the working out of God's will among men.

Had the wisdom shown by his friends been something ex-ceptional, it might have been bearable, but Zophar's shallow agnosticism is infuriating. What of it if a righteous man like Job becomes a laughing-stock? God used to answer his prayers—no matter! Men used to find nothing to criticize in him (*perfect*, 12: 4)—what of it? On the other hand, violent men, who know no other god than their weapons (*that bring their god in their hand*, 12: 6, R.V. mg.), prosper—oh, well, God knows the answer to such anomalies! The all-might of God is something so obvious that even birds and beasts and fishes know that God stands behind all that happens (12: 7)—though modern man has often fallen below the level of the brute creation in this! For Zophar to sug-gest that Job did not know this is a gratuitous insult (13: 1f.).

There is little agreement as to how we should interpret 12: 11–25 R.V. mg., Moffatt, Peake, I.C.C., Strahan all find a contrast between vv. 12 and 13; in other words Job is rejecting the basis of Bildad's confidence (8: 8) and inferentially of his friends as well, and proclaiming that in God alone is wisdom. To me it seems far more likely that Job is continuing his sarcasm. After re-affirming the maxim they had constantly heard, when they had first sat at the feet of the Wise:

> With aged men is wisdom,
>   and in length of days understanding (12: 12),

he heaps afforism on afforism:

> All God's doing; his are the wisdom and the power; to him belong prudence in act and discernment. The ruins he makes, none can rebuild, his imprisonment none can escape; withholds he the rain, all is dried up; sends he rain, it floods all the ground. Yes, he is strong, he is wise; reads the knave's heart as easily as the fool's. He can thwart the counsellor, bemuse the judge, exchange the king's baldrick for the rope of a prisoner, lead the priest away ungowned, dispossess the noble, bewitch the lips

that never erred, rob the elder of his prudence, bring princes into contempt, unman the strong. Things deep hidden in darkness he reveals, kindles the light where death's shadow lay, brings growth or ruin to a people, and what he has ruined restores. The hearts of chieftains he bewilders, leading them by false paths to vain ends, till all light fails, and they grope about in darkness, wander aimless like a drunkard after wine (12: 13–25, Knox).

Yes, of course all this is true, and Job can say it as well or better than his friends, but the unspoken question remains: How much nearer are we to understanding God's ways and works?

But Job cannot believe that God is merely the Unknowable. He wants to speak to the Almighty and argue things out with Him (13: 3). His original cry of "Why?" had been an invitation to his friends to help him in this quest. But he had found them mere windbags, standing up for God with sophistries and empty maxims. The wish to defend God from the attacks and complaints of men may be natural and laudable, but in the case of Job's friends, as so often, there was less concern for God's glory and more for a parade of their own wisdom. But even where the motives are correct it is apt to be love's labour lost. God can look after Himself, and we always run the grave risk of re-creating Him in our own image before we are ready "to justify His ways to men" (13: 4–12).

It had been agony for Job to lose his comfortable, ready-made views of God's providence, and he recognizes that it is taking his life in his hand (13: 14) to seek an interview with God and to argue things out with Him. To this many will say Amen; they will point to those who, unsatisfied with the old orthodoxies, have sought to know more and more fully and have made shipwreck of their faith. This is, alas, all too true, but where this is so, the motive of the search has often been at fault, and they have sought the answer by the wrong means. We must hesitate in judgment, however, for often enough the heresies of yesterday are the orthodoxies of today, and where we have thought of shipwreck, they have been sailing unknown seas and gathering great wealth.

Job is emboldened in his undertaking, for he knows that a godless man would not and could not so come before God (13: 16). So strongly does his faith blaze forth that he assures his genuinely horror-struck friends, *I know I shall be justified* (13: 18), and tells them that if any can bring a justified charge against him, *then would I hold my peace and give up the ghost* (13: 19).   Job is so confident that, if God will but lift his afflictions for the moment and veil His glory, he is content to be either plaintiff or defendant.

JOB PLEADS HIS CAUSE (CHS. 13: 20–14: 22)

20 ONLY do not two things unto me,
then will I not hide myself from thy face:
21withdraw thine hand far from me;
and let not thy terror make me afraid.
22Then call thou, and I will answer;
or let me speak, and answer thou me.
23How many are mine iniquities and sins?
make me to know my transgression and my sin.
24Wherefore hidest thou thy face,
and holdest me for thine enemy?
25Wilt thou harass a driven leaf?
and wilt thou pursue the dry stubble?
26For thou writest bitter things against me,
and makest me to inherit the iniquities of my youth:
27thou puttest my feet also in the stocks, and markest all my paths;
thou drawest thee a line about the soles of my feet:
28though I am like a rotten thing that consumeth,
like a garment that is moth-eaten.

14. Man that is born of a woman
is of few days, and full of trouble.
2He cometh forth like a flower, and is cut down:
he fleeth also as a shadow, and continueth not.
3And dost thou open thine eyes upon such an one,
and bringest me into judgement with thee?
4Who can bring a clean thing out of an unclean?
not one.
5Seeing his days are determined,
the number of his months is with thee,
and thou hast appointed his bounds that he cannot pass;
6look away from him, that he may rest,
till he shall accomplish, as an hireling, his day.
7For there is hope of a tree, if it be cut down, that it will sprout again,
and that the tender branch thereof will not cease.
8Though the root thereof wax old in the earth,
and the stock thereof die in the ground;
9yet through the scent of water it will bud,
and put forth boughs like a plant.
10But man dieth, and wasteth away:
yea, man giveth up the ghost, and where is he?
11*As* the waters fail from the sea,
and the river decayeth and drieth up;
12so man lieth down and riseth not:
till the heavens be no more, they shall not awake,
nor be roused out of their sleep.
13Oh that thou wouldest hide me in Sheol,
that thou wouldest keep me secret, until thy wrath be past,
that thou wouldest appoint me a set time, and remember me!
14If a man die, shall he live *again*?
all the days of my warfare would I wait,
till my release should come.
15Thou shouldest call, and I would answer thee:
thou wouldest have a desire to the work of thine hands.
16But now thou numberest my steps:

dost thou not watch over my sin? 17My transgression is sealed up in a bag, and thou fastenest up mine iniquity. 18And surely the mountain falling cometh to nought, and the rock is removed out of its place; 19the waters wear the stones; the overflowings thereof wash away the dust of the earth: and thou destroyest the hope of man. 20Thou prevailest for ever against him, and he passeth; thou changest his countenance, and sendest him away. 21His sons come to honour, and he knoweth it not; and they are brought low, but he perceiveth it not of them. 22But his flesh upon him hath pain, and his soul within him mourneth.

AFTER his bold declaration of confidence as to the outcome of his hearing before God (13: 20ff.) Job begins by demanding to know what God has against him: *How many are my iniquities and my sins? Make me know my transgression and my sin* (13: 23). This is not in itself a declaration of guilt. All along Job's thesis is that, while he is a sinner, he is not so in a measure that would justify his sufferings. He offers God the unexpressed alternative of revealing sins that would justify his sufferings or of motivating his sufferings on some other ground. Obviously it is the latter that he really expects.

Here we must imagine a dramatic pause. Job looks vainly to the brazen vault of heaven for an answer, while his friends huddle together in startled fear lest a thunderbolt or fire from heaven should silence the blasphemy. But neither hope nor fear is fulfilled.

Job continues by pleading that if there are no such sins to reveal he is too insignificant for God to make such an example of him (13: 24-28). By *the iniquities of my youth* we must not understand that Job had sown his wild oats as a young man. He is rather suggesting that the only conceivable reason for his suffering is as insignificant as the sufferer himself.

Since God will not answer Job's plea, Job turns and arraigns God. He affirms that not only is God's treatment of Job unworthy, but so is His treatment of men in general (14: 1-12). Job cries, *Oh that a clean thing could come out of an unclean! Not one can* (14: 4). Since all the severity of God can never transform man, God should *look away from* man in his frailty, for all too soon he will go to his "long home." Job is not here asking God to cease being from the judge of all the earth. Even when he later questions the morality of God's rule, he does so with fear in his heart, lest by any means he might be correct. He is here concerned with the ordinary man, more sinned against than sinning, more labouring than enjoying the fruits of his lands, more suffering than rejoicing.

The ancient Israelites, or rather those among them from whom sprang the writers of the Old Testament, so lived in consciousness of Jehovah's presence and favour that they were normally able to live in the passing moment, looking neither to the disappointed hopes of yesterday nor to their fears for tomorrow. For them the present, blessed by the presence of God, was essentially good, and so the Old Testament tends to be an optimistic book. From time to time, however, the writer detaches himself from the present and looks on life as a whole. Then a pessimistic note, gilded it is true with the sunshine of God, breaks through. Death stands there in the shadows, bringing to naught all man's efforts and achievements. Job sees the irony that while the cut-down or dying tree may yet live (14: 7ff—a common phenomenon in tropical and sub-tropical climates, cf. Is. 6: 13, 11: 1, R.V., and better R.S.V.) no such hope awaits man.

Western civilization today is essentially optimistic. We can so drug ourselves with luxuries, machine-made entertainment and the "security" of the welfare state that neither the certainty of death nor the threat of nuclear weapons brings us to look on life as a whole. "Life is worth living" is the slogan of our age. Is it mere coincidence that the suicide rate is highest in those lands and among those social classes where it is easiest to refuse to see life as it really is? It is interesting how there is a growing tendency, which reaches its climax in North America, to wrap death in decent obscurity by the skill of the undertaker, the crematorium and the park-cemetery. The modern man revolts against the old hymn:

> Time, like an ever-rolling stream,
> Bears all its sons away;
> They fly forgotten, as a dream
> Dies at the opening day.

For all that there stands written over all life, even more clearly than for Job, "It is appointed unto man once to die, and after this the judgment."

Sheol

We cannot think otherwise of God than as the origin of all wisdom and rational thought. For all that, there is in God's wisdom and logic an element too high for man's mind to grasp; He says, "My ways are higher than your ways, and My thoughts than your thoughts." Logically the view should be correct that when man dies he ceases to exist. Man is above all *nephesh*, which in suitable contexts our older translations consistently render "soul." This is most unfortunate, for neither in popular use nor in the normal understanding of dogmatic theology do the two words approximate in meaning.

Nephesh is the *totality* that results when body and spirit are united. The R.S.V. and Moffatt render Gen. 2: 7 far more satisfactorily by "and man became a living being"; Knox's "a living person" is perhaps even better. When the body returns to the dust and the spirit returns to Him who gave it, logically the *nephesh*, the personality of man, should vanish. In fact the Old Testament teaches that it continues a shadow existence in Sheol (New Testament, Hades). It is a shadow existence because there is no spirit to impel it to action, and no body through which i can act, but for all that the *nephesh* continues to vegetate u impaired.

In 3: 11–26, Job had craved death, but subsequently we the conflict between this longing and the desire for a little p and sunshine before the inevitable end comes. In ch. 1⁴ reacts doubly against death: not merely is there the longi a few peaceful hours, but his natural fear of death and its has reasserted itself. Once more (cf. 7: 8, 21) the thoug that God's anger with him must be some strange passin̄ tion. He fears, however, that he cannot hold out until and so he prays (14: 13) in agony that he may enjoy all t tages of death without its finality. Then, startled, where his thoughts have led him: *If a man die, shall h* The answer implied is clearly "No." We must, h clearly that Job is not thinking of resurrection in Ch but of a continuance of life which death has inter̄ if we were to supply the answer "Yes," the en̄ again would again be death.

Though as yet it is a striking thought regretf away, were it possible for him to have a new sp

under God's smile and favour, he would gladly bear *all the days of my service* (14: 14) in the agony of this life and in the waiting in Sheol. As it is, all he has to hope for is a period of unexplained suffering followed by a name forgotten among men, and the hopeless and purposeless existence of Sheol.

> Thou destroyest the hope of man.
> > Thou prevailest for ever against him, and he passeth;
> > Thou changest his countenance, and sendest him away.
> His sons come to honour, and he knoweth it not;
> > And they are brought low, but he perceiveth it not.

So ends the first round of the debate. Job's three friends have revealed clearly how each, according to his own character and experience, has prejudged him whom he called friend by trying to accommodate his case to his own wonted measuring rod. Job has writhed under his friends' condemnation and lack of sympathy and understanding. The heavens have been silent to reproach and appeal alike. Broken Job collapses on the dung-hill as he accepts that death with all its finality is all that he can expect.

It does not end here, however, for orthodoxy has been outraged and is on the war-path looking for blood.

THE SECOND ROUND

"I am Offended" (Ch. 15)

Then answered Eliphaz the Temanite, and said,

2Should a wise man make answer with vain knowledge,
and fill his belly with the east wind?

3Should he reason with unprofitable talk,
or with speeches wherewith he can do no good?

4Yea, thou doest away with fear,
and restrainest devotion before God.

5For thine iniquity teacheth thy mouth,
and thou choosest the tongue of the crafty.

6Thine own mouth condemneth thee, and not I;
yea, thine own lips testify against thee.

7Art thou the first man that was born?
or wast thou brought forth before the hills?

8Hast thou heard the secret counsel of God?
and dost thou restrain wisdom to thyself?

9What knowest thou, that we know not?
what understandest thou, which is not in us?

10With us are both the grayheaded and the very aged men,
much elder than thy father.

11Are the consolations of God too small for thee,
and the word *that dealeth* gently with thee?

12Why doth thine heart carry thee away?
and why do thine eyes wink?

13That thou turnest thy spirit against God,
and lettest *such* words go out of thy mouth.

14What is man, that he should be clean?
and he which is born of a woman, that he should be righteous?

15Behold, he putteth no trust in his holy ones;
yea, the heavens are not clean in his sight.

16How much less one that is abominable and corrupt,
a man that drinketh iniquity like water!

17I will shew thee, hear thou me;
and that which I have seen I will declare:

18which wise men have told
from their fathers, and have not hid it;

19unto whom alone the land was given,
and no stranger passed among them:

20the wicked man travaileth with pain all his days,
even the number of years that are laid up for the oppressor.

21A sound of terrors is in his ears;
in prosperity the spoiler shall come upon him:

22he believeth not that he shall return out of darkness,
and he is waited for of the sword:

23he wandereth abroad for bread, *saying*, Where is it?
he knoweth that the day of darkness is ready at his hand:

24distress and anguish make him afraid;

they prevail against him, as a king ready to the battle:

25because he hath stretched out his hand against God,
and behaveth himself proudly against the Almighty;

26he runneth upon him with a *stiff* neck,
with the thick bosses of his bucklers:

27because he hath covered his face with his fatness,
and made collops of fat on his flanks;

28and he hath dwelt in desolate cities,
in houses which no man inhabited, which were ready to become heaps.

29He shall not be rich, neither shall his substance continue,
neither shall their produce bend to the earth.

30He shall not depart out of darkness;
the flame shall dry up his branches, and by the breath of his mouth shall he go away.

31Let him not trust in vanity, deceiving himself:
for vanity shall be his recompence.

32It shall be accomplished before his time,
and his branch shall not be green.

33He shall shake off his unripe grape as the vine,
and shall cast off his flower as the olive.

34For the company of the godless shall be barren,
and fire shall consume the tents of bribery.

35They conceive mischief, and bring forth iniquity,
and their belly prepareth deceit.

SILENCE lay for a while over the dung-hill until it was broken by Eliphaz' voice. There is a sharp edge to it now and a spot of red on his cheeks. He is trying hard to keep his temper, and as his words begin to roll out a little of the old graciousness returns. But it is clear that Eliphaz has been really shocked and offended.

"Are you one of the Wise, Job? What wise man would talk like you?" (vv. 2f). Urbanity and moderation, the carefully turned phrase and balanced aphorism, these have always been beloved in the schools of learning. When our Lord looked around Him with anger (Mark 3: 5) or called His opponents "ye serpents, ye offspring of vipers" (Matt. 23: 33), the Pharisees, like so many of their modern descendants, were doubtless shocked that one who was called Rabbi should so lower His dignity. They probably said, "After all He is only one of the *am ha-aretz* (common people) from Galilee." But there are times when the hard facts of life demand the sweeping away of sophistries which try to empty them of true meaning.

"Job, you speak like a godless man and you will encourage others to follow your example" (vv. 4ff). Eliphaz always loves to make his own standards the pattern of behaviour, and he will always be found turning to the alleged perils of the "younger brother" as a good motive for condemning what he does not approve of. In my own experience I have generally found the "younger brother" strangely tough. He is all for a bit of experiment and is apt to think of Eliphaz as an old stick-in-the-mud, if not worse. It is unchristian living by the professedly Christian leader that makes him stumble.

"Job, you are suffering from swelled head, you want to know what only the superhuman could know" (vv. 7f.). The Christian will quite cheerfully discuss the mystery of the Trinity; he will dogmatize how man and God could co-exist in the person of the Messiah; he will peer down the vistas of time and draw up a timetable for the future. But when you take him by the back of the neck and rub his nose on some of the facts of life, he is promptly up in arms, and appeals to the inscrutable wisdom of God.

"Job, you are claiming to know more than *we*, than *I*, who am old enough to be your father"—this is the meaning of verse 10. Here is the rub. Eliphaz, who has based his whole theology on experience, feels that a challenge to his theology is a challenge to his experience, a challenge to his yard-stick, a challenge to his personal integrity, especially when it comes from a much younger man.

I once received a letter from a well-known Christian: How can you write like that to a man of my age and position? That he had wantonly slandered me obviously did not trouble his conscience. That he had no answer to my rebuttal of his charges against me left him unmoved. My sin was that I had ventured to reject his judgment.

So once again Eliphaz repeats the teaching of chs. 4 and 5. But now the shadows have been increased. The picture of the sinfulness of man (vv. 14ff.) is darker, and it is clear enough that Eliphaz would be ill-pleased, if you perversely saw *him* in the picture; it is Job he is thinking of. Then, with a glance at Bildad, he appeals to the things most surely believed, the undiluted traditions of the fathers (vv. 17ff.). Before our eyes is unrolled the tragic life and death of Mr. Badman (vv.20–35); whose first name is, of course, Job, if only he will recognize himself.

It is easy to smile as we picture Eliphaz leaning forward in his eagerness, a little pompously and a little breathlessly reaching a triumphant conclusion in which he sees the wicked not merely going down to a premature grave, but leaving nothing but disaster behind him. But whether it was the pious young man asking me incredulously how there could be "pleasures of sin" (Heb. 11:25), or those who deny that there can be piety and a knowledge of God among the Roman Catholics (or any other denomination they dislike, for that matter), or who affirm that unless you have conformed to something external you cannot be a Christian, or who commiserate with Judaism as being nothing more than sterile legalism, this is always the voice of Eliphaz, who subordinates fact to theory.

JOB SOLILOQUIZES (CHS. 16, 17)

THEN Job answered and said,
²I have heard many such things:
miserable comforters are ye all.
³Shall vain words have an end?
or what provoketh thee that thou answerest?
⁴I also could speak as ye do;
if your soul were in my soul's stead,
I could join words together against you,
and shake mine head at you.
⁵*But* I would strengthen you with my mouth,
and the solace of my lips should assuage *your grief.*
⁶Though I speak, my grief is not assuaged:
and though I forbear, what am I eased?
⁷But now he hath made me weary:
thou hast made desolate all my company.
⁸And thou hast laid fast hold on me, *which* is a witness *against me*:
and my leanness riseth up against me, it testifieth to my face.
⁹He hath torn me in his wrath, and persecuted me;
he hath gnashed upon me with his teeth:
mine adversary sharpeneth his eyes upon me.
¹⁰They have gaped upon me with their mouth;
they have smitten me upon the cheek reproachfully:
they gather themselves together against me.
¹¹God delivereth me to the ungodly,
and casteth me into the hands of the wicked.
¹²I was at ease, and he brake me asunder;
yea, he hath taken me by the neck, and dashed me to pieces:
he hath also set me up for his mark.
¹³His archers compass me round about,
he cleaveth my reins asunder, and doth not spare;
he poureth out my gall upon the ground.
¹⁴He breaketh me with breach upon breach;
he runneth upon me like a giant.
¹⁵I have sewed sackcloth upon my skin,
and have laid my horn in the dust.
¹⁶My face is red with weeping,
and on my eyelids is the shadow of death;
¹⁷although there is no violence in mine hands,
and my prayer is pure.
¹⁸O earth, cover not thou my blood,
and let my cry have no *resting* place.
¹⁹Even now, behold, my witness is in heaven,
and he that voucheth for me is on high.
²⁰My friends scorn me:
but mine eye poureth out tears unto God;
²¹that he would maintain the right of a man with God,
and of a son of man with his neighbour!
²²For when a few years are come,

I shall go the way whence I shall not return.

17. My spirit is consumed, my days are extinct,
the grave is *ready* for me.
²Surely there are mockers with me,
and mine eye abideth in their provocation.
³Give now a pledge, be surety for me with thyself;
who is there that will strike hands with me?
⁴For thou hast hid their heart from understanding:
therefore shalt thou not exalt *them*.
⁵He that denounceth his friends for a prey,
even the eyes of his children shall fail.
⁶He hath made me also a byword of the people;
and I am become one in whose face they spit.
⁷Mine eye also is dim by reason of sorrow,
and all my members are as a shadow.
⁸Upright men shall be astonied at this,
and the innocent shall stir up himself against the godless.
⁹Yet shall the righteous hold on his way,
and he that hath clean hands shall wax stronger and stronger.
¹⁰But return ye, all of you, and come now:
and I shall not find a wise man among you.
¹¹My days are past, my purposes are broken off,
even the thoughts of my heart.
¹²They change the night into day:
the light, *say they*, is near unto the darkness.
¹³If I look for Sheol as mine house;
if I have spread my couch in the darkness;
¹⁴if I have said to corruption, Thou art my father;
to the worm, *Thou art* my mother, and my sister;
¹⁵where then is my hope?
and as for my hope, who shall see it?
¹⁶It shall go down to the bars of Sheol,
when once there is rest in the dust.

ONCE he had answered Eliphaz for the first time (ch. 6), Job had grown ever less interested in what his friends had to say, for they were only repeating the platitudes in which he had been brought up himself. Zophar woke a spark of sarcasm, but Eliphaz' indignation produces only a dignified rebuke. He reminds them that they are only repeating themselves (16: 2a), and that after all they had come to comfort him (16: 2b, cf. 2: 11). As Knox renders it, *Old tales and cold comfort; you are all alike.* After all, if they could not comfort, they were under no compulsion to say anything.

The futility of Eliphaz' pomposity did not stir Job as Zophar's jibes had done, and seated, as it were, between God and his friends he begins a soliloquy in which, while he may address one side or the other, he speaks mainly to himself.

Neither speaking nor silence has had much effect on his condition (16: 6). After all, there was not much purpose in blaming his friends, for it was God who had treated him as though he were guilty (16: 7f.).   If God had acted as though He were a wild animal (16: 9, 12a,b.), he could not blame men for acting similarly (16: 10).   He had been the mark for God's arrows (16: 12c, 13), a fortress attacked by the strongest of warriors (16: 14).   In spite of all, his reply had been humility and prayer (16: 15ff).   *I have sewed sackcloth upon my skin* implies the permanence of his mourning.   Among the Arabs one may under certain circumstances sew oneself into a garment, so that it cannot be removed without cutting the seams.   Job is not referring to his friends in verse 11, but to the great, evil men who have rejoiced at the downfall of a pillar of righteousness.

Job had never doubted that sooner or later God would change His attitude towards him (7: 8, 21, 14: 13ff.), though he had no hope that friends or enemies would.   So he calls on the earth (16: 18) to keep on crying to God till He hears—for He, the just one, is already his witness—and proclaims that he was in spite of all right with God (16: 21).   Perhaps nowhere more strongly than in 17: 3, does Job suggest a contradiction in God Himself: God is to become surety for Job that his cause will be vindicated with God.   Such language may shock us, but in fact there can be few children of God who have not at one time or another faced this very problem.   There IS an apparent contradiction in God's acts, and it is only as our eyes are fixed on the power and love of God that it disappears.

Since the vision of God's power is yet future, Job, left in his perplexity, gives a pitying glance at his friends (17: 4) and maintains that he will *hold on his way* (17: 9)—verses 8f. surely refer to Job himself—even though the hopes of physical recovery held out to him by his friends are false (17: 12–16).

Not only is the translation of 17: 5 very doubtful, but however we render it, it seems almost impossible to give a satisfactory meaning to it in its setting.   A reference to Moffatt *ad loc.* will show to what straits he is driven.

THE FATE OF MR. BADMAN (CH. 18)

THEN answered Bildad the Shuhite, and said,

²How long will ye lay snares for words?
consider, and afterwards we will speak.

³Wherefore are we counted as beasts,
and are become unclean in your sight?

⁴Thou that tearest thyself in thine anger,
shall the earth be forsaken for thee?
or shall the rock be removed out of its place?

⁵Yea, the light of the wicked shall
be put out,
and the flame of his fire shall not
shine.

⁶The light shall be dark in his tent,
and his lamp above him shall be
put out.

⁷The steps of his strength shall be
straitened,
and his own counsel shall cast him
down.

⁸For he is cast into a net by his own
feet,
and he walketh upon the toils.

⁹A gin shall take *him* by the heel,
a snare shall lay hold on him.

¹⁰A noose is hid for him in the
ground,
and a trap for him in the way.

¹¹Terrors shall make him afraid on
every side,
and shall chase him at his heels.

¹²His strength shall be hunger-
bitten,
and calamity shall be ready for his
halting.

¹³It shall devour the members of his
body,
the firstborn of death shall devour
his members.

¹⁴He shall be rooted out of his tent
wherein he trusteth;
and he shall be brought to the king
of terrors.

¹⁵There shall dwell in his tent that
which is none of his:
brimstone shall be scattered upon
his habitation.

¹⁶His roots shall be dried up beneath,
and above shall his branch be cut
off.

¹⁷His remembrance shall perish from
the earth,
and he shall have no name in the
street.

¹⁸He shall be driven from light into
darkness,
and chased out of the world.

¹⁹He shall have neither son nor son's
son among his people,
nor any remaining where he
sojourned.

²⁰They that dwell in the west shall
be astonied at his day,
as they that dwell in the east were
affrighted.

²¹Surely such are the dwellings of
the unrighteous,
and this is the place of him that
knoweth not God.

BILDAD was in his own way as annoyed as Eliphaz; but because
he stood for a cause and not some personal interest he could
control his feelings better. He honestly could not understand the attitude of the man who rejected the wisdom of the
past. It was clear that "there is nothing new under the sun," and
obviously the wisdom of the great saints and theologians must
have taken a case like Job's into consideration.

So he breaks out:

Ah, you wordmongers, you have never had enough! First
grasp our meaning, and we might argue to some purpose; but
no, to men like thee we are worthless as dumb beasts. See
with what fury he tears his own bosom! (18: 2ff, Knox).

It is quite likely that the last remark is looking back to Job's
words in 16: 9. Bildad believes that Job is just trying to keep
his end up by wilfully misunderstanding his friends.

So he takes up the story of Mr. Badman again and turns it with a cold pitilessness against Job. Eliphaz is to go farther (ch. 22), but loses his temper in doing so and makes a fool of himself, thus defeating his own ends. Your traditionalist, however, is too conscious of the weight of the past behind him to allow his feelings to be involved. If Eliphaz was sufficient of a gentleman to describe the fate of Mr. Badman in general, conventional terms (15: 20–35), perhaps Bildad was correct after all in suggesting that Job had not wanted to understand Eliphaz. Well, he will not misunderstand Bildad, who leaves nothing to chance!

He begins, therefore, as did the story of Job's misfortunes, with the extinction of Mr. Badman's family (18: 5ff.). Most commentaries understand the *light* and the *lamp* as referring to prosperity and happiness, but II Sam. 21: 17, I Kings 11: 36, 15: 4, II Kings 8: 19, Psalm 132: 17, all suggest most strongly that it is life and above all descendants that are intended. Where there is life in an oriental dwelling there will be a light at night. Psalm 127: 3ff., is a telling commentary on v. 7a.

In vv. 8–11 we have the unrecorded consequences of 1: 13–22, unrecorded because to an Oriental they were self-evident. The wicked and evil had risen against him (cf. 16: 10f.), and even his own kin had disowned him (cf. 19: 13–19). Then follows (vv. 11ff.) a reference to Job's physical sufferings, and Bildad finishes in cold satisfaction with a picture of his certain end (vv. 14–21). Amen! so shall be the fate of Job!

Eliphaz, after time for reflection, may see that he has been defending his own experience, Zophar may possibly realize that human common sense is inadequate to cope with the divine, and so they may in time come to terms with the world's Jobs, but not so Bildad. The world must conform to his pattern, for it is divinely given; where such things are in fashion he will excommunicate, persecute and even burn the man he considers to be under the judgment of God, in the hope of saving his soul.

"I KNOW THAT MY VINDICATOR LIVETH" (CH. 19)

THEN Job answered and said,
²How long will ye vex my soul,
and break me in pieces with words?
³These ten time have ye reproached me:
ye are not ashamed that ye deal hardly with me.

⁴And be it indeed that I have erred,
mine error remaineth with myself.
⁵If indeed ye will magnify yourselves against me,
and plead against me my reproach:
⁶know now that God hath subverted me *in my cause*,

and hath compassed me with his net.

⁷Behold, I cry out, Violence! but I am not heard:
I cry for help, but there is no judgement.

⁸He hath fenced up my way that I cannot pass,
and hath set darkness in my paths.

⁹He hath stripped me of my glory,
and taken the crown from my head.

¹⁰He hath broken me down on every side, and I am gone:
and mine hope hath he plucked up like a tree.

¹¹He hath also kindled his wrath against me,
and he counteth me unto him as *one of* his adversaries.

¹²His troops come on together, and cast up their way against me,
and encamp round about my tent.

¹³He hath put my brethren far from me,
and mine acquaintance are wholly estranged from me.

¹⁴My kinsfolk have failed,
and my familiar friends have forgotten me.

¹⁵They that dwell in mine house,
and my maids, count me for a stranger:
I am an alien in their sight.

¹⁶I call unto my servant, and he giveth me no answer,
I intreat him with my mouth.

¹⁷My breath is strange to my wife,
and I am loathsome to the children of my *mother's* womb.

¹⁸Even young children despise me;
if I arise, they speak against me.

¹⁹All my inward friends abhor me:
and they whom I loved are turned against me.

²⁰My bone cleaveth to my skin and to my flesh,
and I am escaped with the skin of my teeth.

²¹Have pity upon me, have pity upon me, O ye my friends;
for the hand of God hath touched me.

²²Why do ye persecute me as God,
and are not satisfied with my flesh?

²³Oh that my words were now written!
oh that they were inscribed in a book!

²⁴That with an iron pen and lead they were graven in the rock for ever!

²⁵But I know that my vindicator liveth,
and that he shall stand up at the last upon the earth:

²⁶and after my skin hath been thus destroyed,
yet without my flesh shall I see God:

²⁷whom I shall see on my side,
and mine eyes shall behold, and not another.
My reins are consumed within me.

²⁸If ye say, How we will persecute him!
seeing that the root of the matter is found in me;

²⁹be ye afraid of the sword:
for wrath *bringeth* the punishments of the sword,
that ye may know there is a judgement.

JOB does not deign to answer Bildad's accusation. He tells his friends what he had already boldly said to God (7: 20a), that even if he had sinned his sin was no concern of theirs (19: 4). Sin is a social offence, an offence against individuals, and an offence against God. Those who are called to rule and judgment must deal with sin in its first capacity. If we have been personally sinned against we have a duty to the sinner, at least if he is a member of the Church (Matt. 18: 15ff.). Otherwise we have

no concern with the sins of others, only with the sinner.   Our
purpose should not be to try to persuade men to sin less, a process
that may produce Pharisees, but not saints, but to turn the sinner
to God.   We must preach that men are sinners, but we dare not
sit in judgment and assess the quantity and quality of their sins.

Job's friends had undoubtedly judged Job secretly on the basis
of the scale of his sufferings even before he spoke.   Once he had
implicitly challenged their judgment, they were not concerned
with showing that he was a sinner (Job knew that quite well), but
that he was a great sinner.   They were not concerned so much
with turning him to God as with getting him to acquiesce in their
judgment.   When they spoke of the greatness of God, it was to
bludgeon Job, not to draw him to God.   Job's friends are with
us today, as they have ever been in the Church.   That is why the
worldly man shrinks from the pious but not from saints.   The
open sinners in the time of Christ shrank from the Pharisees but
flocked to our Lord.

The greatest wrong his friends did Job was resolutely to refuse
to see that he was genuine in his efforts to come to terms with
God.   So now he reminded them once again that he really had
a complaint against God (vv. 5–12).   This had been aggravated
by the behaviour of kith and kin (vv. 13f.); his slaves, male and
female, had forgotten their duty (vv. 15f.); his wife had lost her
affection for him (taking *My breath is strange to my wife* metaphorically, as does Stevenson), and his pleas to brothers and sisters
remained unheard (v. 17); even the little children refused him the
honour due to his age (v. 18).   He turned to his friends for a little
sympathy, a little understanding (v. 21), but we may suppose that
he met nothing but the cold glance of bewilderment and anger.

It is hard enough for a Christian to be silent when he is
calumniated, even though he knows that he can trust his Lord
to care for his honour.   For Job, to whom honour meant more
than it does to us, the thought that God and man had joined
together to drag his honour in the dust meant more than physical
suffering or material loss.   He declared that if only he could write
his vindication on a scroll, or better still engrave it in stone, then
surely a generation would come that would vindicate him (vv. 23f.)

But what would be the use of human vindication, when his
controversy was with God?   Suddenly the conviction we have
noted before, the conviction of a strange duality in God, a God
who is temporarily unjust, but who will yet remember His former

mercy and love, flared up into white light. The verses (25ff.) in which Job expressed his new insight have led to much controversy among translators and commentators, but the following seems a fair rendering of them:

> I know that my Vindicator lives
> and will yet stand upon the earth;
> and after my skin has been thus destroyed,
> then without my flesh shall I see God,
> whom I shall see on my side,
> and my eyes shall see to be unestranged.
> My heart fails with longing within me.

Job had no hope of vindication in this life, but now he knew God *must* vindicate him. But (and here is the leap of faith) a vindication in which he did not share would be a hollow mockery, so he knew that he would see this hour, bodiless though he might be; yes, he would see God unestranged! He nearly swooned at the thought.

There is no need to justify the rendering "Vindicator." It is given by R.V. mg., R.S.V., and is accepted explicitly or implicitly by almost all moderns. Job calls God his *go'el*; the *go'el* was a man's near kinsman, whose duty was the avenging of wrong, e.g. as avenger of blood, or the redeeming of the man, when he had become a slave, or of his property. When the term is used of God (either the substantive or the cognate verb), as it is particularly in the Psalms and Isa. 40–66, it obviously receives a much richer meaning. In our context Job is thinking neither of healing nor of resurrection, as A.V. and R.V. tx. might suggest. He is concerned with the clearing of his good name and hence "Vindicator" expresses the sense best—a similar rendering would suit Pr. 23: 11, and it is implicit in a number of passages where we must retain "redeemer."

A vindication that is not shared, we have already said, is a hollow thing and so Job is brought to the confidence of Ps. 139: 8, where David realizes that communion with God is possible in Sheol, and above all to that of Pss. 73: 23f., 17: 15, that death cannot break off a communion with God begun in this life. In other words it is continued conscious communion with God after death rather than the resurrection of the body that Job is proclaiming.

Far more important than an exact definition of Job's hope of

life beyond the grave is his calling God his *go'el*.   The only real
parallel is Ps. 19: 14, for it is a plural in Isa. 47: 4, 63: 16, the
nation and not an individual speaking.   Everywhere else we find
the second or third person.   God can speak of Himself as Israel's
go'el, for He bound Himself to Israel by the choice of Abraham,
the exodus from Egypt and the covenant at Sinai.   God says,
"Israel is My son, My firstborn" (Exod. 4: 22, cf. Hos. 11: 1), but
Israel, and above all the individual Israelite, hesitated to claim
the kinship involved in calling God his *go'el*.   Job, who is not
a member of the chosen people and who does not stand in covenant
relationship with God discovers in the furnace of affliction that
he has been so bound up with his God that he can turn to him
and call on him for vindication as a *right*, for God has made him
His.

This is the turning point in Job's words.   He might have kept
his certainty to himself for all the difference that it made to his
friends.   If they looked on it as anything more than the ravings
of an unhinged mind, it only infuriated them the more.   Though
Job never quite rises to the same heights again, we can sense that
the strain had been relieved, that he could think more calmly,
that he could set his sufferings in a wider framework.

"I AM INSULTED" (CH. 20)

THEN answered Zophar the Naamathite, and said,
²Therefore do my thoughts give
answer to me,
even by reason of my haste that is
in me.
³I have heard the reproof which
putteth me to shame,
but out of my understanding *my*
spirit answereth me
⁴Knowest thou *not* this of old time,
since man was placed upon earth,
⁵that the triumphing of the wicked
is short,
and the joy of the godless but for
a moment?
⁶Though his excellency mount up
to the heavens,
and his head reach unto the clouds;
⁷yet he shall perish for ever like his
own dung:
they which have seen him shall
say, Where is he?

⁸He shall fly away as a dream, and
shall not be found:
yea, he shall be chased away as a
vision of the night.
⁹The eye which saw him shall see
him no more;
neither shall his place any more
behold him.
¹⁰His children shall seek the favour
of the poor,
and his hands shall give back his
wealth.
¹¹His bones are full of his youth,
but it shall lie down with him in
the dust.
¹²Though wickedness be sweet in
his mouth,
though he hide it under his tongue;
¹³though he spare it, and will not
let it go,
but keep it still within his mouth;
¹⁴yet his meat in his bowels is turned,
it is the gall of asps within him.

15He hath swallowed down riches,
and he shall vomit them up again:
God shall cast them out of his
belly.

16He shall suck the poison of asps:
the viper's tongue shall slay him.

17He shall not look upon the rivers,
the flowing streams of honey and
butter.

18That which he laboured for shall
he restore, and shall not swallow
it down;
according to the substance that
he hath gotten, he shall not
rejoice.

19For he hath oppressed and forsaken the poor;
he hath violently taken away an
house, which he builded not.

20Because he knew no quietness in
his greed,
he shall not save aught of that
wherein he delighteth.

21There was nothing left that he
devoured not;
therefore his prosperity shall not
endure.

22In the fulness of his sufficiency he
shall be in straits:
the hand of every one that is in
misery shall come upon him.

23When he is about to fill his belly,
God shall cast the fierceness of his
wrath upon him,
and shall rain it upon him as his
food.

24He shall flee from the iron weapon,
and the bow of brass shall strike
him through.

25He draweth it forth, and it cometh
out of his body:
yea, the glittering point cometh
out of his gall;
terrors are upon him.

26All darkness is laid up for his
treasures:
a fire not blown *by man* shall
devour him;
it shall consume that which is left
in his tent.

17The heavens shall reveal his iniquity,
and the earth shall rise up against
him.

28The increase of his house shall
depart,
his goods shall flow away in the
day of his wrath.

29This is the portion of a wicked
man from God,
and the heritage appointed unto
him by God.

HIS confidence that God would finally vindicate him made Job bold and he carried the war into the enemies' camp. His friends could hardly believe their ears, when they heard him saying:

If you say, "How we will pursue him!"
and, "The root of the matter is found in him";
be afraid of the sword,
for wrath brings the punishment of the sword,
that you may know there is a judgment (19: 28f. R.S.V.).

This left Zophar bursting to answer (20: 2). Approach the man of common sense the right way; ask his opinion on matters he obviously has not noticed and he is likely to veer round to your opinion and perhaps even to forget that he did not hold it all along. Tell him, however, that his common sense will bring disaster to himself or others, and *I hear censure which insults me* (20: 3a, R.S.V.) is likely to be his reaction.

There is little need to occupy ourselves with the details of Zophar's picture of Mr. Badman. He adds little to Eliphaz' picture in ch. 15. The chief new element is his insistence on the brevity of Mr. Badman's enjoyment of the fruits of evil. Here too we see a weakness of common sense. Eliphaz was, after all, generalizing from an imperfect knowledge of God and of human life, but at least he based himself on facts. Zophar, once he has accepted the theories of the Wise, does not need facts; to him it is obvious that if Mr. Badman is under the judgment of God, judgment must fall suddenly and soon. Yes, obvious, but . . .!

One thing Zophar spares Job. He is too annoyed and too little of a man of theory to work out a parallel between his picture of Mr. Badman and the plight of his friend as did Bildad. He does, however, prepare the way for Eliphaz (ch. 22). As a shrewd man of common sense he must have been puzzled by the lack of concrete accusations they could bring against a man who must obviously have been guilty of heinous offences, if they were to judge by his sufferings. So he indirectly accuses him of the commonest of all offences of the rich against the poor (20: 19), i.e. land-grabbing and oppression.

Mr. Badman's Prosperity (Ch. 21)

THEN Job answered and said,
    ²Hear diligently my speech;
and let this be your consolations.
³Suffer me, and I also will speak;
and after that I have spoken, mock on.
⁴As for me, is my complaint of man?
and why should I not be impatient?
⁵Mark me, and be astonished,
and lay your hand upon your mouth.
⁶Even when I remember I am troubled,
and horror taketh hold on my flesh.
⁷Wherefore do the wicked live,
become old, yea, wax mighty in power?
⁸Their seed is established with them in their sight,
and their offspring before their eyes.

⁹Their houses are safe from fear,
neither is the rod of God upon them.
¹⁰Their bull gendereth, and faileth not;
their cow calveth, and casteth not her calf.
¹¹They send forth their little ones like a flock,
and their children dance.
¹²They sing to the timbrel and harp,
and rejoice at the sound of the pipe.
¹³They spend their days in prosperity,
and in a moment they go down to Sheol.
¹⁴Yet they said unto God, Depart from us;
for we desire not the knowledge of thy ways.
¹⁵What is the Almighty, that we should serve him?

and what profit should we have,
if we pray unto him?

16Lo, their prosperity is not in their
hand:
the counsel of the wicked is far
from me.

17How oft is it that the lamp of the
wicked is put out?
that their calamity cometh upon
them?
that *God* distributeth sorrows in
his anger?

18that they are as stubble before
the wind,
and as chaff that the storm carrieth away?

19*Ye say*, God layeth up his iniquity
for his children.
Let him recompense it unto himself, that he may know it.

20Let his own eyes see his destruction,
and let him drink of the wrath of
the Almighty.

21For what pleasure hath he in his
house after him,
when the number of his months is
cut off in the midst?

22Shall any teach God knowledge?
seeing he judgeth those that are
high.

23One dieth in his full strength,
being wholly at ease and
quiet:

24his breasts are full of milk,

and the marrow of his bones is
moistened.

25And another dieth in bitterness of
soul,
and never tasteth of good.

26They lie down alike in the dust,
and the worm covereth them.

27Behold, I know your thoughts,
and the devices which ye wrong-
fully imagine against me.

28For ye say, Where is the house of
the prince?
and where is the tent wherein the
wicked dwelt?

29Have ye not asked them that go
by the way?
and do ye not know their tokens?

30That the evil man is spared in the
day of calamity?
that they are led away in the day
of wrath?

31Who shall declare his way to his
face?
and who shall repay him what he
hath done?

32Yet shall he be borne to the grave,
and shall keep watch over the
tomb.

33The clods of the valley shall be
sweet unto him,
and all men shall draw after him,
as there were innumerable before
him.

34How then comfort ye me in vain,
seeing in your answers there remaineth only falsehood?

JOB was too much under the influence of his vision of God his
Vindicator for Zophar's angry words to touch him as they
would have earlier. Only his *mock on* (singular! 21:3) shows
that the arrow of 20:19 had not left him untouched. He asked
his friends to listen and so give him consolation (21:2)—a touch
of sarcasm this—for he had something to lay before them that
would strike them dumb (v. 5).

The thought that lay hidden under the Why? of ch. 3, under
the glimpse of the universality of human suffering in ch. 7, which
for a moment was openly expressed in 9:22ff., now comes out into
the open. It had been dropped while his friends' accusations had
driven him to self-vindication and to God for vindication. Now
that he knows that God will yet be on his side, he can face the

deeper cause of his agony, his doubt of that moral government of the world on which all the theories of the Wise were based.

Job looks at the wicked, the *resha'im*, at Mr. Badman, who fears neither man nor God, and has no respect for law, whether God's or man's. What he sees makes him deny all he was taught and all his friends have been telling him. Mr. Badman lives to a prosperous old age, and his children flourish after him; when the time comes for death it is a falling asleep: *They go down at last without a struggle to the grave* (21: 13, Knox). Though they flout God (21: 14f.), there is no supernatural intervention in their lives: *Behold, is not their prosperity in their hands?* (21: 16, R.S.V.).

To forestall his friends' angry interruption Job challenges them, "How often do things turn out the way you say (vv. 17f.)? Or, if you are going to push the judgment off on his children (v. 19), what does Mr. Badman care about that, once his life is run (vv. 20f.)?"

Silenced for a moment, they let Job continue. He maintains that things are even worse than he has depicted. Mr. Badman goes down to the grave without knowing an evil hour: Mr. Goodman dies without knowing a good hour, and yet there is the same end for both (vv. 23–26). In fact his friends' arguments pointed to quite opposite conclusions to those they had drawn. Any traveller (v. 29) could tell them *that the wicked man is spared in the day of calamity, that he is rescued in the day of wrath* (v. 30, R.S.V.), and his tomb is honoured in days to come. In fact, so implies Job, he must obviously be a good man, if his friends' theories and the aphorisms of the Wise are correct.

What shall we say to Job before Eliphaz explodes? Is there any truth in his charge? That he exaggerates is obvious, but under other circumstances he would probably have owned up to this himself.

To begin with we must acknowledge that long before the time of Job's friends down to our own the religious man has tended to distort the facts. God is the impartial pourer of His gifts on godly and ungodly alike (Matt. 5: 45), and the great scourges of nature have normally smitten godly and ungodly alike. While from Scripture, Church history and personal experience we can find a goodly number of examples of God's judgment on the wicked, we can as easily find at least as many examples of the sufferings of the righteous. More than that, the reverse is also true. The worst king of Judah, Manasseh, also reigned the longest.

Beside a Hitler and a Mussolini reaping the whirlwind in their deaths, we must place a Lenin and Stalin dying in their beds. Though "Yea, and all that would live godly in Christ Jesus shall suffer persecution" (II Tim. 3: 12) is a New Testament statement, "For Thy sake we are killed all the day long: we are accounted as sheep for the slaughter" (Psalm 44: 22, cf. Romans 8: 36) is equally true for the Old Testament, if we but read between the lines. When a crowded congregation breathes Hallelujah at some outstanding testimony of God's keeping, it is apt to forget the many who have gone to prison, and death with praise in their hearts to God. Lowell exaggerated, as Job did, when he wrote,

> Truth for ever on the scaffold,
> Wrong for ever on the throne,

but with his knowledge of the cross he could balance it, as Job could not, with,

> And, behind the dim unknown,
> Standeth God within the shadow,
> Keeping watch above His own.

When God's will is done and God's law is respected, the righteous are likely to prosper and the wicked to suffer. Indeed, wherever law is at all respected the righteous will profit from it. But since we know that the whole world, i.e. human society, lies in the evil one (I John 5: 19), we must expect that the moral government of God will often not be visible, and in place of prosperity the believer will have to say, "We know that in everything God works for good with those who love Him" (Rom. 8: 28, R.S.V.).

As the second round in the debate closes we find that the initiative has passed to Job. He is still wrestling with his problems, which we are beginning to see in their true proportions. His friends, however, are fighting desperately to salvage some part of their treasured ideas from the onslaught of this savage to whom nothing is sacred. It would have been well for them, if they had left then and there, but Eliphaz is not prepared to confess quite so easily that he has been defeated.

CHAPTER VII

ORTHODOXY CONFOUNDED

"THOU ART THE MAN!" (CH. 22)

THEN answered Eliphaz the Temanite, and said,

²Can a man be profitable unto God? surely he that is wise is profitable unto himself.

³Is it any pleasure to the Almighty, that thou art righteous? or is it gain *to him*, that thou makest thy ways perfect?

⁴Is it for thy fear *of him* that he reproveth thee, that he entereth with thee into judgement?

⁵Is not thy wickedness great? neither is there any end to thine iniquities.

⁶For thou hast taken pledges of thy brother for nought, and stripped the naked of their clothing.

⁷Thou hast not given water to the weary to drink, and thou hast withholden bread from the hungry.

⁸But as for the mighty man, he had the earth; and the honourable man, he dwelt in it.

⁹Thou hast sent widows away empty, and the arms of the fatherless have been broken.

¹⁰Therefore snares are round about thee, and sudden fear troubleth thee,

¹¹Or darkness, that thou canst not see, and abundance of waters cover thee.

¹²Is not God in the height of heaven? and behold the height of the stars, how high they are!

¹³And thou sayest, What doth God know? can he judge through the thick darkness?

¹⁴Thick clouds are a covering to him, that he seeth not; and he walketh on the vault of heaven.

¹⁵Wilt thou keep the old way which wicked men have trodden?

¹⁶who were snatched away before their time, whose foundation was poured out as a stream:

¹⁷who said unto God, Depart from us; and, What can the Almighty do to us?

¹⁸Yet he filled their houses with good things; but the counsel of the wicked is far from me.

¹⁹The righteous see it, and are glad; and the innocent laugh them to scorn:

²⁰*saying*, Surely they that did rise up against us are cut off, and the remnant of them the fire hath consumed.

²¹Acquaint now thyself with him, and be at peace: thereby good shall come unto thee.

²²Receive, I pray thee, instruction from his mouth, and lay up his words in thine heart.

²³If thou return to the Almighty, thou shalt be built up; if thou put away unrighteousness far from thy tents.

²⁴And lay thou *thy* treasure in the dust,

and *the gold of* Ophir among the stones of the brooks;
²⁵and the Almighty shall be thy treasure,
and precious silver unto thee.
²⁶For then shalt thou delight thyself in the Almighty,
and shalt lift up thy face unto God.
²⁷Thou shalt make thy prayer unto him,
and he shall hear thee; and thou shalt pay thy vows.

²⁸Thou shalt also decree a thing, and it shall be established unto thee;
and light shall shine upon thy ways.
²⁹When they cast *thee* down, thou shalt say, *There is* lifting up;
and the humble person he shall save.
³⁰He shall deliver him that is innocent:
yea, he shall be delivered through the cleanness of thine hands.

W E have seen that Eliphaz the Temanite was at heart a good, kindly and God-fearing man. But Job had been dragging him remorsely to the cliff's edge and at last in his picture of Mr. Badman (ch. 21) had forced him to look down on a storm-tossed world in which there was no vestige of Divine rule and justice. In very terror Eliphaz turned on him.

Let us not be too hard on him. He was potentially the best of Job's friends, but the firm ground on which he thought he stood was essentially less secure than that of the others. Bildad relied on the consensus of human wisdom—if he had lived today, it would have been on some traditional scheme of Scripture interpretation or dogmatic theology—and Zophar on common-sense, but Elpihaz' rock was his own experience. Our experience of God may seem the most certain and comforting thing in life, but in the hour of crisis it may fail us completely, as Asaph discovered (Ps. 77: 6–9). Eliphaz was not the last in his position to panic, when his experience seemed to be contradicted.

Eliphaz begins by repeating the main thought of his dream (vv. 2–4, cf. 4: 17–20). When he had first told it, it might have seemed to the hearer as no more than one of those solemn experiences that colour and mould a man's life. Now we see that it had become a tyranny that held him as in a strait-jacket. Not merely Job but also God was to be understood in terms of the dream, and so Job had to become the chief of sinners and God the mere cold embodiment of an idea. This is the ultimate fate of all those who insist on interpreting God wholly in terms of their own experience.

Somewhat reassured by finding his feet once more on his familiar rock, Eliphaz turns in cold fury on the man who had made his universe shake for a moment. From the poor he had taken his outer garment (cf. Exod. 22: 26f., Deut. 24: 12f.) for a derisory loan (*for nought*, v. 6). Though he had been *mighty* and *honourable* (v. 8), he had ignored the needy (v. 7) and refused to help the widow and orphan in the hour of their greatest need (v. 9, cf. Exod. 22: 22ff.).

It might be profitable for us to pause in our reading and mentally to draw our own picture of Mr. Badman. It is bound to be different, for society has not only changed but also grown so much more complex, and the ties of the family group with its loyalties correspondingly weaker. But is our picture the true one? The sin above all others condemned by our Lord is sin against the weak—the sin against the Holy Spirit is an attitude of mind and heart to God and does not come into consideration here—for He said:

> It is impossible but that occasions of stumbling should come: but woe unto him, through whom they come! It were well for him, if a millstone were hanged about his neck, and he were thrown into the sea, rather than that he should cause one of these little ones to stumble (Luke 17: 1f.).

Love is the sign of life, lovelessness of death (I John 3: 14). So, provided we make allowances for the changes in society, the true Mr. Badman of today would bear close resemblance to Eliphaz' picture.

Eliphaz has one more shaft left to fire. He deliberately takes a phrase from Job's picture of Mr. Badman (21: 14f.) and applies it to Job (22: 12–17). Job is not merely bad, he IS Mr. Badman.

The typical modern atheist is the product of that intellectual pride of humanism that makes man the measure of all things and of the self-confidence of modern science. At his best there is something noble but pathetic about him. We have only to compare Psa. 23 with Henley's

> "Out of the night that covers me,
>   Black as the pit from pole to pole,
> I thank whatever gods may be
>   For my unconquerable soul"

to realize the vanity and emptiness of human pride.

But the atheist of the Old Testament is the fool (*nabal*) who says in his heart, "There is no God" (Psa. 10: 4, 14: 1, 53: 1). He crosses our path again and again in Scripture and in our daily lives. It is not that he denies the existence of God by word or intellectual argument; it is his life that denies it. He thinks that if there is a God He is not concerned with him (Psa. 10: 11, 73: 11), or even that God is like him in character (Psa. 50: 21). As a result the only check upon his behaviour is self-interest. Such a one, according to Eliphaz, is Job!

There is nothing vindictive about all this once Eliphaz has regained his equilibrium. Let Job but vindicate Eliphaz' experience and judgment, and he holds out to him in genuine warmth the riches of God's mercy (vv. 21–30) in language that reminds us of his earlier appeal in 5: 17–26. I am sure that, by the time he had finished, the hard feelings had evaporated, and that he was fully expecting Job to take his place on the penitent form. Once again we see how the self-centredness of the "good" man takes "Let God be found true, but every man a liar" (Rom. 3: 4) and makes it run "Let my understanding of God be found true, but every man that disagrees with it a liar."

"I Cannot Understand" (Ch. 23)

THEN Job answered and said,
²Even to-day is my complaint bitter:
his hand is heavier than my groaning.
³Oh that I knew where I might find him,
that I might come even to his seat!
⁴I would order my cause before him,
and fill my mouth with arguments.
⁵I would know the words which he would answer me,
and understand what he would say unto me.
⁶Would he contend with me in the greatness of his power?
Nay; but he would give heed unto me.
⁷There the upright might reason with him;
so should I be delivered for ever from my judge.
⁸Behold, I go forward, but he is not *there*;
and backward, but I cannot perceive him:
⁹on the left hand, when he doth work, but I cannot behold him:
he hideth himself on the right hand, that I cannot see him.
¹⁰But he knoweth the way that I take;
when he hath tried me, I shall come forth as gold.
¹¹My foot hath held fast to his steps;
his way have I kept, and turned not aside.
¹²I have not gone back from the commandment of his lips;
I have treasured up the words of his mouth more than my necessary food.
¹³But he is one, and who can turn him?
and what his soul desireth, even that he doeth.
¹⁴For he performeth that which is appointed for me:
and many such things are with him.
¹⁵Therefore am I troubled at his presence;
when I consider, I am afraid of him.

¹⁶For God hath made my heart faint,
and the Almighty hath troubled me:

¹⁷because I was not cut off before the darkness,
neither did he cover the thick darkness from my face.

I CAN see the ghost of a smile flit over Job's face marked with the scars of disease and suffering. At long last innuendoes and hints had come to an end and Job knew what they had been thinking all along, even though they might not have said it even to one another. As long as there seemed to be a shred of justification in the accusation, the desire for self-justification rose in his heart, but this nonsense could be ignored.

Eliphaz had capped Job's exaggeration about Mr. Badman with even greater exaggeration. This must have helped to restore Job's balance, and I get the impression that he had been quietly telling God that he knew that he had been drawing the long bow a trifle; but, for all that, he could not understand God's ways among men, for—and here he begins to speak aloud, to God, not to his friends—he could not understand God's ways with him.

The atmosphere and confidence of ch. 19 are still with us. There is no doubt in Job's mind that if he could only have a face-to-face talk with God he would be able to clear up the mystery. The progress of Job's thought is fascinating, but to understand it we must think of this chapter as a soliloquy with pauses from time to time. In vv. 2–7 it is not the old rebellious wish to argue out his case with God that we hear, but rather the sequel to 19: 27. The A.V. and R.V. mg. are correct as against R.V. text in v. 2, which we should, however, render with the R.S.V. (Moffatt essentially concurs):

Today also my complaint is bitter,
His hand is heavy in spite of my groaning.

Vindication after death is all very well, but the wronged heart of man yearns for it in this life. Let it be even in private, but *I should be acquitted for ever by my judge* (v. 7, R.S.V.).

Alas, there was no such finding of Him (vv. 8f.), but instead of this reducing Job to despair, as it did formerly, it only led him on spiritually. No longer do we get the strange picture of a duality in God, of a God who contradicts Himself (cf. 7: 8, 21; 16: 19). Now Job realized, even if only for a passing moment, that the mystery of darkness that had fallen on him was only God's refining fire (v. 10). Since in the days of his prosperity

Job had set himself to know God's will and to do it (vv. 11f.), he had no doubt as to the outcome.

In any case, he realized, the wish to find God was foolish, for *He is unchangeable* (v. 13, R.S.V., a translation that gives much the same sense as the emendation supported by most modern scholars, "He hath chosen"), and so all Job's arguments would be wasted. He must await the working out of God's will (v. 14); with that he sinks back temporarily into his misery (vv. 15ff.).

For those who from their childhood have known God only as seen in the face of Jesus Christ, it is hard to realize to what extent the Incarnation has made God more humanly comprehensible to us, and how, for this very reason, the Gospel is such a stumbling block to both Judaism and Islam. But this very comprehensibility constantly leads us into a hopelessly superficial outlook on life around us, and on God's ways with it.

There are not a few who assure us that it is comparatively easy to come to the throne of God and to talk things out with Him and so to obtain complete clarity on our own problems and often on those of others. Some claim to be able to do this by a correct use of the Scriptures, others by a technique of prayer or "listening," yet others by due attention to "the inner light." I do not want to seem to deny the strong element of truth in this, but it is a most serious exaggeration. Even our Lord on the cross cried out, "My God, My God, why . . .?" Though God graciously allows Himself to be found in measure by those who seek Him, He remains the God who hides Himself, and not until we see Him shall we know fully as we have been fully known.

So we find that today, as in the days of Job, while good men insist on the greatness of God and on the inscrutability of His sovereign purpose, they are convinced, for all that, that His purposes are easily discernible in the daily round of life, in spite of the fact that experience repeatedly denies their assertions. To affirm that "we know that in everything God works for good with those who love Him" (Rom. 8: 28, R.S.V.) is an expression of faith, not of understanding. To count it all joy, when we meet various trials (James 1: 2) is to recognize with joy God's working, but it does not imply knowledge of the extent or of the immediate purpose of the trial. In spite of the superficial optimism of our pundits, God does bring Himself glory by early death, ill-health, poverty, inability to use the gifts of God's own giving and the many other things which we are often assured should have at the most a transient place in the Christian's life. It is our failure to realize this that brings so many of God's afflicted ones to the verge of despair, and sometimes beyond it.

THE EVILS OF SOCIETY (CH. 24)

WHY are times not laid up by the Almighty?
and why do not they which know him see his days?

²There are that remove the landmarks;
they violently take away flocks, and feed them.

³They drive away the ass of the fatherless,
they take the widow's ox for a pledge.

⁴They turn the needy out of the way:
the poor of the earth hide themselves together.

⁵Behold, as wild asses in the desert they go forth to their work, seeking diligently for meat;
the wilderness *yieldeth* them food for their children.

⁶They cut their provender in the field;
and they glean the vintage of the wicked.

⁷They lie all night naked without clothing,
and have no covering in the cold.

⁸They are wet with the showers of the mountains,
and embrace the rock for want of a shelter.

⁹There are that pluck the fatherless from the breast,
and take a pledge of the poor:

¹⁰they go about naked without clothing,
and being an-hungred they carry the sheaves;

¹¹they make oil within the walls of these men;
they tread *their* winepresses, and suffer thirst.

¹²From out of the populous city men groan,
and the soul of the wounded crieth out:

yet God imputeth it not for folly.

¹³These are of them that rebel against the light;
they know not the ways thereof, nor abide in the paths thereof.

¹⁴The murderer riseth with the light, he killeth the poor and needy;
and in the night he is as a thief.

¹⁵The eye also of the adulterer waiteth for the twilight,
saying, No eye shall see me:
and he disguiseth his face.

¹⁶In the dark they dig through houses:
they shut themselves up in the daytime;
they know not the light.

¹⁷For the morning is to all of them as the shadow of death;
for they know the terrors of the shadow of death.

¹⁸*Ye say*, He is swift upon the face of the waters;
their portion is cursed in the earth:
he turneth not by the way of the vineyards.

¹⁹Drought and heat consume the snow waters:
so doth Sheol *those which* have sinned.

²⁰The womb shall forget him; the worm shall feed sweetly on him;
he shall be no more remembered:
and unrighteousness shall be broken as a tree.

²¹He devoureth the barren that beareth not;
and doeth not good to the widow.

²²Yet *God* by his power maketh the mighty to continue:
he riseth up, and no man is sure of life.

²³*God* giveth them to be in security, and they rest thereon;

and his eyes are upon their ways.
²⁴They are exalted; yet a little while,
and they are gone;
yea, they are brought low, they
are taken out of the way as all
other,

and are cut off as the tops of the
ears of corn.
²⁵And if it be not so now, who will
prove me a liar,
and make my speech nothing
worth?

ALREADY in our study of chs. 7 and 14 we saw how Job's suffering gave him a truer picture of human life as a whole than that possessed by his friends. With the slackening of tension brought by the rise of hope Job was able to look at the suffering around him more objectively. In answering Zophar the second time (ch. 21) Job had merely challenged and denied his friends' fundamental outlook on life. Now he works out the implications of his challenge. He looks on life and cries out:

Why has not the Almighty sessions of set justice?
Why do His followers never see Him intervening? (24: 1, Moffatt).

Many scholars feel that this chapter is an anti-climax after the very strong language of ch. 21 and suggest that Job did in fact express himself so vigorously about the fate of the righteous that some pious scribe felt compelled to replace what he considered blasphemy by relatively harmless platitudes. Quite apart from the inherent objection to such a view, it is to ignore the change in mood that set in in ch. 19, and also the background of the whole book. It is true that Job had become one of the great and mighty, but the whole discussion is on the level of the Wise. These were in ancient society, together with many of the priests, the nearest approach to our modern middle class. Except where they dabbled in plots, or where the state went down in blood and fire, they were more cushioned against sudden adversity than others.

They were peculiarly prone to the besetting weakness of the middle classes: an undue respect for the rich and powerful, and a blind eye for the need and suffering of the poor. This was strengthened by a tendency we find throughout ancient society, which is reflected in the Old Testament.

When John the Baptist wished to know of a certainty what he had to think of Jesus, the supreme proof of His Messiahship was "the poor have the gospel preached to them" (Matt. 11: 5). Though we seldom recognize the fact, the Old Testament, quite in keeping with its historic background, is concerned mainly with the full citizen in Israel.   The landless and broken man, the slave, and the hired servant, the harlot and the outcast, the bastard and the leper leave their mark on its pages, but it is seldom that the prophetic message is addressed to them, and often they had no place within the cultus of Israel.

It was not until the Son of God came in utter poverty, and, after having grown up in a place from which nothing good could be expected (John 1: 46) and having consorted with the outcast and the notorious sinner, became an outcast by being hanged on a tree (Deut. 21: 23), that the average man could even conceive that God was concerned with the outcast.   By the educating work of the Holy Spirit during the inter-testamental period the Pharisees had come to realize clearly enough that riches were not a guide to whether a man enjoyed God's favour, but the hard words, "This multitude which knoweth not the law are accursed" (John 7: 49) show how little true understanding most of them had for the outcast.   It was not until Jewry knew itself as an outcast in exile that there grew up in many hearts a truer understanding for the broken and despised.

But do not let us criticize the men of the Old Testament or the Pharisees too readily.   Though it could doubtless have been said of all the early churches as it was said to the Christians in Corinth, "Ye see your calling, brethren, how that not many wise men after the flesh, not many mighty, not many noble are called" (1 Cor. 1: 26), yet already James (2: 1ff.) had to warn against undue deference to the rich.   It has not been so much false doctrine or antinomianism that have been the great enemies of the Church in every period, but rather an undue respect for riches and intellect, which has made the poor and outcast feel strangers in what should have been their home.   Though there have been repeated movements inside and outside the organized Church to alter this, they have always succumbed sooner or later to the prevailing atmosphere.

Job had shared the prevailing feelings of the Wise.   Not until he became an outcast did he see his fellow outcasts as his fellow men rather than as objects of charity or condemnation.   He now saw that the fate of the weak (vv. 2–4) was due to the evil character of the strong and not to the sin of those they oppressed; equally, the bitter life of the landless and wronged (vv. 5–12) could not be imputed to their fault.   Yet for all that there was no sign of God's judgment (vv. 1, 12c.).   Because his friends assumed that the outcasts must be suffering for their own sin, they entirely failed to realize that even if the fate of the wicked was what they described, it would mean no relief for those whom they had wronged the most deeply. It was just here that Job saw the clearest proof of a lack of Divine rule in the world, and we fail to see the problem at our peril. The fact that we cheerfully assign the great and evil leaders of Fascism and Communism and the conscienceless controllers of world finance to hell does not answer the problem of their victims, godly and godless alike.

From the victims of wrongdoing Job turns (vv. 13–17) to a type of wrongdoer who plays little part in the thinking of his friends, but who, for all that, does more real harm to individuals and society than does the *rasha'*, the arrogantly wicked man, *viz.* the thief who is prepared to murder in cold blood, and the adulterer prepared to break up homes to satisfy his lusts. They shun the light of day, unlike the *rasha'*, and so escape detection, while they undermine society. Note the R.S.V. rendering in v. 17b, *For they are friends with the terrors of deep darkness.* It is given to few to see sin where it really is. The sinner is all too often profoundly comfortable at church services, for the sins denounced there have little relevance to his own life. Apart from that, however, we should realize that the real threat to society comes not from those who serve more than half a lifetime of penal servitude or even meet their end on the scaffold, but from those who make their own desires their god, but are normally sufficiently astute to keep within the letter of the law, while achieving their purposes.

Apparently the R.V. mg. and R.S.V. give the only acceptable sense when they render v. 18, *Ye say, He is swift . . .*; vv. 18ff. must apparently represent the opinions of Job's friends. The meaning and text of v. 24 are far from clear, but in the context it must mean that while death overtakes the wicked it is only the common fate of all. With his survey of life completed Job challenges his friends to prove him wrong (v. 25). They do not really try, for they know that Job has laid his finger on the mystery of God's providential dealings with men.

CONFUSION (CHS. 25–27)

THEN answered Bildad the Shuhite, and said,
²Dominion and fear are with him; he maketh peace in his high places.

³Is there any number of his armies?
and upon whom doth not his light arise?

⁴How then can man be just before God?
or how can he be clean that is born of a woman?
⁵Behold, even the moon hath no brightness,
and the stars are not pure in his sight:
⁶how much less man, that is a worm!
and the son of man, which is a worm!

26. Then Job answered and said,
²How hast thou helped him that is without power!
how hast thou saved the arm that hath no strength!
³How hast thou counselled him that hath no wisdom,
and plentifully declared sound knowledge!
⁴To whom hast thou uttered words?
and whose spirit came forth from thee?
⁵The shades tremble
beneath the waters and the inhabitants thereof.
⁶Sheol is naked before him,
and Abaddon hath no covering.
⁷He stretcheth out the north over empty space,
and hangeth the earth upon nothing.
⁸He bindeth up the waters in his thick clouds;
and the cloud is not rent under them.
⁹He closeth in the face of his throne,
and spreadeth his cloud upon it.
¹⁰He hath described a boundary upon the face of the waters,
unto the confines of light and darkness.
¹¹The pillars of heaven tremble
and are astonished at his rebuke.
¹²He stilleth the sea with his power,
and by his understanding he smiteth through Rahab.
¹³By his spirit the heavens are garnished;
his hand hath pierced the swift serpent.

¹⁴Lo, these are but the outskirts of his ways:
and how small a whisper do we hear of him!
but the thunder of his power who can understand?

27. And Job again took up his parable and said,
²As God liveth, who hath taken away my right;
and the Almighty, who hath vexed my soul;
³all the while my breath is in me,
and the spirit of God is in my nostrils;
⁴surely my lips shall not speak unrighteousness,
neither shall my tongue utter deceit.
⁵God forbid that I should justify you:
till I die I will not put away mine integrity from me.
⁶My righteousness I hold fast, and will not let it go:
my heart shall not reproach *me* so long as I live.
⁷Let mine enemy be as the wicked,
and let him that riseth up against me be as the unrighteous.
⁸For what is the hope of the godless,
when God cutteth him off,
when God taketh away his soul?
⁹Will God hear his cry,
when trouble cometh upon him?
¹⁰Will he delight himself in the Almighty,
and call upon God at all times?
¹¹I will teach you concerning the hand of God;
that which is with the Almighty will I not conceal.
¹²Behold, all ye yourselves have seen it;
why then are ye become altogether vain?
¹³This is the portion of a wicked man with God,
and the heritage of oppressors, which they receive from the Almighty.
¹⁴If his children be multiplied, it is for the sword;

and his offspring shall not be satisfied with bread.

15Those that remain of him shall be buried in death,
and his widows shall make no lamentation.

16Though he heap up silver as the dust,
and prepare raiment as the clay;

17he may prepare it, but the just shall put it on,
and the innocent shall divide the silver.

18He buildeth his house as the moth,
and as a booth which the keeper maketh.

19He lieth down rich, but he shall not be gathered;
he openeth his eyes, and he is not.

20Terrors overtake him like waters;
a tempest stealeth him away in the night.

21The east wind carrieth him away, and he departeth;
and it sweepeth him out of his place.

22For *God* shall hurl at him, and not spare:
he would fain flee out of his hand.

23Men shall clap their hands at him,
and shall hiss him out of his place.

WE have already seen in ch. II that the text of this section is almost certainly in confusion and that part may well have been lost. This suits the position of the speakers well enough, for it mirrors their own confusion of mind. The obstinacy of his friends has gradually driven Job to a position he hates and does not really want to defend. His friends on the other hand can only maintain their traditional positions by shutting their eyes to facts and by repeating platitudes in a loud voice.

We need not hesitate to hear Bildad in ch. 25, though it may well be that ch. 26 belongs to him too. If Bildad were, like the writer of Ecclesiastes, taking up an agnostic position and claiming that God's ways are beyond man's understanding, his contrast of God's greatness (25: 2f.) with man's sinfulness and insignificance (25: 4ff.) would be valid. But he entirely overlooks that the argument that is intended to crush Job's impious views is equally effective against his own confident picture of God's moral rule as seen in the prosperity of the good and destruction of the wicked. One of the commonest fallacies that beset good men is the idea that because a theory is "edifying" it must be true.

It could be that Job replies with an even stronger affirmation of God's all-might and concludes with an affirmation of complete agnosticism (26: 14). Since, however, this would be an implicit retraction of his arguments of ch. 24, which is most unlikely, we would do well to base no arguments on ch. 26.

There is no doubt that it is Job we hear in 27: 2–5. The witness of his conscience is too strong for him to bow to his friends' affirmations of his sinfulness or of the all-might of God. The voice of God will yet prostrate him in humility and penitence, but the purely human measuring rods used by his friends merely drive him to even deeper anguish.

Unless we are to plead for a sustained note of sarcasm, of which there is no indication and which we could hardly justify in the setting, it seems impossible to ascribe 27: 7-23 to Job. The passage is an affirmation of all the three friends have been proclaiming and a flat contradiction of Job's own views. We shall probably do best to see Zophar speaking here, making dogmatism take the place of evidence and vehemence that of proof. It may be that Job's answer is lost, or more probably he looks on such statements as unworthy of being refuted again and deals with them by implication in his summing up (chs. 29–31).

So the third round ends in inevitable confusion, the confusion that must arise when orthodoxy turns its back on experience and creates a world to suit its theories, and when experience ignores revelation and seeks to make itself the measure of truth.

CHAPTER VIII

JOB SUMS UP

An Interlude in Praise of Wisdom (Ch. 28)

So far as we were able to interpret ch. 27, we heard Job ending his answers to his friends with a fierce and passionate self-vindication:

As God liveth, who hath taken away my right,
  and the Almighty, who hath made my life bitter;
as long as my breath is in me,
  and the spirit of God is in my nostrils;
my lips shall not speak falsehood,
  neither shall my tongue utter deceit.
God forbid that I should justify you:
  till I die I will not put away my integrity from me.
My righteousness I hold fast, and will not let it go;
  my heart doth not reproach me for any of my days (27: 2–6).

Note how often "me" and "my" recur in these few verses.

Silence fell on the dunghill, broken only by the call of playing children and the hum of the nearby town. Along the horizon the first hint of thunderclouds showed, while Job's friends looked at one another in terrified anger, and the young man Elihu drew a little nearer.

For twenty-five chapters of thrust and counter-thrust we have heard all the wisdom of the schools and the dogmatism of experience break over Job, only to leave him more unconvinced than at the first and the wisdom of the Wise confounded. To break the tension, to turn our attention from the clash of passion, and to prepare us for God's intervention, the author now introduces a poem on Wisdom. It would seem to be completely false to picture ch. 28 as Job's own words; it would be completely out of character, and 29: 1 should act as a warning against the supposition. We should rather think of a curtain descending for a brief interval at the tensest point of the drama.

SURELY there is a mine for silver,
and a place for gold which they
refine.

[2]Iron is taken out of the earth,
and brass is molten out of the stone.

[3]*Man* setteth an end to darkness,
and searcheth out to the furthest
bound
the stones of thick darkness and
of the shadow of death.

[4]He breaketh open a shaft away
from where men sojourn;
they are forgotten of the foot *that
passeth by*;
they hang afar from men, they
swing to and fro.

[5]As for the earth, out of it cometh
bread:
and underneath it is turned up as
it were by fire.

[6]The stones thereof are the place of
sapphires,
and it hath dust of gold.

[7]That path no bird of prey knoweth,
neither hath the falcon's eye seen it:

[8]the proud beasts have not trodden
it,
nor hath the fierce lion passed
thereby.

[9]He putteth forth his hand upon the
flinty rock;
he overturneth the mountains by
the roots.

[10]He cutteth out channels among
the rocks;
and his eye seeth every precious
thing.

[11]He bindeth the streams that they
trickle not;
and the thing that is hid bringeth
he forth to light.

[12]But where shall wisdom be found?
and where is the place of understanding?

[13]Man knoweth not the price thereof;
neither is it found in the land of
the living.

[14]The deep saith, It is not in me:

and the sea saith, It is not with me.

[15]It cannot be gotten for gold,
neither shall silver be weighed for
the price thereof.

[16]It cannot be valued with the gold
of Ophir,
with the precious onyx, or the
sapphire.

[17]Gold and glass cannot equal it:
neither shall the exchange thereof
be jewels of fine gold.

[18]No mention shall be made of coral
or of crystal:
yea, the price of wisdom is above
rubies.

[19]The topaz of Ethiopia shall not
equal it,
neither shall it be valued with pure
gold.

[20]Whence then cometh wisdom?
and where is the place of understanding?

[21]Seeing it is hid from the eyes of all
living,
and kept close from the fowls of
the air.

[22]Abaddon and Death say,
We have heard a rumour thereof
with our ears.

[23]God understandeth the way thereof,
and he knoweth the place thereof.

[24]For he looketh to the ends of the
earth,
and seeth under the whole heaven;

[25]to make a weight for the wind;
yea, he meteth out the waters by
measure.

[26]When he made a decree for the rain,
and a way for the lightning of the
thunder:

[27]then did he see it, and declare it;
he established it, yea, and searched
it out.

[28]And unto man he said,
Behold the fear of the Lord, that
is wisdom;
and to depart from evil is understanding.

THE poem divides into three parts: (*a*) vv. 1–11. The skill of
man in discovering the hidden riches of the earth (this portion
is almost unintelligible in the A.V.; the translators obviously

did not know what to make of it); (*b*) vv. 12–22, Wisdom can neither be found nor purchased; (*c*) vv. 23–28, God is the possessor of Wisdom.

In the first section we have a remarkable picture of mining operations in the author's time. He is fascinated by the thought of the miner deep underground, while corn grows far above him on the surface (v. 5). and the passing traveller has no conception of what is happening under his feet (v. 4). In his pursuit of these hidden treasures neither difficulty nor danger daunts the spirit of man.

When we turn to Wisdom, *man does not know the way to it, and it is not found in the land of the living* (v. 13, R.S.V.). Neither in the depths of the ocean (v. 14) nor in those of Sheol (v. 22) is its home to be found. Even if we could find its abode, all the riches, of the world could not buy it (vv. 15–19).

In poetic imagery God is pictured as knowing Wisdom's dwelling, for the whole world is known to Him (v. 24). In fact He *saw* and *searched out* Wisdom at the creation (vv. 26f.). *To man, He has told this much, that wisdom is fearing the Lord; here lies discernment, in refusing the evil path* (v. 28, Knox).

For the Wise this is a commonplace and self-evident (cf. Prov. 1: 7, 3: 7, 9: 10, 14: 16, 15: 33, 16: 6, Eccles. 12: 13), but sometimes we are very apt to forget the commonplace and self-evident. Neither Job's friends nor Job had been particularly concerned with *the fear of the Lord*. Self-vindication, the vindication of orthodoxy, yes, but no one had laid "his hand upon his mouth" (40: 2) and listened to what God had to say. In their zeal for orthodoxy, for their conception of God, Job's friends had gone far down the evil path, while they slandered him. Now the curtain goes up on the second part of the drama, and we are to see whether they can find true Wisdom in spite of their disastrous start.

Job's Concluding Monologue (Chs. 29–31)

Job had introduced the whole discussion by his great impassioned "Why?" in ch. 3. Now that his friends had been silenced, he summed up the whole situation in a long and poignant soliloquy. He can hardly be addressing his friends. Though the formal notice of their default is not given till 32:1, it is clear that they had been dragged out of their depth and broken on Job's stubborn refusal to bow to authority. In the second half of the drama they are reduced to little more than decorative pieces of the background, as they gnaw their fingers in impotent anger and then look on in growing amazement as Job reacts to God's voice, which they could not understand though they heard it. Though Job addresses God directly only in 30:20–23, it seems clear that ultimately the whole of these chapters is a rehearsal for God's ears.

There is, however, more to be said. Both in 29:1 and 27:1 Job is said to take up his *mashal*. A.V. and R.V. render "his parable," on which the kindest comment would be that it is lacking in intelligence, for nothing farther from a parable could well be imagined than these two sections. R.S.V. and I.C.C. have "discourse," which, though rather pompous, is intelligible, though it is no translation of *mashal*. This is used of didactic poems, e.g. Pss. 49, 78, and so we may perhaps render "instruction." If Job's friends, and for that matter we, have ears to hear, they will learn both from Job's defiant challenge and from his solemn recital of his life how inadequate is their superficial judgment based merely on a strictly selective observation of God's ways with men.

THE MEMORY OF HAPPIER DAYS (CH. 29)

AND Job again took up his parable, and said,

2 Oh that I were as in the months of old,
as in the days when God watched over me;

3 when his lamp shined above my head,
and by his light I walked through darkness;

4 as I was in the ripeness of my days,
when the friendship of God was upon my tent;

5 when the Almighty was yet with me,
and my children were about me;

6 when my steps were washed with butter,
and the rock poured me out rivers of oil!

7 When I went forth to the gate unto the city,
when I prepared my seat in the broad place,

8 the young men saw me and hid themselves,
and the aged rose up and stood;

9 the princes refrained talking,
and laid their hand on their mouth;

10 the voice of the nobles was hushed,
and their tongue cleaved to the roof of their mouth.

11 For when the ear heard *me*, then it blessed me;
and when the eye saw *me*, it gave witness unto me:

12 because I delivered the poor that cried,
the fatherless also, that had none to help him.

13 The blessing of him that was ready to perish came upon me:
and I caused the widow's heart to sing for joy.

14 I put on righteousness, and it clothed me:
my justice was as a robe and a turban.

¹⁵I was eyes to the blind,
and feet was I to the lame.
¹⁶I was a father to the needy:
and the cause of him that I knew
not I searched out.
¹⁷And I brake the jaws of the un-
righteous,
and plucked the prey out of his
teeth.
¹⁸Then I said, I shall die in my
nest,
and I shall multiply my days as
the sand:
¹⁹my root is spread out to the waters,
and the dew lieth all night upon
my branch:
²⁰my glory is fresh in me,
and my bow is renewed in my
hand.

²¹Unto me men gave ear, and waited,
and kept silence for my counsel.
²²After my words they spake not
again;
and my speech dropped upon
them.
²³And they waited for me as for the
rain;
and they opened their mouth wide
as for the latter rain.
²⁴I smiled on them when they had
no confidence;
and the light of my countenance
they cast not down.
²⁵I chose out their way, and sat *as*
chief,
and dwelt as a king in the army,
as one that comforteth the mour-
ners.

J OB began by sketching his former happiness and prosperity.
It is most striking that it was his fellowship with God that
stood out in his memory; all the rest was derived and received
its meaning from this.

He thought of *the days of my ripeness* (v. 4, I.C.C.)—"my autumn
days" (R.S.V.) is more literal but misses the point, as does "my
prime" (Moffatt). Job did not think back, as do so many, to the
dreams and illusive promises of youth and young manhood. By
the grace of God Job's life had borne fruit, and he was thinking
of this solid reality. God had guarded him (v. 2), He had given
him His guidance (v. 3, *above my head*, R.V. mg., is obviously
correct) and friendship (v. 4, *when the friendship of God was upon
my tent*, R.S.V.); in brief, *the Almighty was . . . with me* (v. 5a).

This had had as its inevitable result family happiness (v. 5b),
prosperity (v. 6) and respect (vv. 7–10). But since prosperity
will always command superficial respect, Job stressed that there
was genuine reason for it (vv. 11–17). Moffatt renders v. 14
interestingly: *I wore the robe of charity and kindness, my justice
was a tunic and a turban.* The verse brings together righteousness
(*tsedeq*) and justice (*mishpat*, more literally·the verdict spoken).
But righteousness in the Old Testament, when used of God, refers
not merely to His doing right, but to His doing it in the right way
with compassion and understanding. Since the earthly judge was
God's representative, it was always hoped that he would reflect
God's righteousness in his exercise of human righteousness. As

Moffatt has rightly understood it, Job not only held the scales of justice evenly, but also knew how to interpret the rigour of law with love to the oppressed and needy. He found that he became what he practised: *I clothed myself with righteousness, and it clothed itself with me* (v. 14, I.C.C.).

This the real Job, the same through and through, without contradiction between profession and practice, theology and life. Dare we blame him, if he expected that his old age would be the climax of his prime? He would die in the bosom of a happy family, *I shall die with my nestlings* (v. 18, I.C.C.; "among my brood," Moffatt)—in a ripe old age. Does not our own conception of God lead us to expect this, unless indeed the righteous man has become involved in a general catastrophe? Moreover catastrophe in old age is generally far harder to understand and bear.

THE MISERY OF THE PRESENT (CH. 30)

BUT now they that are younger than I have me in derision,
whose fathers I disdained to set with the dogs of my flock.

2Yea, the strength of their hands, whereto should it profit me? men in whom vigour is perished.

3They are gaunt with want and famine;
they gnaw the dry ground, in the gloom of wasteness and desolation.

4They pluck salt-wort by the bushes;
and the roots of the broom *are* to warm them.

5They are driven forth from the midst *of men*;
they cry after them as after a thief.

6In the clefts of the valleys must they dwell,
in holes of the earth and of the rocks.

7Among the bushes they bray;
under the nettles they are gathered together.

8*They are* children of fools, yea, children of base men;
they were scourged out of the land.

9And now I am become their song, yea, I am a byword unto them.

10They abhor me, they stand aloof from me,
and spare not to spit in my face.

11For he hath loosed my cord, and afflicted me,
and they have cast off the bridle before me.

12Upon my right hand rise the rabble;
they thrust aside my feet,
and they cast up against me their ways of destruction.

13They break up my path,
they set forward my calamity,
even men that have no helper.

14As through a wide breach they come:
in the midst of the ruin they roll themselves *upon me*.

15Terrors are turned upon me,
they chase mine honour as the wind;
and my welfare is passed away as a cloud.

16And now my soul is poured out within me;
days of affliction have taken hold upon me.

17In the night season my bones are pierced in me,
and the *pains* that gnaw me take no rest.

18By *his* great force is my garment disfigured:

it bindeth me about as the collar
of my coat.

¹⁹He hath cast me into the mire,
and I am become like dust and
ashes.

²⁰I cry unto thee, and thou dost not
answer me:
I stand up, and thou lookest at me.

²¹Thou art turned to be cruel to me:
with the might of thy hand thou
persecutest me.

²²Thou liftest me up to the wind,
thou causest me to ride *upon it*;
and thou dissolvest me in the
storm.

²³For I know that thou wilt bring
me to death,
and to the house appointed for all
living.

²⁴Surely against a ruinous heap he
will not put forth his hand;
though *it be* in his destruction, *one
may utter* a cry because of these
things.

²⁵Did not I weep for him that was in
trouble?
was not my soul grieved for the
needy?

²⁶When I looked for good, then evil
came;
and when I waited for light, there
came darkness.

²⁷My bowels boil, and rest not;
days of affliction are come upon
me.

²⁸I go mourning without the sun:
I stand up in the assembly, and cry
for help.

²⁹I am a brother to jackals,
and a companion to ostriches.

³⁰My skin is black, *and falleth* from
me,
and my bones are burned with
heat.

³¹Therefore is my harp *turned* to
mourning,
and my pipe into the voice of
them that weep.

THAT the respect paid to money lasts no longer than the money
is a constant theme in world literature. Job himself would
have expected no less, but he found that respect for true
merit does not outlive the prosperity either. Now that he was
weighing his sufferings more dispassionately, he felt that this was
the greatest evil of all.

Already when considering ch. 19 we saw that, when he found
his friends shared in his neighbours' and relatives' scorn and condemnation of him, it drove him to cry for vindication, a cry that
led him to trust in God as his Vindicator. How deeply this
attitude of scorn had hurt Job we are now allowed to see. In the
New Testament we find Paul proclaiming that we find the example
of our Lord supremely in the fact that He did not consider His
divine glory as a thing to be grasped and held on to, but that He
emptied Himself, taking the form of a slave (Phil. 2: 5–8), and a
slave has no honour.

It is hard enough to forgo the accidental and unmerited prestige
of birth, rank and wealth for Christ's sake. It becomes a heavier
price than many are prepared to pay when they see that true
attainments, nobility of character, and even the gifts of the Spirit
remain unrecognized, as often as not, by their fellow Christians.

The context of Paul's description of the apostles,

> Being reviled, we bless; being persecuted, we endure; being defamed, we intreat; we are made as the filth of the world, the offscouring of all things even until now (1 Cor. 4: 12f.),

is worth pondering. Indeed some of the language in 2 Cor. 10–13 reveals how deeply some of the dishonouring attacks made by the Judaizers had hurt Paul.

In ch. 19 Job was moved by the failure of his nearest to support him, now his thoughts are fixed on the baseness of some of the scum of society who ventured to turn on him. Today we are unfortunately all too familiar with the gutter press and the licence given to muck-raking reporters to hound the man who is down. In the far more rigid social structure of oriental society this was only possible, if the whole of society had turned against Job. What made the attack of the rabble all the more bitter was their lack of gratitude, for it was just they whom he had helped all he could (29: 15ff.).

There are those, e.g. Moffatt, Strahan, Peake, who find too great a contrast between 30: 2–8 in their present setting and the sympathy of 24: 2–12 and especially of 31: 15; hence they move these verses to ch. 24 (cf. Moffatt *ad loc.*), where they become part of the description of the plight of the poor. The suggestion is very attractive, but with our complete lack of knowledge about the transmission of the book it should not be lightly accepted, even though the theory is not impossible. There is, however, a more likely explanation of the apparent contradiction. Job was a very human man under intense stress, and there are many apparent inconsistencies in his words. What is even more important is that Job never fell into the Marxist fallacy of thinking that because some of the proletariat—those "who have nothing to lose but their chains"—are the victims of injustice and oppression they all are. Job knew that some of them had reached the depths because their character had taken them there.

It seems best to interpret v. 11a as a plural: *They have unstrung me and undone me* (Moffatt). Then vv. 9–14 are a consistent description how Job had been treated by base men; the behaviour of others may be inferred from it. In vv. 15–19 Job looks inward. The suggestion that he is thinking particularly of his illness is most doubtful. As the italics suggest, the A.V. and R.V. translation of v. 18a is unjustified; we should render with R.V. mg., *By His great force is my garment disfigured*, or with R.S.V., *With violence it seizes my garment*.   In fact, as we have seen before, his bodily state is merely the outward expression of far greater inner anguish, but it reminds him that men were only persecuting him whom God had first *cast into the mire* (v. 19).

So Job's heart turned once again in appeal to the inscrutable Deity, who seemed to have shut up the fountains of mercy (vv. 20–24), even though Job himself had been merciful (vv. 25f.).   It seems likely that Knox has found the meaning of the difficult picture in v. 22: *Didst Thou exalt me, lift me so high in the air, only to hurl me down in ruin?*   But there was no voice that answered, and so Job ended the picture of misery by describing his sufferings once again (vv. 26–31).

A closer examination of these verses will suggest once again that Job's disease played little part in his anguish.   In v. 27 we have the description of intense emotional suffering; there is no suggestion here of fever; R.S.V., Knox and Moffatt all give the modern idiom by using *heart* instead of "bowels."   His appeal in the assembly for help (v. 28) was doubtless because of the wrong that base men had done him.   The first half of this verse should probably be rendered with Moffatt and Strahan, *I wail, with none to comfort me*.   The meaning of vv. 29f. should be clear enough, when we remember that Job had been cast out of the city, and that his only home was the dunghill outside the gate, where he was exposed to all the powers of the elements.

If we have been tempted to judge Job harshly, it may be that we are being forced to modify our verdict.   It had been the presence and blessing of God that had poured radiance on the past; it was the veiling of God's face that had turned the present into night.

With that deep subtle intuition that suffering brings in its train, Job began to sense that his problem must be the problem of many others.   As Strahan has written on v. 31: "The parallel phrase 'my harp is turned to mourning' leads one simply to expect 'and my pipe to wailing,' which would leave us thinking of Job in his lonely sorrow.   But the poet hears, and lets his reader hear, 'the voice of them that weep,' making Job speak here, as so often elsewhere, not as an individual, but in the name of all who ever shed a bitter tear."

"I Am Innocent!' (Ch. 31)

I MADE a covenant with mine eyes;
how then should I look upon a
maid?

²For what portion *should I have* of
God from above,
and what heritage of the Almighty
from on high?

³Is it not calamity to the unrighteous,
and disaster to the workers of
iniquity?

⁴Doth not he see my ways,
and number all my steps?

⁵If I have walked with vanity,
and my foot hath hasted to deceit;

⁶(let me be weighed in an even balance,
that God may know mine integrity;)

⁷if my step hath turned out of the
way,
and mine heart walked after mine
eyes,
and if any spot hath cleaved to
mine hands:

⁸then let me sow, and let another
eat:
yea, let the produce of my field be
rooted out.

⁹If mine heart have been enticed
unto a woman,
and I have laid wait at my neighbour's door:

¹⁰then let my wife grind unto
another,
and let others bow down upon
her.

¹¹For that were an heinous crime;
yea, it were an iniquity to be
punished by the judges:

¹²for it is a fire that consumeth unto
Destruction,
and would root out all mine increase.

¹³If I did despise the cause of my
manservant or of my maid-
servant,
when they contended with me:

¹⁴what then shall I do when God
riseth up?
and when he visiteth, what shall I
answer him?

¹⁵Did not he that made me in the
womb make him?
and did not one fashion us in the
womb?

¹⁶If I have withheld the poor from
their desire,
or have caused the eyes of the
widow to fail;

¹⁷or have eaten my morsel alone,
and the fatherless hath not eaten
thereof;

¹⁸(nay, from my youth he grew up
with me as with a father,
and I have been her guide from
my mother's womb;)

¹⁹if I have seen any perish for want
of clothing,
or that the needy had no covering;

²⁰if his loins have not blessed me,
and if he were not warmed with
the fleece of my sheep;

²¹if I have lifted up my hand against
the fatherless,
because I saw my help in the
gate:

²²then let my shoulder fall from the
shoulder blade,
and mine arm be broken from the
bone.

²³For calamity from God was a
terror to me,
and by reason of his excellency I
could do nothing.

²⁴If I have made gold my hope,
and have said to the fine gold,
Thou art my confidence;

²⁵if I rejoiced because my wealth
was great,
and because mine hand had gotten
much;

²⁶if I beheld the sun when it shined,
or the moon walking in brightness;

²⁷and my heart hath been secretly
enticed,
and my mouth hath kissed my
hand:

²⁸this also were an iniquity to be
punished by the judges:
for I should have lied to God that
is above.

²⁹If I rejoiced at the destruction of
him that hated me,

or lifted up myself when evil found
him;

30(yea, I suffered not my mouth to
sin

by asking his life with a curse;)

31if the men of my tent said not,
Who can find one that hath not
been satisfied with his flesh?

32the stranger did not lodge in the
street;

but I opened my doors to the
traveller;

33if like Adam I covered my transgressions,

by hiding mine iniquity in my
bosom;

34because I feared the great multitude,

and the contempt of families terrified me,

so that I kept silence, and went
not out of the door—

35Oh that I had one to hear me!

(lo, here is my signature, let the
Almighty answer me;)

and the indictment which mine
adversary hath written!

36Surely I would carry it upon my
shoulder;

I would bind it unto me as a
crown.

37I would declare unto him the
number of my steps;

as a prince would I go near unto
him.

38If my land cry out against me,
and the furrows thereof weep together;

39if I have eaten the fruits thereof
without money,

or have caused the owners thereof
to lose their life:

40let thistles grow instead of wheat,
and cockle instead of barley.

The words of Job are ended.

In 13: 13–22 Job had challenged God to argue things out with him in whatever way He wished. Now he stood up and solemnly took the role of the accused. If God would not show Himself, would not bring an accusation, then Job would none the less, according to the court procedure of the time, clear himself with a solemn oath, listing all the conceivable crimes that might be charged against him and calling for dreadful penalties to fall on him, if he were lying.

From one point of view this is the climax of the book. Broken though he may be and an outcast, forsaken by God and despised by man, he will yet clear himself before God and man. Some commentators seek to rearrange the text. While their result is doubtless tidier, I doubt that Job was feeling in a tidy mood. One rearrangement is, however, unavoidable. It is impossible to believe that vv. 38–40 stood originally in their present position, though we cannot suggest with certainty the point in the chapter from which they have been displaced.

Job began (vv. 1–4) by affirming that since he recognized God's knowledge of his life (v. 4) and His punishment of the wicked (v. 3), *I imposed a covenant on my eyes; how then could I [even] look on a virgin?* (v. 1, I.C.C.). In other words, he had brought even his wayward sight under control, and he would not permit it to beguile his thoughts even to the most venial of sins.

The first group of sins he denied are insincerity—*vanity*—and deceit (v. 5), the leaving of the path of God's law, the yielding to covetous wishes, and the staining of his hands with wrong (v. 7). The imprecation (v. 8) is an almost proverbial one (cf. Deut. 28: 30, 33).

From the general Job passed to the particular, from the venial to the gross. In v. 9 he denied the sin of adultery, which weakens the whole foundation of society. The hypercritical have suggested that in v. 10 Job called down punishment on his wife instead of on himself. But there was no greater indignity, no greater confession of impotence, than to be unable to prevent the forcible carrying away of one's wife. Where honour ranked above all else, this dishonour was worse than death. There follow (vv. 13–23) a number of sins against the weak and helpless (cf. Exod. 22: 21–24, 23: 9; Deut. 24: 17, 27: 19). The point is that the weak and helpless were considered to be particularly under God's protection, so to wrong them was to defy God. In v. 13 Job denied that he had ever *rejected* (R.S.V.) any claim of his slaves against him. The slave had few rights before the law, but he did not take advantage of this fact, for both he and his slaves were equally the wonderful work of God (v. 15). The whole modern tendency is to affirm the equality of men; Job on the other hand would have denied this as folly. He stresses that men with all their manifold differences are equally the creation of an all-wise God, and hence all deserve the same respect and justice, which are worth far more than any theoretical equality that so many cannot use to advantage.

From this principle comes the affirmation (vv. 16f., 19f.) that those from whom God had withheld the prosperity He had granted Job had always shared in Job's prosperity. Nor had he used his rank and money to influence the judges (v. 21b—*the gate* was the scene of public justice, cf. Ruth 4) and so permit him to show violence to and oppress *the perfect* or unoffending (this, and not "fatherless," based on a different division of the Hebrew consonants, seems to be correct in v. 21a, see Strahan, I.C.C., Moffatt, etc.).

Job next denied all idolatry, inner and outer, the worship of money (vv. 24f.) and the worship of nature (vv. 26f.). He affirmed that he had been forgiving and hospitable (vv. 31f.—the A.V. has strangely inverted the sense in v. 31b; Job's servants are portrayed as hyperbolically suggesting that all the world had been feasted at Job's table). If even, like most men (v. 33 mg.—possibly "from men," R.S.V., Moffatt), he had simply and hypocritically hidden his faults out of fear of men, then——

But why should Job continue? He had claimed a standard that many Christians could not honestly pretend to have attained *Oh that I had one* [i.e. God] *to hear me! Here is my signature!* Job was picturing his protestations and imprecations not merely pronounced, but written down and solemnly signed.

Let the Almighty answer me! Before the accusations could be made, Job had answered them and challenged God to find something else to charge him with.

> Oh that I had the scroll of indictment which mine accuser hath
>   written!
> Surely I would carry it on my shoulder;
>   I would bind it on me as a crown—

i.e. he would make it public property and consider it his highest honour, for it would become clear that God had nothing to charge him with.

> I would give Him an account of all my steps;
>   like a ruler of men I would approach Him.

And so the words of Job are ended. His friends are speechless (32: 1), for he has shown himself greater than they had ever imagined. Even if the book were to end here, Job's sufferings would not have been in vain. God had "winnowed out his path" (Psa. 139: 3), and all unknowingly Job was re-echoing the divine word to Satan, *Hast thou considered My servant Job . . . a perfect and an upright man?*

CHAPTER IX

ELIHU

So these three men ceased to answer Job, because he was righteous in his own eyes. ²Then was kindled the wrath of Elihu the son of Barachel the Buzite, of the family of Ram: against Job was his wrath kindled, because he justified himself rather than God. ³Also against his three friends was his wrath kindled, because they had found no answer, and yet had condemned Job. ⁴Now Elihu had waited to speak unto Job, because they were elder than he. ⁵And when Elihu saw that there was no answer in the mouth of these three men, his wrath was kindled.

⁶And Elihu the son of Barachel the Buzite answered and said,

I am young, and ye are very old;
wherefore I held back, and durst not shew you mine opinion.
⁷I said, Days should speak,
and multitude of years should teach wisdom.
⁸But there is a spirit in man,
and the breath of the Almighty giveth them understanding.
⁹It is not the great that are wise,
nor the aged that understand judgement.
¹⁰Therefore I said, Hearken to me;
I also will shew mine opinion.
¹¹Behold, I waited for your words,
I listened for your reasons,
whilst ye searched out what to say.
¹²Yea, I attended unto you,

and behold, there was none that convinced Job,
or that answered his words, among you.
¹³Beware lest ye say, We have found wisdom;
God may vanquish him, not man:
¹⁴for he hath not directed his words against me;
neither will I answer him with your speeches.
¹⁵They are amazed, they answer no more:
they have not a word to say.
¹⁶And shall I wait, because they speak not,
because they stand still, and answer no more?
¹⁷I also will answer my part,
I also will shew mine opinion.
²⁸For I am full of words;
the spirit within me constraineth me.
¹⁹Behold, my belly is as wine which hath no vent;
like new wine-skins it is ready to burst.
²⁰I will speak, that I may be refreshed;
I will open my lips and answer.
²¹Let me not, I pray you, respect any man's person;
neither will I give flattering titles unto any man.
²²For I know not to give flattering titles;
else would my Maker soon take me away.

As Job's last impassioned words rang out, his friends looked at each other and nodded almost imperceptibly. Their task was finished: they had vindicated the wisdom of the Wise, but all in vain. With heavy hearts at the impenitence of their old friend they prepared to leave, when they were startled by a new voice vibrant with passion: *I am young in years, and you are aged; therefore I was timid and afraid to declare my opinion to you* (32: 6, R.S.V.).

Modern commentators and writers are agreed by a large majority that chs. 32–37, containing the speeches of Elihu, are a later interpolation, though a few would see in them an after-thought by the original author. It may be frankly admitted that, superficially at least, their arguments are strong. But we must remember that, though he has since changed his mind, the American scholar Pfeiffer could write, "These arguments did not seem convincing to the present writer in 1915,"* and they have only become valid to him now because he has found a new and doubtful interpretation for Elihu's views. In addition different scholars mutually contradict one another in the purpose they suggest for the interpolation. If the book is in any sense a drama, the non-mention of Elihu at an earlier stage can be reasonably explained. Had the reader been waiting all the time for Elihu's cue, he might have missed much of the drama and tension in the speeches of Job and his friends. Were it true, as so many (but not Pfeiffer) maintain, that Elihu adds virtually nothing to the debate, it is difficult to see why anyone should have troubled to interpolate him.

The introduction of Elihu in prose (32: 2–5) indicates that a new element is being introduced. He is given a brief genealogy, something that is lacking in the case of Job and his friends. As was stressed at the beginning of this study, Job and his friends are introduced, irrespective of whether they were of good family or not, as representatives of the Wise. Their position in society rested on their own merits, not on those of their fathers. Elihu, however, is introduced as a young aristocrat. He does not share in the vested interests of the Wise, and he begins by challenging their whole position:

I said, 'Let days speak,
 and many years teach wisdom.'
But it is the spirit in a man,
 the breath of the Almighty,
 that makes him understand.
It is not the old that are wise,
 nor the aged that understand right (32: 7ff., R.S.V.).

* Pfeiffer: *Introduction to the Old Testament* (1948), p. 673.

The Wise were not godless men; their goal was the understanding of the divine rule of the world, that they might direct their own and their pupils' footsteps accordingly. But they believed that provided God gave them the right start—for Eliphaz, as we have seen, it was religious experience, for Bildad the voice of tradition, for Zophar sound common sense—their own reason was ample and would bring them to their goal. Elihu challenges them with the claim that man needs the inspiration of the Spirit for this—*Yet God inspires a man, 'tis the Almighty who breathes knowledge into him* (32: 8, Moffatt).

Beyond a doubt Elihu stands on firmer ground than the three friends. With one burning phrase he has laid bare the inner weakness of those who have spoken before him. Human reason cannot grasp the depths of God's work in heaven or on earth (cf. 28: 20–28), but the sequel is to show that Elihu's claim to inspiration is as shallow as the three friends' claim to divine Wisdom.

A hint as to the outcome is given us already in the prose introduction to Elihu: *Against Job was his wrath kindled, because he justified himself rather than God* (32: 2), which Moffatt rightly interprets, "for making himself out to be better than God." Even more than in the arguments of Job's friends we find in Elihu the inability to bring together God's sovereign rule and His loving concern for the individual. As a result he has even less sympathy and understanding for Job's "Why?" than the others, though of course there is more excuse for him than for the older men.

We are apt to find in Elihu a noble, youthful indignation, with which, in fact, 32: 3 does not credit him. If we retain the Hebrew text, we must render it with I.C.C., *because they had found no answer, and had not shown Job to be unrighteous.* It is, however, more probable that the rabbinic tradition, which makes this verse one of the *tiqqune sopherim* (corrections of the scribes), eighteen passages deliberately changed to avoid objectionable expressions, is correct. In that case Job has been substituted for God, and the original form will have been, "because they had found no answer, and so had condemned God." We can see that Elihu's "inspiration" was merely a true realization that the friends were lacking in something, but not a revelation of what that lack was.

In fact Elihu represents a phenomenon we constantly meet for good in our church life. The self-satisfaction of an older generation finally drives young men to revolt. In practice they seldom say much that is new and seldom say it well, but there are almost invariably glimpses of valuable truth which the older generation had missed to its loss.

Much in Elihu's speeches is strongly reminiscent of Eliphaz and Bildad, but it does not seem that Zophar appealed to him. He was genuinely shocked by three features in Job's words and he deals with them in turn. This gives us a useful criterion for the division of his answer.

ELIHU'S FIRST ANSWER (CH. 33)

Howbeit, Job, I pray thee, hear my speech,
and hearken to all my words.
²Behold now, I have opened my mouth,
my tongue hath spoken in my mouth.
³My words *shall utter* the uprightness of my heart:
and that which my lips know they shall speak sincerely.
⁴The spirit of God hath made me,
and the breath of the Almighty giveth me life.
⁵If thou canst, answer thou me;
set *thy words* in order before me, stand forth.
⁶Behold, I am toward God even as thou art:
I also am formed out of the clay.
⁷Behold, my terror shall not make thee afraid,
neither shall my pressure be heavy upon thee.
⁸Surely thou hast spoken in mine hearing,
and I have heard the voice of *thy* words, *saying*,
⁹I am clean, without transgression;
I am innocent, neither is there iniquity in me:
¹⁰Behold, he findeth occasions against me,
he counteth me for his enemy:
¹¹He putteth my feet in the stocks,
he marketh all my paths.
¹²Behold, I will answer thee, in this thou art not just;
for God is greater than man.
¹³Why dost thou strive against him,
for that he giveth not account of any of his matters?

¹⁴For God speaketh once,
yea twice, *though man* regardeth it not.
¹⁵In a dream, in a vision of the night,
when deep sleep falleth upon men,
in slumberings upon the bed;
¹⁶then he openeth the ears of men,
and sealeth their instruction,
¹⁷that he may withdraw man *from his* purpose,
and hide pride from man:
¹⁸he keepeth back his soul from the pit,
and his life from perishing by the sword.
¹⁹He is chastened also with pain upon his bed,
and with continual strife in his bones:
²⁰so that his life abhorreth bread,
and his soul dainty meat.
²¹His flesh is consumed away, that it cannot be seen;
and his bones that were not seen stick out.
²²Yea, his soul draweth near unto the pit,
and his life to the destroyers.
²³If there be with him an angel,
an interpreter, one among a thousand,
to shew unto man what is right for him.
²⁴then he is gracious unto him, and saith,
Deliver him from going down to the pit,
I have found a ransom.
²⁵His flesh shall be fresher than a child's;
he returneth to the days of his youth:

²⁶He prayeth unto God, and he is favourable unto him;
so that he seeth his face with joy:
and he restoreth unto man his righteousness.
²⁷He singeth before men, and saith, I have sinned, and perverted that which was right,
and it profited me not:
²⁸he hath redeemed my soul from going into the pit,
and my life shall behold the light.

²⁹Lo, all these things doth God work, twice, *yea* thrice, with a man,
³⁰to bring back his soul from the pit, that he may be enlightened with the light of living.
³¹Mark well, O Job, hearken unto me: hold thy peace, and I will speak.
³²If thou hast anything to say, answer me:
speak, for I desire to justify thee.
³³If not, hearken thou unto me: hold thy peace, and I will teach thee wisdom.

ELIHU turns first to Job's protestations of innocence (vv. 8–11). He prefaces his answer, however, with a rather disingenuous claim to be doing what Job had wanted all along. In 9: 32–35 and 13: 20–22, Job in his anguish had called on God to remove His heavy hand from him, so that he might be able to stand and answer Him. Elihu, catching the words but not the sense, offers himself as God's spokesman without the dread of God surrounding him. If the language of vv. 2–7 seems rather involved, it is because he is making oblique references to Job's own words. He had completely failed to see that Job's agony had driven him to the point where only the voice of God Himself would satisfy him. (It is to be noted that the A.V. in v. 6a is impossible and completely distorts the picture.)

For the quotations in v. 9 compare 9: 21, 10: 7, 16: 17, 23: 10–12 and 27: 5, 6. This has been the way of the heresy-hunter down the ages; expressions are snapped up out of their factual and emotional contexts, and balancing statements like 7: 21 and 13: 26 are conveniently forgotten. In vv. 10, 11 Elihu goes on to summarize some of Job's complaints against God (cf. 10: 13–17, 19: 6–12, 13: 24, 27). He is undoubtedly correct when he sums up, *Behold, in this you are not right* (v. 12, R.S.V.), but he immediately dodges the issue by adding, *For God is greater than man*, i.e. "the moral loftiness of God's nature made it impossible that He should act in the arbitrary, hostile manner charged against Him by Job" (Davidson, *ad loc.*).

It is repeatedly stressed in Scripture that the character of God is known from His words and acts. We know Him not merely from what He claims to be but even more from what He has done. Job has claimed to depict God's character from the way He has treated him, but he has yet to realize that to argue from human finiteness to divine infinity on the basis of part of one's own experience (Job conveniently forgot the experiences of his earlier life), with a few hand-picked facts thrown in as a make-weight, is a perilous process. But Elihu has embarked on a much more perilous path. He dismisses Job's explanation of his experience with an airy wave of his hand as being incompatible with his *a priori* concept of God and goes on to give a completely arbitrary explanation of it.

But let us be fair to Elihu. If Job's sufferings mean very little to him, it is because he is a young man and they lie outside his experience. Although he has been genuinely shocked by Job's words (cf. 34: 7ff.), it has been shock, not the personal hurt that Job's friends felt. His view of God's character and ways may be somewhat theoretical, but it is noble. Instead of thinking of punishment he sees God active in salvation. He did not deny that men were punished for their sins (cf. 36: 13f.), but in his thoughts punishment took second place to restoration. Job had himself had a glimpse of this truth on a higher level (23: 10); what marks out Elihu from Job's friends is that his explanation (vv. 14–28) does not establish a ratio between sin and suffering. Who knows? Had the others been as wise as Elihu, the whole discussion might have flowed in other channels.

Elihu seems to envisage two methods of divine warning. The former (vv. 14–20), strongly influenced by Eliphaz' words (4: 12–19), is that of the warning dream. The latter (vv. 21–28) is illness. He uses popular ideas of angels of death (*the destroyers*, v. 22) and angels of mercy (v. 23). The *if* (v. 23) does not express doubt: Elihu's whole point is that there are a thousand, i.e. very many, angels of mercy available. It is not clear whether the speaker in v. 24 is the angel or God; the latter seems more natural. The "ransom" (*kopher*) is probably to be understood metaphorically of that which covered the sick man's sin, i.e. his repentance. Elihu was no more an inspired theologian than were Job's friends.

ELIHU'S SECOND ANSWER (Ch. 34)

MOREOVER Elihu answered and said,

²Hear my words, ye wise men;
and give ear unto me, ye that have knowledge.

³For the ear trieth words,
as the palate tasteth meat.

⁴Let us choose for us that which is right:
let us know among ourselves what is good.

⁵For Job hath said, I am righteous,
and God hath taken away my right:

⁶notwithstanding my right I am *accounted* a liar;

my wound is incurable, *though I am* without transgression.

⁷What man is like Job,

who drinketh up scorning like water?

⁸which goeth in company with the workers of iniquity,

and walketh with wicked men.

⁹For he hath said, It profiteth a man nothing

that he should delight himself with God.

¹⁰Therefore hearken unto me, ye men of understanding:

far be it from God, that he should do wickedness;

and from the Almighty, that he should commit iniquity.

¹¹For the work of a man shall he render unto him,

and cause every man to find according to his ways.

¹²Yea, of a surety, God will not do wickedly,

neither will the Almighty pervert judgement.

¹³Who gave him a charge over the earth?

or who hath disposed the whole world?

¹⁴If he set his heart upon himself,

if he gather unto himself his spirit and his breath;

¹⁵all flesh shall perish together,

and man shall turn again unto dust.

¹⁶If now *thou hast* understanding, hear this:

hearken to the voice of my words.

¹⁷Shall even one that hateth right govern?

and wilt thou condemn him that is just *and* mighty?

¹⁸Is it *fit* to say to a king, *Thou art* vile?

or to nobles, *Ye are* wicked?

¹⁹*How much less to* him that respecteth not the persons of princes,

nor regardeth the rich more than the poor?

for they all are the work of his hands.

²⁰In a moment they die, even at midnight;

the people are shaken and pass away,

and the mighty are taken away without hand.

²¹For his eyes are upon the ways of a man,

and he seeth all his goings.

²²There is no darkness, nor shadow of death,

where the workers of iniquity may hide themselves.

²³For he needeth not further to consider a man,

that he should go before God in judgement.

²⁴He breaketh in pieces mighty men without inquisition,

and setteth others in their stead.

²⁵Therefore he taketh knowledge of their works;

and he overturneth them in the night, so that they are destroyed.

²⁶He striketh them as wicked men in the open sight of others;

²⁷because they turned aside from following him,

and would not have regard to any of his ways:

²⁸so that they caused the cry of the poor to come unto him,

and he heard the cry of the afflicted.

²⁹When he giveth quietness, who then can condemn?

and when he hideth his face, who then can behold him?

whether *it be done* unto a nation, or unto a man, alike:

³⁰that the godless man reign not,

that there be none to ensnare the people.

³¹For hath any said unto God,

I have borne *chastisement*, I will not offend *any more*:

³²That which I see not teach thou me:

if I have done iniquity, I will do it no more?

³³Shall his recompence be as thou wilt, that thou refusest it?

for thou must choose, and not I:

therefore speak what thou knowest.

³⁴Men of understanding will say unto me,

yea, every wise man that heareth me:

35 Job speaketh without knowledge, and his words are without wisdom.

36 Would that Job were tried unto the end,

because of his answering like wicked men.

37 For he addeth rebellion unto his sin,

he clappeth his hands among us, and multiplieth his words against God.

JUST as his first answer had contained a deliberate allusion to Eliphaz' position, so his second takes up Bildad's attitude. He appeals to the consensus of the Wise (vv. 2, 34) as Bildad had to tradition (8: 8ff.).

In his first answer, for all his weakness, we saw Elihu at his best; here he is at his worst. There we obviously have his own reflections, here he is mouthing the shibboleths he has learnt from his childhood. He sets up a completely *a priori* picture of God's rule in the world. We have seen that one of the outstanding features of Job's spiritual progress was his learning to look on life in a new way and to see things that had been hidden from him and his friends by the blinkers of preconceived ideas. But for all we can gather from Elihu's words he might have been away at lunch when Job was describing the world as he had come to see it. We must not forget that in the setting of the book of Job it is not a question whether Elihu is right or not—obviously he is right, at least in large measure—but whether he contributes anything to the solution of Job's "Why?" Obviously he does not. Equally today the Christian who merely repeats theological truths will seldom meet the needs of those who, battered in life, are asking "Why?"

It would seem that Elihu, being a young man of rank and riches, had grown up with a vested interest in the maintenance of society as it was. He believed not only that "the powers that be are ordained of God" (Rom. 13: 1), but also that the powers that be must be good. As a result he was more shocked by Job's challenge to the accepted order than by his apparent denial of sinfulness. This goes far to account for the complete lack of sympathy for Job in this chapter.

Elihu's attitude is the worse because of its emptiness. However much he may refuse to follow Bildad in his appeal to tradition, we have the feeling that here is a learned man whose views have been carefully thought through and elaborated and who knows all the arguments. His tragedy is that he has become the prisoner of a theory. With Elihu we gain the impression that he has never thought of applying the theories he has learnt off by heart to life around him.

This is a constant danger in any church, where the theological manual threatens to displace the Bible as the text-book for the young. It is always easier to teach the adolescent theology than the Bible. The danger is that he will become as orthodox but as empty as Elihu shows himself in this chapter.

Elihu's Third Answer (Chs. 35–37)

Moreover Elihu answered and said,

²Thinkest thou this to be *thy* right, *or* sayest thou, My righteousness is more than God's,

³that thou sayest, What advantage will it be unto thee?
What profit shall I have, more than if I had sinned?

⁴I will answer thee,
and the companions with thee.

⁵Look unto the heavens, and see;
and behold the skies, which are higher than thou.

⁶If thou hast sinned, what doest thou against him?
and if thy transgressions be multiplied, what doest thou unto him?

⁷If thou be righteous, what givest thou him?
or what receiveth he of thine hand?

⁸Thy wickedness *may hurt* a man as thou art;
and thy righteousness *may profit* a son of man.

⁹By reason of the multitude of oppressions they cry out;
they cry for help by reason of the arm of the mighty.

¹⁰But none saith, Where is God my Maker,
who giveth songs in the night:

¹¹who teacheth us more than the beasts of the earth,
and maketh us wiser than the fowls of heaven?

¹²There they cry, but none giveth answer,
because of the pride of evil men.

¹³Surely God will not hear vanity,
neither will the Almighty regard it.

¹⁴How much less when thou sayest thou beholdest him not,
the cause is before him, and thou waitest for him!

¹⁵But now, because he hath not visited in his anger,
neither doth he greatly regard arrogance;

¹⁶therefore doth Job open his mouth in vanity;
he multiplieth words without knowledge.

36. Elihu also proceeded, and said,

²Suffer me a little, and I will shew thee:
for I have yet somewhat to say on God's behalf.

³I will fetch my knowledge from afar,
and will ascribe righteousness to my Maker.

⁴For truly my words are not false:
one that is perfect in knowledge is with thee.

⁵Behold, God is mighty, and despiseth not any:
he is mighty in strength of understanding.

⁶He preserveth not the life of the wicked:
but giveth to the afflicted *their* right.

⁷He withdraweth not his eyes from the righteous:
but with kings upon the throne
he setteth them for ever, and they are exalted.

⁸And if they be bound in fetters,
and be taken in the cords of affliction;

⁹then he sheweth them their work,

and their transgressions, that they have behaved themselves proudly.

¹⁰He openeth also their ear to instruction,
and commandeth that they return from iniquity.

¹¹If they hearken and serve *him*,
they shall spend their days in prosperity,
and their years in pleasures.

¹²But if they hearken not, they shall perish by the sword,
and they shall die without knowledge.

¹³But they that are godless in heart lay up anger:
they cry not for help when he bindeth them.

¹⁴They die in youth,
and their life *perisheth* among the unclean.

¹⁵He delivereth the afflicted by his affliction,
and openeth their ear in oppression.

¹⁶Yea, he would have led thee away out of distress
into a broad place, where there is no straitness;
and that which is set on thy table should be full of fatness.

¹⁷But thou art full of the judgement of the wicked:
judgement and justice take hold *on thee*.

¹⁸Because there is wrath, beware lest thou be led away by *thy* sufficiency;
neither let the greatness of the ransom turn thee aside.

¹⁹Will thy riches suffice, *that thou be* not in distress,
or all the forces of *thy* strength?

²⁰Desire not the night,
when peoples are cut off in their place.

²¹Take heed, regard not iniquity:
for this hast thou chosen rather than affliction.

²²Behold, God doeth loftily in his power:
who is a teacher like unto him?

²³Who hath enjoined him his way?
or who can say, Thou hast wrought unrighteousness?

²⁴Remember that thou magnify his work,
whereof men have sung.

²⁵All men have looked thereon;
man beholdeth it afar off.

²⁶Behold, God is great, and we know him not;
the number of his years is unsearchable.

²⁷For he draweth up the drops of water,
which distil in rain from his vapour:

²⁸which the skies pour down
and drop upon man abundantly.

²⁹Yea, can any understand the spreadings of the clouds,
the thunderings of his pavilion?

³⁰Behold, he spreadeth his light around him;
and he covereth the bottom of the sea.

³¹For by these he judgeth the peoples;
he giveth meat in abundance.

³²He covereth his hands with the lighting;
and giveth it a charge that it strike the mark.

³³The noise thereof telleth concerning him,
the cattle also concerning *the storm* that cometh up.

37. At this also my heart trembleth,
and is moved out of its place.

²Hearken ye unto the noise of his voice,
and the sound that goeth out of his mouth.

³He sendeth it forth under the whole heaven,
and his lightning unto the ends of the earth.

⁴After it a voice roareth;
he thundereth with the voice of his majesty:
and he stayeth them not when his voice is heard.

⁵God thundereth marvellously with his voice;
great things doeth he, which we cannot comprehend.

⁶For he saith to the snow, Fall thou on the earth;

likewise to the shower of rain,
and to the showers of his mighty
rain.
[7]He sealeth up the hand of every
man;
that all men whom he hath made
may know *it*.
[8]Then the beasts go into coverts,
and remain in their dens.
[9]Out of the chamber *of the south*
cometh the storm:
and cold out of the north.
[10]By the breath of God ice is given:
and the breadth of the waters is
straitened.
[11]Yea, he ladeth the thick cloud
with moisture;
he spreadeth abroad the cloud of
his lightning:
[12]and it is turned round about by
his guidance,
that they may do whatsoever he
commandeth them
upon the face of the habitable
world:
[13]whether it be for correction, or for
his land,
or for mercy, that he cause it to
come.
[14]Hearken unto this, O Job:
stand still, and consider the wondrous works of God.
[15]Dost thou know how God layeth
his charge upon them,
and causeth the lightning of his
cloud to shine?

[16]Dost thou know the balancings of
the clouds,
the wondrous works of him which
is perfect in knowledge?
[17]Thou   whose   garments   are
warm,
when the earth is still by reason of
the south *wind*,
[18]canst thou with him spread out
the sky,
which is strong as a molten mir-
ror?
[19]Teach us what we shall say unto
him;
for we cannot order *our speech* by
reason of darkness.
[20]Shall it be told him that I would
speak?
or should a man wish that he were
swallowed up?
[21]And now men cannot look on the
light when it is bright in the
skies:
when the wind has passed, and
cleanseth them.
[22]Out of the north cometh golden
splendour:
God hath upon him terrible
majesty.
[23]The Almighty, we cannot find him
out; he is excellent in power:
and in judgement and plenteous
justice he will not afflict.
[24]Men do therefore fear him:
he regardeth not any that are wise
of heart.

As Elihu saw it, Job had not merely made baseless claims for himself and denied God's righteous rule of the world; he had also denied that there was any profit in serving God (35: 3, cf. 9: 22f., 30f., 21: 15, 24: 1), though it is questionable whether Job had ever intended his words to be so understood.

When Karl Marx declared that religion was opium for the people and that all promises of blessing for the keeping of the moral law were only means for making the proletariat satisfied with their chains, he put his finger on an all-too-frequent misuse of religion. All too often some subtle shift of emphasis has brought the official Church on to the side of the dominant classes. In Job's day the virtual equation of poverty and sin, not unknown in the Victorian age, was most comforting to the rich and powerful.

We do not doubt that Elihu was genuinely shocked by the suggestion that God would not reward those who served him, but equally certainly the shock was increased by the uneasy knowledge that, if Job was right, he would have to reconsider his whole outlook on the world.   This probably explains the rather malicious reference to Job's *companions* (35: 4), literally "friends"; he is probably thinking of the rich, careless wicked whom Job had so graphically described, e.g. 21: 14f., and he suggests that Job for all his outward godliness was at heart one of them.

In the earlier part of his answer (35: 5–9) Elihu takes up and expands Eliphaz' aphorism in 22: 2–4, but what was just within the bounds of truth in the mouth of the older man becomes a travesty of Scriptural truth as it is exaggerated by the younger. But it is clear that he does not really believe his own picture of God, for the one who gives "songs in the night" (35: 10f.) is not the transcendent Deity, unmoved by the acts of His creation, whom he had earlier depicted.   We need not be surprised or distressed by this.   There is little hope for the young man with a fully co-ordinated theology; he is only a copy-cat or a poll-parrot. True enough, Elihu was teaching when he should have been learning, but he shows enough good for us to hope great things for him.

He goes on to reveal this dichotomy in thought by expanding in 36: 2–12 his thought of the drawing and teaching of God in suffering.   He goes so far as to call it a *ransom* (36: 18), presumably in the sense that it will be accepted as such by God, if the sinner bows under it and accepts it (cf. 33: 24).   Even though Elihu is as convinced as Job's friends that Job is a great sinner— not, as with them, because of the greatness of his sufferings, but because of the evil of his words—the R.V. translation of 36: 18f., is so wildly inappropriate to Job's position that we should probably follow the R.S.V. rendering of a very difficult passage:

Beware lest wrath entice you into scoffing;
    and let not the greatness of the ransom turn you aside.
Will your cry avail to keep you from distress,
    or all the force of your strength?

For a moment Elihu strikes true Scriptural balance: *Behold, God doeth loftily in His power: who is a teacher like unto Him?* (36. 22). Then, however, he turns again to his concept of God All-Sovereign, above the finding out and understanding of men (36: 26—37: 24).

It may well be that he was stung to the quick by a look of amusement on the faces of Job's friends.   After all, with all his self-assurance he had ended up very much where they had and with even less result.   He had not even stung Job into answering.   So he launches out into a description of the wonders of God in nature to cover his confusion.   But though he uses many words, and at times strikes genuinely poetic notes, he does not really add anything to what Job himself had said, viz. 9: 4–10; 12: 13–25, and perhaps 26: 6–14.

Is it too much to think that, as he describes the greatness of God, Elihu gradually realizes that he has rushed into a subject far too great for him?   As his voice tails off there is no need for anyone to answer him; he has realized that after all righteous emotion need not be inspiration.

CHAPTER X

GOD REPLIES TO JOB

THE THUNDERSTORM (38: 1)

THEN the LORD answered Job out
of the whirlwind, and said ...

ELIHU's many and brave words tailed out feebly with a final
thrust both at Job and his friends: *The Almighty ... regardeth
not any that are wise of heart* (37: 24), which the R.S.V.
interprets correctly as "wise in their own conceit." This is
essentially a repetition of his challenge to the Wise in 32: 7–10.

While he had been speaking, the storm clouds had covered the
sky and blotted out the sun. It is quite possible that the distant
thunder had coloured Elihu's third answer, cf. 36: 29 – 37: 5.
Now the full thunder-roll was heard overhead, and the gloom was
lit up by the lightning's flash. For the men crouching in fear on
the dunghill it seemed as though God had at last bestirred Himself to punish Job's blasphemies. They edged still further away
from him, lest they be consumed with him. But as they glanced
fearfully at him, instead of a look of fear and despair on Job's face
they saw a joyous, humble awe. The Almighty had come to
him, clothed in all the dread majesty of nature, but He had come
and was speaking to Him!

The how of God's direct speaking should little concern us. Too
many have heard the voice of God in thunder or in a still small
voice for us to doubt that He speaks even in our days to men.
But he who hears that voice has little time or wish to think of
how it may be coming to him. In Job's case his friends almost
certainly found themselves in the same position as Paul's travel-
ling companions, "hearing the sound, but beholding no man"
(Acts 9: 7, R.V. mg.), while for Job the storm became the voice
of God speaking clearly to him.

God passes over the words of Elihu in silence (for it is merely
a curiosity of interpretation to apply, *Who is this that darkeneth
counsel by words without knowledge* to him) and this is seen by

many as proof positive that Elihu's words are a later addition,
But He equally passes over the words of Job's friends in silence,
even though there is an almost parenthetical mention of them
later (42: 7). God does not intervene to sum up and decide the
debate; He speaks because behind all the multitude of words Job
has been trying to storm the gates of heaven, and at last He has
pity on His sorely tried servant and answers him.

THE ALL-MIGHT OF GOD

If we look away from some special passage like 19: 25ff., God's
answer to Job is the best known portion of the book. Our
familiarity with it helps to hide from us how entirely unexpected
it is—but then we so seldom read through the book. It would
seem as though God wishes by sledge-hammer blow after sledge-
hammer blow to break down His already broken servant to
nothing. In blazing poetry all the gamut of nature's wonders is
passed before Job's eyes, but nothing is said about his agonized
Why? But is all this as irrelevant as it seems?

To understand God aright we must remember that chs. 38–41
are ultimately only a repetition, more detailed and on a poetically
much higher level, of what has already been said by Elihu
(36: 22 – 37: 24) and by Job himself (9: 4–14, 12: 13–25 and
perhaps 26: 4–14), and their thought underlies much that his
friends have declared, e.g. Bildad in 25: 2–6. If we could accept
Stevenson's view and completely separate the prose introduction
and conclusion from the verse drama, then we could see in these
chapters God's condemnation of Job's foolish words and an
affirmation on a *higher level* of the views of his friends. But we
are not entitled to do this, and in their setting, cf. 42:7, God's
words are ultimately a vindication of Job and a condemnation of
his friends.

In Rom. 1: 18–23 Paul described the reaction of man when
faced by the all-might of God as seen in His creation. We in our
spiritual superiority are apt to say,

> "The heathen in his blindness
> Bows down to wood and stone,"

and fail to realize that we too find means of coming to terms with
God's all-might, which save us from taking it too seriously.
There is a reverent freedom with God which is one of the noblest

fruits of sonship, but there is also an irreverent freedom which is one of the worst weeds in the Christian's garden.

The Rabbinic Jew never for a moment doubted that the giving of the Law at Sinai was an even greater act of grace than the bringing up of Israel out of Egypt, of which it was a logical sequel. But he was profoundly convinced that once God had given it, the consensus of religious men's opinions about the Law established God's will for the individual and people. God had in measure abdicated His freedom of action by His giving of the Law.

In the Church the theologian has tended to take the place of the casuist. We have always recognized that in the incarnation, crucifixion and resurrection of the Son of God we have the supreme evidence of God's grace, but we have all too often believed that we have the right, and even the duty, to make our understanding of these events the measure by which we judge the acceptability of other men to God. It matters not how much of the fruit of the Spirit may be seen in them, if they will not or cannot say Shibboleth, we lay the command of silence upon them, or even thrust them from our midst as unclean.

This is only one of the ways in which we claim to be able to control God. The attitude of the various characters in *Job* may well suggest other ways in which we too are guilty.

For Job's friends the contemplation of God's all-might produced merely a comforting conviction that it provided that immutability which served as a firm foundation for their theories about life. They remind me of the many modern scientists—I am thinking of men who claim to believe in God—who base their denial of all miracle precisely on the wonder of God's creating. They wish to limit Him by that portion of His power and work that they are able to grasp.

For Elihu the all-might of God was a handy weapon to smite Job's presumption with. As we read 36: 22 – 37: 24, we never get the impression that the wonders of nature which he describes so eloquently have ever created humility in him. He may say, *At this also my heart trembleth, and is moved out of its place* (37: 1), but if there was any outward sign of it, it was the conventional one of the actor.

Even Job did not take God's power really seriously. Paul explains that it is revealed in nature, that men might glorify Him as God and give thanks (Rom. 1: 21). With Job we feel, as with his friends, that it is little more than a handy weapon in controversy; it was an intellectual concept to be appealed to in case of need, not the foundation of all his living.   As a result, when Job faces it more seriously from time to time, in his discussion, it drives him to distraction rather than leading him on to confidence.

When God spoke out of the thunderstorm, intellectual conviction become a vital reality.   It broke Job down, but it also brought him peace.   A God, greater than Job had ever pictured Him, was deigning to speak to His sorely tried servant, and that sufficed.

The Casting Out of Fear

I am convinced, though, that we can go further.   All the motives given hitherto for Job's anguish are doubtless valid, but behind them all lay a deeper cause we must now consider. We have already said of Job, "He finds that the firm moorings of his life have vanished, that the ship of his life is adrift on the dark ocean, without chart, without light, being carried he knows not where."   God is now speaking to deeper need, to the hidden fear, hardly realized by Job and certainly unconfessed, that there might be somewhere where the writ of God did not run, where God was not all-sovereign.

Are we not all like Job in this respect?   In his *Nineteen Eighty-Four* George Orwell makes his inquisitor, O'Brien, say to the hero, "You asked me once what was in Room 101.   I told you that you knew the answer already.   Everyone knows it.   The thing that is in Room 101 is the worst thing in the world . . .   The worst thing in the world varies from individual to individual.   It may be burial alive, or death by fire, or by drowning, or by impalement, or fifty other deaths.   There are cases where it is some quite trivial thing, not even fatal."

How true this is!   Deep down in each one of us, unconfessed, and perhaps not even realized, there lies a fear, a fear that just here God's power is inadequate to triumph.   Strangely enough it is all too often "some quite trivial thing."   It is these deep, hidden fears that are the cause of so much disappointment in the Christian life, that give the lie to so much talk on sanctification and victory.   It is only when we grasp the unique combination of love and power in the manger, the cross and the empty tomb that we can say with life as well as with lip, "We know that in everything God works for good with those who love Him" (Rom. 8: 28,

R.S.V.), and we experience the truth of the word, "Perfect love casteth out fear" (I John 4: 18).

This probably explains why God's answer to Job is such a fascinating combination of the great and the small. God's power is not affected by the scale it has to work on; the infinitely great and the microscopically small are equally under His control.

GOD'S ANSWER (CHS. 38–41)

²WHO is this that darkeneth counsel
by words without knowledge?
³Gird up now thy loins like a man;
for I will demand of thee, and declare thou unto me.
⁴Where wast thou when I laid the foundations of the earth?
declare, if thou hast understanding.
⁵Who determined the measures thereof, if thou knowest?
or who stretched the line upon it?
⁶Whereupon were the foundations thereof fastened?
or who laid the corner stone thereof;
⁷when the morning stars sang together,
and all the sons of God shouted for joy?
⁸Or *who* shut up the sea with doors, when it brake forth,
and issued out of the womb;
⁹when I made the cloud the garment thereof,
and thick darkness a swaddling band for it,
¹⁰and prescribed for it my boundary, and set bars and doors,
¹¹and said, Hitherto shalt thou come, but no further;
and here shall thy proud waves be stayed?
¹²Hast thou commanded the morning since thy days *began,*
and caused the dayspring to know its place;
¹³that it might take hold of the ends of the earth,
and the wicked be shaken out of it?
¹⁴It is changed as clay under the seal;

and *all things* stand forth as a garment:
¹⁵and from the wicked their light is withholden,
and the high arm is broken.
¹⁶Hast thou entered into the springs of the sea?
or hast thou walked in the recesses of the deep?
¹⁷Have the gates of death been revealed unto thee?
or hast thou seen the gates of the shadow of death?
¹⁸Hast thou comprehended the breadth of the earth?
declare, if thou knowest it all.
¹⁹Where is the way to the dwelling of light,
and as for darkness, where is the place thereof;
²⁰that thou shouldest take it to the bound thereof,
and that thou shouldest discern the paths to the house thereof?
²¹*Doubtless,* thou knowest, for thou was then born,
and the number of thy days is great!
²²Hast thou entered the treasuries of the snow,
or hast thou seen the treasuries of the hail,
²³which I have reserved against the time of trouble,
against the day of battle and war?
²⁴Which is the way *to the place where* the light is parted,
or the east wind scattered upon the earth?
²⁵Who hath cleft a channel for the waterflood,
or a way for the lightning of the thunder;

²⁶to cause it to rain on a land where
no man is;
on the wilderness, wherein there is
no man;
²⁷to satisfy the waste and desolate
ground;
and to cause the tender grass to
spring forth?
²⁸Hath the rain a father?
or who hath begotten the drops of
dew?
²⁹Out of whose womb came the ice?
and the hoary frost of heaven,
who hath given it?
³⁰The waters are hidden as *with* stone,
and the face of the deep is frozen.
³¹Canst thou bind the cluster of the
Pleiades,
or loose the bands of Orion?
³²Canst thou lead forth the signs of
the Zodiac in their season?
or canst thou guide the Bear with
her train?
³³Knowest thou the ordinances of
the heavens?
canst thou establish the dominion
thereof in the earth?
³⁴Canst thou lift up thy voice to the
clouds,
that abundance of waters may
cover thee?
³⁵Canst thou send forth lightnings,
that they may go,
and say unto thee, Here we are?
³⁶Who hath put wisdom in the dark
clouds?
or who hath given understanding
to the meteor?
³⁷Who can number the clouds by
wisdom?
or who can pour out the bottles of
heaven,
³⁸when the dust runneth into a mass,
and the clods cleave fast together?

³⁹Wilt thou hunt the prey for the
lioness?
or satisfy the appetite of the young
lions,
⁴⁰when they couch in their dens,
and abide in the covert to lie in
wait?

⁴¹Who provideth for the raven his
food,

when his young ones cry unto God,
and wander for lack of meat?

39. Knowest thou the time when
the wild goats of the rock bring
forth?
canst thou mark when the hinds
do calve?
²Canst thou number the months
that they fulfil?
or knowest thou the time when
they bring forth?
³They bow themselves, they bring
forth their young,
they cast out their sorrows.
⁴Their young ones are in good lik-
ing, they grow up in the open
field;
they go forth, and return not
again.

⁵Who hath sent out the wild ass
free?
or who hath loosed the bands of
the wild ass?
⁶whose house I have made the
wilderness,
and the salt land his dwelling
place.
⁷He scorneth the tumult of the city,
neither heareth he the shoutings of
the driver.
⁸The range of the mountains is his
pasture,
and he searcheth after every green
thing.

⁹Will the wild-ox be content to
serve thee?
or will he abide by thy crib?
¹⁰Canst thou bind the wild-ox with
his band in the furrow?
or will he harrow the valleys after
thee?
¹¹Wilt thou trust him, because his
strength is great?
or wilt thou leave to him thy
labour?
¹²Wilt thou confide in him, that he
will bring home thy seed,
and gather *the corn of* thy thresh-
ingfloor?

¹³The wing of the ostrich rejoiceth:
are her pinions and feathers
kindly?

¹⁴For she leaveth her eggs on the earth,
and warmeth them in the dust,

¹⁵and forgetteth that the foot may crush them,
or that the wild beast may trample them.

¹⁶She dealeth hardly with her young ones, as if they were not hers:
though her labour be in vain, *she is* without fear;

¹⁷because God hath deprived her of wisdom,
neither hath he imparted to her understanding.

¹⁸What time she lifteth up herself on high,
she scorneth the horse and his rider.

¹⁹Hast thou given the horse *his* might?
hast thou clothed his neck with the quivering mane?

²⁰Hast thou made him to leap as a locust?
the glory of his snorting is terrible.

²¹He paweth in the valley, and rejoiceth in his strength:
he goeth out to meet the armed men.

²²He mocketh at fear, and is not dismayed;
neither turneth he back from the sword.

²³The quiver rattleth upon him,
the flashing spear and the javelin.

²⁴He swalloweth the ground with fierceness and rage;
neither believeth he that it is the voice of the trumpet.

²⁵As oft as the trumpet *soundeth* he saith, Aha!
and he smelleth the battle afar off,
the thunder of the captains, and the shouting.

²⁶Doth the hawk soar by thy wisdom,
and stretch her wings toward the south?

²⁷Doth the eagle mount up at thy command,
and make her nest on high?

She dwelleth on the rock, and hath her lodging *there*,
upon the crag of the rock, and the strong hold.

²⁹From thence she spieth out the prey;
her eyes behold it afar off.

³⁰Her young ones also suck up blood:
and where the slain are, there is she.

40. Moreover the LORD answered Job, and said,

²Shall he that cavilleth contend with the Almighty?
he that argueth with God, let him answer it.

³Then Job answered the LORD, and said,

⁴Behold, I am of small account;
what shall I answer thee?
I lay mine hand upon my mouth.

⁵Once have I spoken, and I will not answer;
yea twice, but I will proceed no further.

⁶Then the LORD answered Job out of the whirlwind, and said,

⁷Gird up thy lions now like a man:
I will demand of thee, and declare thou unto me.

⁸Wilt thou even disannul my judgement?
wilt thou condemn me, that thou mayest be justified?

⁹Or hast thou an arm like God?
and canst thou thunder with a voice like him?

¹⁰Deck thyself now with excellency and dignity;
and array thyself with honour and majesty.

¹¹Pour forth the overflowings of thine anger:
and look upon every one that is proud, and abase him.

¹²Look on every one that is proud, *and* bring him low;
and tread down the wicked where they stand.

¹³Hide them in the dust together;
bind their faces in the hidden *place*.

¹⁴Then will I also confess of thee

that thine own right hand can save thee.

¹⁵Behold now behemoth, which I made with thee;
he eateth grass as an ox.
¹⁶Lo now, his strength is in his loins,
and his force is in the muscles of his belly.
¹⁷He moveth his tail like a cedar:
the sinews of his thighs are knit together.
¹⁸His bones are *as* tubes of brass;
his limbs are like bars of iron.
¹⁹He is the chief of the ways of God:
he *only* that made him can make his sword to approach *unto him*.
²⁰Surely the mountains bring him forth food;
where all the beasts of the field do play.
²¹He lieth under the lotus trees,
in the covert of the reed, and the fen.
²²The lotus trees cover him with their shadow;
the willows of the brook compass him about.
²³Behold, if a river overflow, he trembleth not:
he is confident, though Jordan swell even to his mouth.
²⁴Shall any take him when he is on the watch,
or pierce through his nose with a snare?

41. Canst thou draw out leviathan with a fish hook?
or press down his tongue with a cord?
²Canst thou put a rope of rushes into his nose?
or pierce his jaw through with a spike?
³Will he make many supplications unto thee?
or will he speak soft words unto thee?
⁴Will he make a covenant with thee,
that thou shouldest take him for a servant for ever?
⁵Wilt thou play with him as with a bird?

or wilt thou bind him for thy maidens?
⁶Shall the bands of *fishermen* make traffic of him?
shall they part him among the merchants?
⁷Canst thou fill his skin with barbed irons,
or his head with fish spears?
⁸Lay thine hand upon him;
remember the battle, and do so no more.
⁹Behold, the hope of him is in vain:
shall not one be cast down even at the sight of him?
¹⁰None is so fierce that he dare stir him up:
who then is he that can stand before me?
¹¹Who hath first given unto me, that I should repay him?
whatsoever is under the whole heaven is mine.
¹²I will not keep silence concerning his limbs,
nor his mighty strength, nor his comely proportion.
¹³Who can strip off his outer garment?
who shall come within his double bridle?
¹⁴Who can open the doors of his face?
round about his teeth is terror.
¹⁵*His* strong scales are *his* pride,
shut up together *as with* a close seal.
¹⁶One is so near to another,
that no air can come between them.
¹⁷They are joined one to another;
they stick together, that they cannot be sundered.
¹⁸His neesings flash forth light,
and his eyes are like the eyelids of the morning.
¹⁹Out of his mouth go burning torches,
and sparks of fire leap forth.
²⁰Out of his nostrils a smoke goeth,
as of a seething pot and *burning* rushes.
²¹His breath kindleth coals,
and a flame goeth forth from his mouth.

²²In his neck abideth strength,
and terror danceth before him.
²³The flakes of his flesh are joined together:
they are firm upon him; they cannot be moved.
²⁴His heart is as firm as a stone;
yea, firm as the nether millstone.
²⁵When he raiseth himself up, the mighty are afraid:
by reason of consternation they are beside themselves.
²⁶If one lay at him with the sword, it cannot avail;
nor the spear, the dart, nor the pointed shaft.
²⁷He counteth iron as straw, and brass as rotten wood.
²⁸The arrow cannot make him flee:
slingstones are turned with him into stubble.
²⁹Clubs are counted as stubble:
he laugheth at the rushing of the javelin.
³⁰His underparts are *like* sharp potsherds:
he spreadeth *as it were* a threshing wain upon the mire.
³¹He maketh the deep to boil like a pot:
he maketh the sea like ointment.
³²He maketh a path to shine after him;
one would think the deep to be hoary.
³³Upon earth there is not his like, that is made without fear.
³⁴He beholdeth everything that is high:
he is king over all the sons of pride.

GOD's answer to Job has by some been grievously misinterpreted as a catalogue of scientific marvels beyond man's understanding, and as a revelation of scientific truth that would be discovered only in the nineteenth or twentieth century of our era. Nothing could be further from the truth. God is here speaking to Job in terms of Job's knowledge and ignorance. It is quite secondary whether modern man has or has not found the answers to God's questions. As for the foreshadowings of modern scientific knowledge, they are, at least in part, due more to "eisegesis," i.e. reading in, than to exegesis.

Today God will speak to the thinking man in terms of *his* knowledge and ignorance. God's creation challenges the modern biologist or atomic physicist with other questions than those Job could not answer, but the challenge is as real.

It is typical of the attitude of the Bible that God's questions virtually restrict themselves to this world, in which man was placed as God's vice-regent (Gen. 1: 28, Psa. 8: 6). God scarcely asks Job about the mysteries of the stars on their silent way, but He faces him with everyday things of this world, in which man is ever tempted to speak Himself free of his Creator.

God's questions range from the earth's mysterious uniqueness in the universe (38: 4–7) and the power that maintains the nightly star pattern, as typified in the Pleiades, Orion and the signs of the Zodiac, constant in its risings and settings (38: 31f) to the forces that maintain animal life in all its manifestations (38: 39 – 39: 4). He is questioned as to his control of the sea, of light and darkness, of snow, hail and ice (38: 8–30). These last refer especially to those sudden and incalculable phenoma of nature which overthrow all the power and forethought of man. Though man has been set to rule the animal creation, there are those he cannot control: the wild ass (39: 5–8), the wild ox (39: 9–12)—the A.V. "unicorn" is as imaginary as the beast itself —the ostrich (39: 13–18), the hawk and the eagle (39: 26–30), or if he does control, it may be at his peril as with the horse (39: 19–25).

When Job confesses himself overwhelmed and convinced (40: 3ff), God points out the futility and negative character of his criticism of the moral rule of the world (40: 11ff), for he cannot do anything about it himself. Then God turns to the apparently irrational in His creation. This has already been indicated in passing in 38: 25ff—why should it rain, where it does no one any good? Now Job is asked to consider a couple of God's "jokes." However much our cold northern minds may resent the fact, the Bible is an oriental book and from time to time bursts out into the glorious, unrestrained hyperbole of the east. Though they may not appear so to our minds—are we perhaps the losers thereby?—behemoth (40: 15–24) is the hippopotamus and leviathan (41: 1–34) the crocodile. Quite candidly I prefer this hyperbole to the perverted ingenuity that can see a prophecy of the modern battleship in the description of leviathan.

Why did God make the hippopotamus and the crocodile? If you have never asked yourself this question, you may find a couple of hours spent in the nearest zoo a worth-while investment. Some of us have a private list to which we have added a few more names. The Wise prided themselves that they were basing their views on the fundamental rationality of God's acts. So God faces Job with a couple of His "jokes," and Job repents in dust and ashes (42: 6).

CHAPTER XI

JOB'S VINDICATION

THEN Job answered the LORD, and said,
²I know that thou canst do all things,
and that no purpose of thine can be restrained.
³Who is this that hideth counsel without knowledge?
therefore have I uttered that which I understood not,
things too wonderful for me, which I knew not.
⁴Hear, I beseech thee, and I will speak;
I will demand of thee, and declare thou unto me.
⁵I had heard of thee by the hearing of the ear;
but now mine eye seeth thee.
⁶wherefore I loathe my words, and repent in dust and ashes.

⁷And it was so, that after the LORD had spoken these words unto Job, the LORD said to Eliphaz the Temanite, My wrath is kindled against thee, and against thy two friends: for ye have not spoken of me the thing that is right, as my servant Job hath. ⁸Now therefore, take unto you seven bullocks and seven rams, and go to my servant Job, and offer up for yourselves a burnt offering; and my servant Job shall pray for you; for him will I accept, that I deal not with you after your folly; for ye have not spoken of me the thing that is right,

as my servant Job hath. ⁹So Eliphaz the Temanite and Bildad the Shuhite and Zophar the Naamathite went, and did according as the LORD commanded them: and the LORD accepted Job. ¹⁰And the LORD turned the captivity of Job, when he prayed for his friends: and the LORD gave Job twice as much as he had before. ¹¹Then came there unto him all his brethren, and all his sisters, and all they that had been of his acquaintance before, and did eat bread with him in his house: and they bemoaned him, and comforted him concerning all the evil that the LORD had brought upon him: every man also gave him a piece of money, and every one a ring of gold. ¹²So the LORD blessed the latter end of Job more than his beginning: and he had fourteen thousand sheep, and six thousand camels, and a thousand yoke of oxen, and a thousand she-asses. ¹³He had also seven sons and three daughters. ¹⁴And he called the name of the first, Jemimah; and the name of the second, Keziah; and the name of the third, Kerenhappuch. ¹⁵And in all the land were no women found so fair as the daughters of Job: and their father gave them inheritance among their brethren. ¹⁶And after this Job lived an hundred and forty years, and saw his sons, and his sons' sons, *even* four generations. ¹⁷So Job died, being old and full of days.

SATAN had said to God, *Doth Job fear God for nought? ... Put forth Thine hand now, and touch all that he hath, and he will renounce Thee to Thy face* (1: 9, 11). Job has lost all, but he has found God and is content. Even without the knowledge of

God's love that comes from Golgotha, he finds Him more than suf-
ficent. The passionate cry for vindication has been forgotten, for it
matters not what men may say, if he knows that his fellowship
with God has been restored.

The vindication of some of God's saints must wait until they
stand before His throne. Job, however, has been more than just
an individual who through suffering and loss has reached the bliss
of communion with God; he is also an object lesson from whom
generations to come were to learn a lesson of God's dealings with
men. He had therefore to be vindicated there and then. This
comes in two stages.

Though nothing we have said about Job's friends has been too
hard, they were for all that men who sought the truth, even though
they wished to force it into their own moulds, so God was able
to speak to them. It is not surprising that He chose Eliphaz
(42: 7), for his distorting medium was more pardonable than that
of the others. That it was Job who had to pray for them (42: 8),
Job the outcast, the chief of sinners, was something that could
break down even the common-sense of Zophar. It was clear that
only a man accepted by God and righteousness in His sight could
mediate for his fellow-men.

But what of Job's fellow-townsmen, the fickle mob that had
thrust him out of their town as unclean and accursed, when the
hand of Satan was upon him? There was only one answer they
could understand, the only answer the mob will ever understand,
and so *the Lord restored the fortunes of Job . . . and gave Job twice
as much as he had before* (v. 10, R.S.V.). Success and prosperity
form the language the world understands, so they all flocked back
to the man they had abandoned in the hour of his bitterest need
(42: 11). He might well have thanked God that they had treated
him as they did, for had he known their comfort and care in his
adversity, he might never have been thrown back on God and
so have learnt to know Him in this new way.

Many have found the end of *Job* disappointing, for, so they say,
it is ultimately no more than a vindication of the views that Job's
friends had put forward all along. Even if this were true, what
of it? It is not Job's words, but Job, who is vindicated; it is
Job's friends rather than their theology that stands condemned.
The force of 42: 7 is that however foolishly he may have said it,
Job was looking for a God big enough to comprehend his experience. On the other hand, however wisely they may have put

it into words, his friends were upholding a God small enough to conform to their theories.   Could the discussion have been carried on in a vacuum, it may well be that we should have been forced to adjudge the friends victors.   But theological discussions cannot be carried on in a vacuum.   We have to bow before what God has done in history, before what He has done to individual men and women, of whom Job was but one.

But that is not all.   God is never concerned that some insist on misunderstanding Him.   There was only one way in which He could vindicate Job that the mob would understand.   If that way could be interpreted as a vindication of the theory that Job had by his sufferings so signally refuted, that was of no concern to God.   Experience shows us that sinful man is happily capable of misinterpreting anything that God has said and done.

The doubling of all Job's possessions was intended to show that there was nothing fortuitous about it all; his contemporaries had to be made to acknowledge that God's hand was at work.   Only his children were not doubled (42: 13).   In the hour of Job's greatest desperation he had been driven to the hope of life beyond the grave.   Now God says Amen to it.   All earthly things are transient, and so his lost possessions could not be restored, but only replaced and doubled.   But by giving him only ten new children God assured him that he would yet meet those he had lost beyond the grave.